THE UNIVERSITY OF CHICAGO
DEPARTMENT OF GEOGRAPHY
RESEARCH PAPERS (Lithographed, 6×9 Inches)

(Available from Department of Geography, The University of Chicago, 5828 S. University Ave., Chicago, Illinois 60637. Price: $5.00 each; by series subscription, $4.00 each.)

48. BOXER, BARUCH. *Israeli Shipping and Foreign Trade*   1957. 176 pp.
53. ACKERMAN, EDWARD A. *Geography as a Fundamental Research Discipline*   1958. 40 pp. $1.00
56. MURPHY, FRANCIS C. *Regulating Flood-Plain Development*   1958. 216 pp.
62. GINSBURG, NORTON, editor. *Essays on Geography and Economic Development*   1960. 196 pp.
71. GILBERT, E. W. *The University Town in England and West Germany*
    1961. 79 pp. 4 plates. 30 maps and diagrams. (Free to new subscribers)
72. BOXER, BARUCH. *Ocean Shipping in the Evolution of Hong Kong*   1961. 108 pp.
74. TROTTER, JOHN E. *State Park System in Illinois*   1966. 152 pp.
84. KANSKY, K. J. *Structure of Transportation Networks: Relationships between Network Geometry and Regional Characteristics*   1963. 155 pp.
91. HILL, A. DAVID. *The Changing Landscape of a Mexican Municipio, Villa Las Rosas, Chiapas*
    NAS-NRC Foreign Field Research Program Report No. 26. 1964. 121 pp.
94. MC MANIS, DOUGLAS R. *The Initial Evaluation and Utilization of the Illinois Prairies, 1815–1840*
    1964. 109 pp.
97. BOWDEN, LEONARD W. *Diffusion of the Decision To Irrigate: Simulation of the Spread of a New Resource Management Practice in the Colorado Northern High Plains*   1965. 146 pp.
98. KATES, ROBERT W. *Industrial Flood Losses: Damage Estimation in the Lehigh Valley*
    1965. 76 pp.
102. AHMAD, QAZI. *Indian Cities: Characteristics and Correlates*   1965. 184 pp.
103. BARNUM, H. GARDINER. *Market Centers and Hinterlands in Baden-Württemberg*   1966. 172 pp.
105. SEWELL, W. R. DERRICK, *et al. Human Dimensions of Weather Modification*   1966. 423 pp.
106. SAARINEN, THOMAS F. *Perception of the Drought Hazard on the Great Plains*   1966. 183 pp.
107. SOLZMAN, DAVID M. *Waterway Industrial Sites: A Chicago Case Study*   1967. 138 pp.
108. KASPERSON, ROGER E. *The Dodecanese: Diversity and Unity in Island Politics*   1967. 184 pp.
109. LOWENTHAL, DAVID, ET AL. *Environmental Perception and Behavior.*   1967. 88 pp.
110. REED, WALLACE E. *Areal Interaction in India: Commodity Flows of the Bengal-Bihar Industrial Area*   1967. 210 pp.
112. BOURNE, LARRY S. *Private Redevelopment of the Central City: Spatial Processes of Structural Change in the City of Toronto*   1967. 199 pp.
113. BRUSH, JOHN E., and GAUTHIER, HOWARD L., JR. *Service Centers and Consumer Trips: Studies on the Philadelphia Metropolitan Fringe*   1968. 182 pp.
114. CLARKSON, JAMES D. *The Cultural Ecology of a Chinese Village: Cameron Highlands, Malaysia*   1968. 174 pp.
115. BURTON, IAN, KATES, ROBERT W., and SNEAD, RODMAN E. *The Human Ecology of Coastal Flood Hazard in Megalopolis*   1968. 196 pp.
117. WONG, SHUE TUCK. *Perception of Choice and Factors Affecting Industrial Water Supply Decisions in Northeastern Illinois*   1968. 96 pp.
118. JOHNSON, DOUGLAS L. *The Nature of Nomadism*   1969. 200 pp.
119. DIENES, LESLIE. *Locational Factors and Locational Developments in the Soviet Chemical Industry*   1969. 285 pp.
120. MIHELIC, DUSAN. *The Political Element in the Port Geography of Trieste*   1969. 104 pp.
121. BAUMANN, DUANE. *The Recreational Use of Domestic Water Supply Reservoirs: Perception and Choice*   1969. 125 pp.
122. LIND, AULIS O. *Coastal Landforms of Cat Island, Bahamas: A Study of Holocene Accretionary Topography and Sea-Level Change*   1969. 156 pp.
123. WHITNEY, JOSEPH. *China: Area, Administration and Nation Building*   1970. 198 pp.
124. EARICKSON, ROBERT. *The Spatial Behavior of Hospital Patients: A Behavioral Approach to Spatial Interaction in Metropolitan Chicago*   1970. 198 pp.
125. DAY, JOHN C. *Managing the Lower Rio Grande: An Experience in International River Development*   1970. 277 pp.

126. MAC IVER, IAN. *Urban Water Supply Alternatives: Perception and Choice in the Grand Basin, Ontario* 1970. 178 pp.

127. GOHEEN, PETER G. *Victorian Toronto, 1850 to 1900: Pattern and Process of Growth* 1970. 278 pp.

128. GOOD, CHARLES M. *Rural Markets and Trade in East Africa* 1970. 252 pp.

129. MEYER, DAVID R. *Spatial Variation of Black Urban Households* 1970. 127 pp.

130. GLADFELTER, BRUCE. *Meseta and Campiña Landforms in Central Spain: A Geomorphology o· the Alto Henares Basin* 1971. 204 pp.

131. NEILS, ELAINE M. *Reservation to City: Indian Urbanization and Federal Relocation* 1971. 200 pp.

132. MOLINE, NORMAN T. *Mobility and the Small Town, 1900–1930* 1971. 169 pp.

133. SCHWIND, PAUL J. *Migration and Regional Development in the United States, 1950–1960* 1971. 170 pp.

134. PYLE, GERALD F. *Heart Disease, Cancer and Stroke in Chicago: A Geographical Analysis with Facilities Plans for 1980* 1971. 292 pp.

135. JOHNSON, JAMES F. *Renovated Waste Water: An Alternative Source of Municipal Water Supply in the U.S.* 1971. 155 pp.

136. BUTZER, KARL W. *Recent History of an Ethiopian Delta: The Omo River and the Level of Lake Rudolf* 1971. 184 pp.

137. HARRIS, CHAUNCY D. *Annotated World List of Selected Current Geographical Serials in English, French, and German* 3rd edition 1971. 77 pp.

138. HARRIS, CHAUNCY D., and FELLMANN, JEROME D. *International List of Geographical Serials* 2nd edition 1971. 267 pp.

139. MC MANIS, DOUGLAS R. *European Impressions of the New England Coast, 1497–1620* 1972. 147 pp.

140. COHEN, YEHOSHUA S. *Diffusion of an Innovation in an Urban System: The Spread of Planned Regional Shopping Centers in the United States, 1949–1968* 1972. 136 pp.

141. MITCHELL, NORA. *The Indian Hill-Station: Kodaikanal* 1972. 199 pp.

142. PLATT, RUTHERFORD H. *The Open Space Decision Process: Spatial Allocation of Costs and Benefits* 1972. 189 pp.

143. GOLANT, STEPHEN M. *The Residential Location and Spatial Behavior of the Elderly: A Canadian Example* 1972. 226 pp.

144. PANNELL, CLIFTON W. *T'ai-chung, T'ai-wan: Structure and Function* 1973. 200 pp.

145. LANKFORD, PHILIP M. *Regional Incomes in the United States, 1929–1967: Level, Distribution, Stability, and Growth* 1972. 137 pp.

146. FREEMAN, DONALD B. *International Trade, Migration, and Capital Flows: A Quantitative Analysis of Spatial Economic Interaction* 1973. 202 pp.

147. MYERS, SARAH K. *Language Shift Among Migrants to Lima, Peru* 1973. 204 pp.

148. JOHNSON, DOUGLAS L. *Jabal al-Akhdar, Cyrenaica: An Historical Geography of Settlement and Livelihood* 1973. 240 pp.

149. YEUNG, YUE-MAN. *National Development Policy and Urban Transformation in Singapore: A Study of Public Housing and the Marketing System* 1973. 204 pp.

150. HALL, FRED L. *Location Criteria for High Schools: Student Transportation and Racial Integration* 1973. 156 pp.

151. ROSENBERG, TERRY J. *Residence, Employment, and Mobility of Puerto Ricans in New York City* 1974. 230 pp.

152. MIKESELL, MARVIN W., EDITOR. *Geographers Abroad: Essays on the Problems and Prospects o, Research in Foreign Areas* 1973. 296 pp.

153. OSBORN, JAMES. *Area, Development Policy, and the Middle City in Malaysia* 1974. 273 pp.

154. WACHT, WALTER F. *The Domestic Air Transportation Network of the United States* 1974. 98 pp.

155. BERRY, BRIAN, J. L., et al. *Land Use, Urban Form and Environmental Quality* 1974. 464 pp.

156. MITCHELL, JAMES K. *Community Response to Coastal Erosion: Individual and Collective Adjustments to Hazard on the Atlantic Shore* 1974. 209 pp.

157. COOK, GILLIAN P. *Spatial Dynamics of Business Growth in the Witwatersrand* 1974. 143 pp.

158. STARR, JOHN T., JR. *The Evolution of Unit Train Operations in the United States: 1960–1969—A Decade of Experience* 1974.

159. PYLE, GERALD F. *The Spatial Dynamics of Crime* 1974. 220 pp

AREA, DEVELOPMENT POLICY
AND THE MIDDLE CITY
IN MALAYSIA

James Osborn
The Center for the Study of Democratic Institutions

THE UNIVERSITY OF CHICAGO
DEPARTMENT OF GEOGRAPHY
RESEARCH PAPER NO. 153

1974

Library of Congress Catalog Card Number: 73-92650

Research Papers are available from:
The University of Chicago
Department of Geography
5828 S. University Avenue
Chicago, Illinois 60637
Price: $5.00 list; $4.00 series subscription

ACKNOWLEDGMENTS

This is the first part of a two-part study of the area/development policy relationship and the rôle of Middle Cities in the development of Malaysia and Indonesia. The research has been supported in the years 1969 through 1972 by grants from The Southeast Asia Development Advisory Group (SEADAG), an undertaking of The Asia Society, New York, and the United States Agency for International Development, from The United States Office of Education (Fulbright-Hays), and from The Jajasan Siswa Lokantara, Djakarta.

Greatest thanks must go to my parents for their unwavering support and encouragement over all the years, and to Professor Norton Ginsburg of the Department of Geography, The University of Chicago for his always thoughtful help, guidance and patience. I have been assisted by consultations with Professors Peter Goheen and Nathan Leites of The University of Chicago, and by Professor Warren Hunsberger of the Department of Economics, American University.

The greatest field problem in Malaysia has been the collection of data and views, primarily from government sources at various levels. In this connection, I acknowledge with thanks the great help of Dr. Carroll Shaw, Dr. Donald Snodgrass, and Dr. V. Barnett of the Harvard Development Advisory Service, Kuala Lumpur, T. Kandasami of the Economic Planning Unit, and Anwar Fasal of the Chief Minister's office, Negeri Pulau Pinang. It is impossible to name all the government officers who helped and always showed courtesy and interest; to the civil services of the Federal, State, and local governments of Malaysia I offer profound thanks. I am greatly indebted to the librarians of the Penang, Ipoh, Universities of Malaya and Singapore and New York Public libraries.

In the years of development of this research, the following people have been particularly inspirational, helpful and kind: Clifford C. Matlock and Dr. Alexander Shakow of AID, Hon. Kenneth T. Young and Lionel Landry of The

Asia Society, and Professors George Borden and Kenneth Frandsen of The Pennsylvania State University. I would like to add my special thanks to Linda Vandegrift for execution of the maps in this paper.

James Osborn
Chicago
September 1, 1972

CONTENTS

LIST OF TABLES

LIST OF ILLUSTRATIONS

CHAPTER I

INTRODUCTION

National development is the major problem and preoccupation of almost all countries in the world today. Central government policy is the major device by which development is induced and channeled in most of these countries. It is often observed, however, that development policies in particular countries rarely change significantly in concept, goals, or administration over time-- perhaps because of the timelessness of certain problems, the unlikelihood of radical change in economic theory, and a continuity of relevant internal and external leadership. Only by seeing what has been tried and how it has worked can real policy lessons be learned and the history of national development be written. Thus an examination of what has been tried and, in the case of Malaysia, has worked can be a crucial and, at once, the best means of informing future policy.

The geographer asks where things are, why they are there, and what difference it makes. These matters are reducible to, but infinitely complex in, the dimension of area. The first question of this Malaysian study, then, is: what is the relationship of area to development and development policy? If there is none, or it is a simple one, those observations would be valuable both for development policy studies and for the science of human geography.

The second question is: what place have cities in area and development?; specifically, what functions can and do cities, as units of areal organization, perform in national development, particularly as affected by development policy? This follows from question one as a case of the area/development policy relationship. It is of added importance because of the world-wide trend towards urbanization, and because rapid urbanization is usually seen as a plague.

Hence the last question is: where should development policy be located for national development?; what areal strategies need to be evolved? The Malaysian development experience is singular for its success, the comparative richness of the country, and the tractability of the problems. Malaysia also has a relatively long history of active and well-documented development policy and several special conditions (the joining of Malaya to the Borneo States and

1

racial economic imbalance associated with a rural/urban dichotomy, for example) that make its case particularly attractive for study.

This is a study in political geography. Political geography concerns itself with political phenomena (including institutional action, but also political actors) interacting with area;[1] that is interaction with both the contents (or ecological system) and environments of areas and the distribution of terrestrial phenomena.[2]

Following Ginsburg, one speaks of area to mean a bounded space, and not of "space" or "spatial administration, economy, interaction" or "national space," which are in themselves meaningless expressions.[3] One looks beyond region and regionalization, which suggest only one of several types of areal form, to the broadest meaning of locational possibilities and associations within a country.[4]

The political phenomenon at issue here is policy. Policy has been defined as "strategic moves that direct an organization's critical resources toward

---

[1] This definition is similar to that of the Ad Hoc Committee on Geography which, in "Studies in Political Geography," calls political geography the study of "the interaction of geographical area and political process" except that it is redundant to say "geographical area," and there are political phenomena which may not be conveniently subsumed in processes, for example political assassination. (Committee Report reprinted in The Structure of Political Geography, ed. Roger E. Kasperson and Julian V. Menghi [Chicago: Aldine, 1969], p. 58.) Kasperson and Menghi, and more recently Cohen and Rosenthal in an unnecessarily incomprehensible paper, also adopt the currently popular but not demonstrably useful large-scale political process approach in defining political geography. (Kasperson and Menghi, eds., p. xi; and Saul B. Cohen and Lewis D. Rosenthal, "A Geographical Model for Political Systems Analysis," Geographical Review, LXI [January, 1971], 6.)

[2] For clear discussions of the development of political geography and the evolution of space-polity studies see Marvin Mikesell, "The Borderlands of Geography as a Social Science," Interdisciplinary Relationships in the Social Sciences, ed. Musafer Sherif and Carolyn Sherif (Chicago: Aldine, 1969), pp. 233-34; and Joseph B. R. Whitney, China: Area, Administration and Nation Building, Research Paper No. 123 (Chicago: University of Chicago, Department of Geography, 1970), pp. 7-9.

[3] See Norton S. Ginsburg, "Areas, Regions, and Human Organization" (Delhi: International Geographical Union, 1968), fugitive, p. 7; and "Area" in International Encyclopedia of the Social Sciences, I (New York: Macmillan, 1969), 398-401.

[4] Others include points and lines, nul area, areal masses, and various types of conceptual area. See below. It may be noted, too, that adherence to the concept of region may have stifled geographical enquiry into policy studies. (Cf. N. S. Ginsburg, "The Regional Concept and Planning Regions," Regional Planning [New York: United Nations, Department of Economic and Social Affairs, 1959], pp. 38-42).

perceived opportunities in a changing environment."[1] More broadly it is called "a set of decisions on goals and strategy, as well as actions."[2] Most succinctly it is called "the relationship of a governmental unit to its environment."[3] It is possible to identify at any time both what the policy of an organization is toward an issue, and the circumstances conditioning choice. For development policy, for example, a plan may exist. In foreign affairs there may be policies which indicate what the government's perceptions and goals are and what acts would be taken if the conditioning circumstances relating to those policies were to change. With regard to national development--or with foreign affairs--there is a set of actions, feedbacks, which are determined by the prior plan or policy, but which, unlike with a static plan, have a very broad set of interactions with the outside world. It is this aspect of policy that can be viewed most profitably in its complex relationship to area.

Policy interacting with area, then, is the subject matter of the Geography of Policy.[4] Four relationships, two, with reciprocals, comprise its content: (1) the effects of policy on the distribution and areal organization of phenomena; (2) the effects of policy on ecological relationships in particular areas; (3) the effect of distribution and areal organization of phenomena on policy; and (4) the effect of areal content on policy. This conception departs from larger but more diffuse "space-polity"[5] studies in concentrating on policy, while retaining wide areal approach.

---

[1]Raymond A. Bauer and Kenneth J. Gergen, The Study of Policy Formation (New York: Free Press, 1968), p. 2.

[2]See Joseph Frankel, The Making of Foreign Policy: An Analysis of Decision Making (London: Oxford University Press, 1963), p. 1.

[3]See Heinz Eulau and Robert Eyestone, "Policy Maps of City Councils and Policy Outcomes: A Developmental Analysis," The American Political Science Review, LXII (March, 1968), 126.

[4]Cf. Saul B. Cohen, "Toward a Geography of Policy," Economic Geography, XLI, No. 1 (January, 1966), iii.

[5]See Whitney, pp. 7-11; see N. J. G. Pounds, Political Geography (New York: McGraw Hill, 1963); and Richard Hartshorne, "The Functional Approach in Political Geography," Annals Association of American Geographers, XL (April, 1950), 95-130. Outside of geography some sporadic and casual work has been done on the area-government relationship, notably Arthur Maass, ed., Area and Power (Glencoe: The Free Press, 1959); and James W. Fesler, Area and Administration (Tuscaloosa: University of Alabama Press, 1949). Neither, to my knowledge was followed up. See also Albert Wohlstetter, "Illusions of Distance," Foreign Affairs, XLVI (January, 1968), 242-55. Seemingly the "policy sciences" of Lasswell and their theory have never developed very far. In

4

Development Policy

Development policy is the specific type of policy analyzed here. It consists of decisions and actions aimed at achieving development goals, as for a nation-state. It is one part, and not necessarily a coherent whole in itself, of a set of policies which the government of a country creates in response to a set of perceived functions. Milton Esman identifies twelve tasks of a national government. Among them are achievement of security against external aggression and ensurance of internal order, protection of the legitimacy of the regime, mobilization of savings and of current financial resources, constitution-making, and activization of participation in modernizing activities.[1] By various means, in short, a government attempts to perpetuate itself, promote the growing welfare of its citizens hence the health of the systems that support them, and enhance the comparative welfare of the country as a whole vis à vis other countries.

Clearly these tasks and functions can conflict with one another. Where the general expression "development" is employed by the government to group

---

geography there has even been a basic misunderstanding of the nature of policy as a complex phenomenon. What pass for policy studies in geography are generally case studies of particular policy projects, for examples dams, examination of some physical-geographic production factors in development, or vaguely modernized geo-politics. See Daniel Lerner and Harold Lasswell, eds., The Policy Sciences (Stanford: Stanford University Press, 1959), pp. 3-15, and Harold Lasswell, "Policy Sciences," International Encyclopedia of Social Sciences, XII (New York: Macmillan, 1968), 181-89. In fact, Warren F. Ilchman and Norman Thomas Uphoff assert that "social scientists can at present contribute little of value to the making of policy choices" (in The Political Economy of Change [Berkeley: The University of California Press, 1969], p. 257). While these authors argue mainly for a policy science which concentrates, ex ante, on improving choices of policy-makers, this can only be to a degree corrupting for the scientist. Where it is possible to make clear the history, mechanisms, and impact of a policy, however, there may lie the opportunity to be both helpful to policy-makers and additive to the theory-building process in the social sciences. Cf. Robert K. Merton and Daniel Lerner, "Social Scientists and Policy Research," The Policy Sciences, pp. 282-307. See also J. R. V. Prescott, The Geography of State Policies (London: Hutchinson University Library, 1968). Although Prescott outlines the political geographer's concern for policy in a way similar to my own (i. e. for "geographical factors which influenced the formation of such [development] policies; . . . the geographical circumstances which influence the operation of the policies; and . . . the geographical results of policy implementation" [p. 142]), his implicit definition of geography does not contain an analytical approach to area; his geographical factors are largely physical; he ignores significant policy attributes, such as administration; and he evidences no awareness of work on policy, however limited, outside of geography.

[1]Milton J. Esman, "The Politics of Development Administration," Approaches to Development: Politics, Administration and Change, ed. John D. Montgomery and William J. Siffin (New York: McGraw-Hill, 1966), pp. 60-64.

the objectives of economic, social, and political growth (at best, per capita), particular discrepancies have been observed, as between stability and growth, and between welfare and economic growth.[1] The politics of choice among such conflicting goals is not the subject of this study; for Malaysia, that is not a particular problem: "development" is set out with a capital budget and a Plan in both of which the choices are made fairly explicit.[2]

Since the Pacific War, national governments in Asia, as elsewhere in the Third World, have commonly redefined their purposes in terms of this development responsibility.[3] Increases in gross national product per capita, accompanied by higher or more productive employment, integration of diverse areal, communal, or employment groups, and general modernization or Westernization of the social, political and economic systems, are taken as indications of positive development. Overall development policies emerge for such countries, which comprise many of Mr. Esman's functions. Thus governments act, according to goals, seeking to control those contents of a country which they think yield "development," and to move them in a positive direction. Where control is not possible or otherwise not desirable (as in the private sector of an accepted free or partially free-enterprise economy, for example), the development policy contains certain expectations as to performance. These provoke a series of governmental actions designed to facilitate or ameliorate the private actors' expected performance.[4]

---

[1] See Mancur Olson, "Rapid Growth as a Destabilizing Force," Journal of Economic History, XXVII (December, 1963), 529-52; Charles Wolf, United States Policy and the Third World (Boston: Little, Brown, 1967), esp. pp. 112-26; and John Friedmann, Regional Development Policy (Cambridge: MIT Press, 1966), pp. 48-49.

[2] Still, it is proper to observe that a portion of Malaysian "development" policy is certainly aimed primarily at welfare rather than striding ahead on a broad front. See Gayl Ness, "Economic Development and Goals of Government in Malaysia," Malaysia: A Survey, ed. Wang Gung-wu (New York: Praeger, 1964), pp. 307-8.

[3] Ibid. And see, for the example of Indonesia, Yearbook 1968 (Hong Kong: Far Eastern Economic Review, 1969), pp. 181-84; and Mubyarto, "Domestic Price Policies: Indonesia," SEADAG Discussion Paper (New York: The Asia Society, 1969), fugitive, p. 4.

[4] Development thus means a congeries of change goals, forces, and acts. We may separate the goals initially. First, there is national development, that is to say integrated and "balanced" growth in the national economic systems. This is usually measured in aggregate terms--optimization of population growth, distribution, and training, capital accumulation, rise in GNP/capita and productivity, and an improved balance of payments. Areally it suggests the need for

Understanding of a government's own definition of development is essential, since from it follow the content and means of policy implementation. As noted, Malaysia, and before it the Federation of Malaya and the governments of Sarawak and North Borneo, since the late 1950's have approached development planning by economic sector and the adoption of a development budget emphasizing capital expenditures. This is understandable in a country with money and international credits to spend; although much important development activity rests with the private sector. Development based on this strategy has been a great success: political, social, and areal problems have, at least until lately, been of secondary importance. The goals of national development and national stability have been met in aggregate terms; national integration and balanced growth is still elusive. (See Chapter III.) But living levels have moved far enough ahead of the aspirations of the population that discontent, instability, and/or other special ills seem to have been minimized. [1]

However two objections have been raised to Malaysia's approach, which will take on importance in the analysis below. First, the sectoral approach in centralized planning is incapable of treating or creating what are specifically termed the "external economies which [are] the fundamental contribution of urbanization to the development process" [2] and may more generally be called the "areal dynamics of development." Second, viewing output (the development goal, i.e. a rise in aggregate output or income) as a function solely of investment can be invalid because "there are numerous inhibitions and obstacles to development other than inadequate investment." [3] To these objections may be

---

economically sound locations of productive capital investments, particularly circulation infra-structure. A second development goal is the development of particular national sectoral and regional units. This may be a particularly desirable approach when a truncated or depressed national economy is faced. It suggests specialized attention to certain areally discrete income-producing activities (e.g. primary products, and export) or areas (leading regions) for a given period of time. A third goal may countervail: national stability and integration. This may necessitate attention to backward sectors and areas and to welfare, defense, and political concerns which must be balanced with more purely economic ones.

[1] The successful obliteration of what was a highly organized, well supported and dynamic communist insurgency during the ten-year "Emergency" (1948-58) can be taken as evidence of this.

[2] See Malcolm D. Rivkin, "Urbanization and National Development, " in United Nations, Urbanization: Development Policies and Planning (New York: United Nations, 1968), pp. 79-88, especially p. 87.

[3] See Gunnar Myrdal, Asian Drama, Vol. III, Appendix 4 (New York: Pantheon, 1968), pp. 2005-29, especially pp. 2005-9.

added the general observation that development plans, supposedly the real specification of development policy goals and intentions, are often highly unrealistic
and deceptive. Greater stress on lists of and targets for specific projects may
indicate greater reliability. In Malaysia, comprehensive project lists are not
compiled, but great attention is given to project performance by those responsible for development.

Area and Development Policy

National Area

Geographers have for some time worked on and refined location theory
and techniques for measuring the relative economic and demographic character
of areas. But only occasionally are location theorists asked to deal with development problems in the Third World. William Alonso is discouraging on the
matter. He identifies several important ways in which the conditions assumed
by classical location theory fail to correspond with conditions in developing
countries. Among them are: (1) greater than assumed scarcity of information;
(2) greater than assumed structural fluidity because of the relatively small economic base--hence less validity to the traditional ceteris paribus assumptions;
and (3) greater than assumed shortages of entrepreneurial, managerial, and
technical personnel in and out of government.[1] Despite such observations,
development planning often pays lip service to classical location theory,[2] as
recently in South Korea:

> Choices of activity location are determined in the [planning] model by
> market locations, resource locations, interregional transportation costs,
> infrastructure capital costs, water-system capacities, and economies of
> scale, in accord with standard location theory.[3]

How this will have worked, as either a predictive exercise with respect to firm

---

[1]William Alonso, "Industrial Location and Regional Policy in Economic
Development," Working Paper No. 74 (Berkeley: Department of City and Regional Planning and Center for Planning and Development Research, 1968), fugitive, p. 39.

[2]Frequently the city hierarchical aspect of location theory is invoked,
although with little substantive success so far, as in Kingsley E. Haynes,
"Growth Poles and the Hierarchy of Cities: Some References to Malaysia,"
SEADAG Discussion Paper (New York: The Asia Society, 1970), fugitive. This
is discussed below.

[3]Irma Adelman, Practical Approaches to Development Planning: Korea's
Second Five Year Plan (Baltimore: Johns Hopkins Press, 1969), p. 186.

and individual behavior, or as a guide to government economic development policy is problematical.

John Friedmann and Walter Stohr wrote in 1966 that, "the bulk of academic literature on regional science . . . remains irrelevant for practical purposes."[1] Nevertheless, the most popular areal approach to the problems of development in underdeveloped countries has been that concerned with regional planning. The literature divides into two groups. One concentrates on the processes of Western economic development through which areal pattern, and occasionally areal policy, have had historical association with national development.[2] The other parallels the economists' concern for leading sectors and considers the notion of "balanced" versus "leading" regions for investment. More generally it focuses upon the dilemma between dispersing economic and social investments on the basis of equity considerations (area or inter-regional balance) and concentrating such investments in limited areas (leading regions).[3] This has blended into the French school of regional input-output and "growth-pôles" analysis whose efficacy is now a matter of some debate.[4]

Governments of underdeveloped countries are attracted to a regional approach in their development policy in varying degrees.[5] However integration

---

[1] In "The Uses of Regional Science: Policy Planning in Chile," Regional Science Association, Papers, Vol. XVIII, Vienna Congress (1966), p. 219.

[2] For example see Harvey S. Perloff, Edgar S. Dunn, Jr., Eric E. Lampard, and Richard F. Muth, Regions, Resources, and Economic Growth (Baltimore: Johns Hopkins Press, 1960); and Benjamin Ward, Greek Regional Development, Research Monograph Series No. 1 (Athens: Center of Economic Research, n. d.).

[3] Here is the potential developmental goal conflict noted above. See Albert O. Hirschman, The Strategy of Economic Growth (New Haven: Yale University Press, 1958), pp. 183-201; John Friedmann, Regional Development Policy, passim; and the essays of Hirschman, Lefebre, Rahman, and Chenery in Regional Development and Planning, ed. John Friedmann and William Alonso (Cambridge: MIT Press, 1964).

[4] See N. M. Hansen, ed., Growth Centers in Regional Economic Development (New York: Free Press, 1972), and Antoni Kuklinski, Growth Poles and Growth Centres in Regional Planning (Hague: Mouton, 1972).

[5] Clearly there is interest in Chile, Brazil, and Venezuela, Turkey, Indonesia, and even Thailand. See John Friedmann, Regional Development Policy; Friedmann and Stohr; Stefan H. Robock, Brazil's Developing Northeast (Washington: Brookings Institution, 1963); Malcolm D. Rivkin, Area Development for National Growth: The Turkish Precedent (New York: Praeger, 1965); Government of Indonesia, Rantjana Pembangunan Lima Tahun (Djakarta: Department of Information, 1969); and P. Uathavikul, "Regional Planning as a Tool for Develop-

of regional concern into national overall planning has been a problem. As
Friedmann notes,

> The traditional approach has been to view regional development planning
> (and associated planning for urbanization) as a concern with local issues
> primarily by local people and more especially by those who live in the
> economically distressed parts of a country.[1]

Thus not only has regional concern been directed primarily to problem areas,
but the tendency has been to treat them separately, and to leave them to their
own administrative devices, even though they may occupy inordinately (by Western standards) large amounts of the national area.[2]

Use of the expression "regional planning" has led, naturally, to a concentration on conceptions of and planning for areal problems on an intra- and
sometimes inter-regional basis.[3] Regional planning has meant planning for and
of regions, rather than on a broader and more diversified areal basis.[4] And

---

ment: The Case of Thailand" (Bangkok: National Institute of Development Administration, 1969), fugitive, p. 2.

[1] Regional Development Planning, p. 3.

[2] See Lloyd Rodwin, "Choosing Regions for Development," Regional Development and Planning, ed. Friedmann and Alonso, p. 40. Malaysia is a case in
point: the recognized underdeveloped regions are the East Coast of Malaya and
East Malaysia. All have comparatively greater state government autonomy,
especially Sabah and Sarawak; and although "balanced regional development" is
a development plan objective, it is not actively pursued. (See below, and John C.
Beyer, "Regional Inequalities and Economic Growth in Malaysia," Yorkshire
Bulletin of Economic and Social Research, XXI [May, 1969], 17-30).

[3] This returns perhaps to Hartshorne, and others' conception of geography
as having region as its central organizing construct. (Cf. David Harvey's discussion in Explanation in Geography [New York: St. Martin's Press, 1969], p.
125, et passim.) Even in the Soviet Union, regionalism in industrial location
policy and administration seems to take precedence over that "territorial principle" by which the economy can be viewed as a whole. In India, there have been
attempts at industrial location control, but they have been founded on a poorly
conceived central government conception of "proper" regional distribution. See
P. J. D. Wiles, The Political Economy of Communism (Cambridge: Harvard
University Press, 1962), pp. 148-65; Irwin Roth, "Industrial Location and
Indian Government Policy," Asian Survey, X (May, 1970), 383-96; and L. S.
Bhat, Some Aspects of Regional Planning in India (New Delhi: Indian Statistical
Institute, 1963); and see also N. S. Ginsburg, "The Regional Concept and Plan-
ning Regions," Regional Planning (New York: United Nations, Department of
Economic and Social Affairs, 1959), pp. 38-42; and United Nations, Decentraliza-
tion for National and Local Development (New York: United Nations, 1962), p.
19, for general considerations.

[4] This despite T. A. Reiner's weak definition of regional planning as "efforts which lead to allocation consciously, if not very scientifically, made on a
spatial basis," in "Sub-National and National Planning: Decision Criteria,"

despite the exhortations of Friedmann and others the governments of developing
countries, except where they perceive momentous regionalized political problems, have been unimpressed with the need for considering areal elements, so
conceived, in development planning. Regional approaches have not seemed particularly useful for central planning, while sophisticated areal planning has not
been developed. Explicit full-blown areal policy in national plans is virtually
unknown. One searches practically in vain in the political science and geographical literatures for discussions of the relationship between area and policy. [1]
Only development administration, a sub-field, offers areally oriented asser-
tions. Here there is a practical interest in the problem of concentration versus
deconcentration, especially of power. [2]

Regional Science Association, Papers, Vol. XIV, Ghent Congress (1964), pp.
107-36. A good example of the limited areal conception of development planning to date is found in L. B. M. Mennes, Jan Tinbergen, and J. George Waardenburg, The Element of Space in Development Planning (Amsterdam: North
Holland, 1969), in which the authors remark: "In national planning the element
of space will show itself first of all if it is desired to split up a national plan
into plans for parts of the country, which we call regions" (p. 49).

[1]Three partial exceptions are Friedmann's Regional Development Policy;
Malcolm Rivkin's Area Development for National Growth; and Roy I. Wolfe,
Transportation and Politics (Princeton: Van Nostrand, 1963).

[2]However no profound help is forthcoming, viz. "the power to achieve
significant progress can be obtained only through some combination of centralization and decentralization." Bertram Gross, The Administration of Economic
Development Planning: Principles and Fallacies (New York: United Nations,
1966), p. 50. Henry Maddick observes with no great utility, that "whilst development needs point to decentralization in both under-developed and developed
countries alike the trend is toward centralization," in Democracy, Decentralization and Development (Bombay: Asia Publishing House, 1963), p. 28. There
has been some theoretical and empirical work in the analysis of the nature of
areal administration in geography too, including that of Christaller, Losch,
Philbrick, Robert H. Brown (Political Areal-Functional Organization: With
Special Reference to St. Cloud, Minnesota, Research Paper No. 51 [Chicago:
University of Chicago, Department of Geography, 1957]), and J. B. R. Whitney
(China: Area, Administration, and Nation Building). None of these treats the
use of areal administrative units for particular central government policy purposes. Nor does Maass, in Area and Power. Studies concentrating on regional
administrative problems include: United States Natural Resources Committee,
Regional Factors in National Planning (Washington: United States Government
Printing Office, 1945); and the United Nations' Regional Planning; and Handbook
of Public Administration (New York: United Nations, 1961). See also Decentralization for National and Local Development. In this and the above sources
are to be found generally unsupported recommendations on the use of intermediate regional units for the administration of certain programs, for instance the
dubious assertion that "A plan of administration which will permit the greatest
possible number of actions to be taken in the areas, states, provinces, districts,
towns and villages where the people reside is an inherent need of an effective

Cities

Urbanization, as both a process and a policy problem in relation to development, has become the exception to this generalized broad absence of discussion of area in policy. Cities throughout the world have lately been recognized as units of areal organization having problems of national significance. They are increasingly seen as a burden in the Third World, including Malaysia, because of rapid growth rates, unaccompanied by concomitant industrial development.[1] Cities and towns are said to have become repositories of underemployment, shared-poverty, social discontent, and environmental malaise. Urban policy such as it exists concentrates on limiting or reversing metropolitan growth and on creating new settlement points.[2] Yet, most recently urban areas have been described as possibly desirable targets of specific development (as opposed to welfare) policies, owing to certain unique attributes which are essential to national modernization. D. W. Fryer writes:

---

government" (my emphasis, in United Nations, Handbook of Public Administration, p. 36).

[1]Not all industrialization is an answer to urban problems, of course: modern industry, as noted by Norton Ginsburg, is a relatively light employer, especially of poorly-skilled labor. "Here lies one of the major problems of economic development in Asian countries, the evolution of a pattern of industrial activity which provides productive employment for rapidly expanding labor forces" (in "Planning the Future of the Asian City," The City as a Center of Change in Asia, ed. D. W. Dwyer [Hong Kong: University of Hong Kong, in press]). W. F. Wertheim points out the even more dramatic connection between urban popular welfare and economic development in Indonesia in remarking, "if a great proportion of the urban population is not to starve, a much larger number of jobs has to be created than is reconcilable with efficient management" (in East-West Parallels [Hague: Hoeve, 1964], p. 173). See also David R. Kamerschen in "Further Analysis of Overurbanization," Economic Development and Cultural Change, XVII (January, 1969), 235-53, who has found no significant positive relationship between industrialization and urbanization in a large number of countries treated.

[2]See especially The New Urban Debate (Washington: Agency for International Development, 1968), p. 2, in which it is written: "National development entails change, and cities are primarily agents of change." William Alonso comments, at least, that, "in brief, there is no basis for belief that primacy or over-urbanization per se is detrimental to the efficiency of economic development" ("Urban and Regional Imbalance and Economic Development," Economic Development and Cultural Change, XVII October, 1969 , 4). Four mutually reinforcing links between continued urbanization and industrial development are suggested to be (1) labor supply (it is preferable to have the marginally employed in urban areas), (2) market concentration, (3) availability of capital, and (4) managerial and entrepreneurial talent, all grown and maintained in urban areas. United Nations, Urbanization: Development Policies and Planning (New York: United Nations, 1968), p. 72.

It is, unfortunately, only too true that with a few striking exceptions, the return on public investment in agriculture and rural problems in the Third World has been extremely disappointing; and most would agree that the main agencies promoting modernization originate in the cities, and having arisen thereafter constitute a powerful stimulus to further urban growth, both economically and geographically. Yet their exact nature and modus operandi continue to elude us.[1]

Cities may be the preëminent machines through which development and modernization are achieved. One look at the city/development relationship, however, reveals it to be as complicated as everything else. This is partly because of a confusion in the use of the term "development," as related to cities, confusion on the meaning of city, and partly, too, because research has not yet been concentrated sufficiently on the question. Confusion arises because four interrelated but necessarily separable processes are going on: (1) urbanization, that is growth of cities and urban population absolutely and at the expense of rural or pre-urban populations. This may or may not be accompanied by "urbanism," the dynamic cultural-economic change on which progress seems based; (2) cities acting and reacting in national development terms. They receive development policy impulses (expenditures and administration) and they fulfill (or not) policy expectations, as for instance in their private sectors; (3) the development of cities, whereby cities change in form and function, character and value. This is certainly not synonymous with either urbanization or optimal contribution to or rôle in national development; and (4) city malaise, which is largely a function of urbanization, but also the product of other forces and negative developments. This can become a large problem in a nation and an important object of development policy, even though it is a negative welfare phenomenon and may not be related functionally to national or positive city development.

---

[1]My emphasis, in "National Development Plans and the Budget: Public Sector Resources for Urbanization," SEADAG Discussion Paper (New York: The Asia Society, 1969), p. 1. A contrary view is held by T. G. McGee, who writes ". . . in the context of Southeast Asia, it seems that a theoretical framework which regards the city as the prime catalyst of change must be discarded. Rather, the city must be seen as a symptom of processes operating at a societal level. Thus to accurately diagnose the characteristics of cities, one must investigate the condition of underdevelopment which characterizes these countries. In these terms, the cities only too frequently may be described as cancers not catalysts" (in "The Urbanization Process: Western Theory and Southeast Asian Experience" [Hong Kong: University of Hong Kong, fugitive, 1969], p. 22). This argument is belied in Malaysia. The explicit reverse view is at present carried by the "trickle-down" theorists. See for example V. Nichols, "Growth Poles: An Evaluation of Their Propulsive Effect," Environmental Planning, I (1969).

Confusion persists in the planning and development literature among
these processes. They are often just lumped into a vague problem category
called "urbanization." Thus, the crucial positive functions of cities in development are obscured, and urbanization (with or without urbanism) and city malaise
are confused. Differentiation between the development of cities and national
development in (or through) cities, often competitive, is missed. This is
despite the fact that development policy as steps to achieve goals of change in a
national area, is intimately concerned with cities. Such concern, as with area
in general, is often not explicit.[1] It happens, as will be seen below, that much
national sectoral policy action is located in urban areas and/or administered
from them.[2]

Middle cities have been chosen for examination in this study for two reasons: (1) their possibly pivotal rôle in urbanization and modernization in the
Third World; and (2) the near absence in the policy-oriented literature of mention of their problems and significance. Middle cities should be of importance
for reason of their large numbers and wide distribution throughout underdeveloped countries, including Malaysia. The term "middle" has been adopted,
moreover (instead of "middle-sized," or "intermediate") in order to convey

---

[1]"Urban policy," for example, does not exist as an overt aspect of national policy in Southeast Asia except in Singapore where to call it that is redundant, in Northeast Thailand and South Vietnam where there was a war, and,
lately in Malaysia where there has been insurgency, riots, and racial rancor.
Rarely, anywhere, are there national agencies devoted exclusively to urbanization; nor are they necessarily desirable; although in Latin America "the overhead costs of rapid urbanization--costs of public works, housing, and social
services suited to urban conditions--may absorb such a high proportion of national expenditures that a planning body can hardly avoid the subject" ("Some
Policy Implications of Urbanization," Urbanization in Latin America, ed. Philip
Hauser [Paris: UNESCO, 1961], p. 300. Cf. James F. Guyot, "Creeping
Urbanism and Political Development in Malaysia," Comparative Urban Research:
The Administration and Politics of Cities, ed. Robert T. Daland [Beverly Hills:
Sage Publications, 1969], pp. 124-61).

[2]P. N. Rosenstein-Rodan notes that a large share of all overhead investments come to be channeled into urban areas of underdeveloped countries ("Les
besoins de capitaux dans les pays sous-developpés," Economie Appliqué, VII
[January-June, 1954], pp. 77-87). Fryer, in discussing the national plans of
Thailand and Malaysia remarks: "In sum there is little to indicate any marked
degree of rural bias in the development plans of the two countries" ("National
Development Plans and the Budget," p. 12). This is apparent, respecting Ma-
laysia, also to Lim Tay Boh; see Problems of the Malayan Economy (Singapore:
Donald Moore, 1960), p. 24. For a discussion of urban bias in Indian develop-
ment planning see Michael Lipton, "Strategy for Agriculture: Urban Bias and
Rural Planning," The Crisis of Indian Planning, ed. Paul Streeten and Michael
Lipton (London: Oxford University Press, 1968), pp. 130-45.

more than the notion of relative size. These cities in the Third World are theoretically "middle" in other ways significant to development, ways not made strictly regular or predictable by their relative positions in the city system, and only observable through micro-area or ecological analysis. They seem to be (1) way stations in rural-urban migration patterns and other upward flows; (2) receptacles of important communication and developmental impulses and innovations on the way from the central governments capitals and metropoles to the people and the countryside; (3) at once the outposts of central authority and the nodes of countervailing (peripheral) regional power; and (4) centers where increasing permanent population and economic growth, and administrative-budgetary authority may accrue.

That middle cities have been practically ignored in the literature[1] results from the concentration of research effort on the largest cities of the world, the ones best documented and most convenient to study.[2] Other work on urbanization has stressed national and international city systems and hierarchies, at one extreme,[3] and intensive analysis of very small settlement units on the other.[4]

---

[1] W. A. Withington is the only social scientist to seriously address the question of the importance of Middle Cities (his expression is "intermediate City") in Southeast Asia. His work, as yet uncompleted, stresses comparison of the positions of Middle Cities within the city systems of Southeast Asian countries. His definition can comprise cities of a population as low as 10,000; but for analysis of central government policy cities in the range of 10,000 to 25,000 are too variable as to availability and reliability of data to be useful in an overall analysis. A category of "small city," which grades off into extended villages and then compounds might be explored separately. (See "The Intermediate City in the Developing World of Southeast Asia," SEADAG Discussion Paper [New York: The Asia Society, 1970], fugitive.) See also Leighton W. Hazelhurst, "The Middle-Range City in India," Asian Survey, VIII (July, 1968), 539-52. Here the stress is on an economic functional and structural definition, rather than position in national flows or population size.

[2] For example, the work of R. J. W. Neville on Singapore; of Laurence Sternstein on Bangkok; and of H. J. Heeren on Djakarta.

[3] For example N. S. Ginsburg, "The Great City in Southeast Asia," American Journal of Sociology, LX (March, 1955), 455-62; Hamzah Sendut, "Patterns of Urbanization in Malaya," The Journal of Tropical Geography, XVI (October, 1962), 114-30; and Pauline Milone, Urban Areas in Indonesia: Administrative and Census Concepts (Berkeley: University of California, Institute of International Studies, 1966).

[4] For example, Barrington Kaye, Upper Nankin Street Singapore: A Sociological Study of Chinese Households Living in a Densely Populated Area (Singapore: University of Malaya Press, 1960); and Koentjaraningrat, ed., Villages in Indonesia (Ithaca: Cornell University Press, 1967).

A clearer view is needed of the relative potential importance of Middle Cities in the creation and implementation of government development policies.[1]

The Geography of Development Policy

The four associations in a geography of policy discussed above may be recast into two sets. The first, consists of explicit and implicit locational decisions of a government. These include concerns for areal scale of management as well as pointal, lineal, and areal location of activity, and are based on perceptions of areal pattern and its significance in the country. These decisions form Area in Policy. Second, there are the actual policy acts and interactions within and among areas, points, and lines. They comprise Policy in Area. There may well be discrepancies between the areal perceptions, designs, and management in a development policy and the actual location and areal interactions of policy activities on the ground. That will be explored in Malaysian development policy below.

Area in Development Policy

This study posits an areal logic to development (or any) policy consisting of three classes of decisions and actions which, taken together, are exhaustive and are underlain by a set of assumptions about process. These classes are:

(1) where[2] things are wanted,

(2) where things are put, and

(3) where things are believed to be.

---

[1] For a preliminary attempt to get at one aspect of this problem, see Stanford Research Institute, Costs of Urban Infrastructure for Industry as Related to City Size in Developing Countries: India Case Studies (Menlo Park: Stanford Research Institute, 1968). The authors conclude, for the specific region of India on which they concentrated (and in the 18 cities that cluster analysis showed had similar relevant characteristics) that:

Unit costs of an increment of infrastructure, in terms of public investment and for a large industrial expansion, are virtually equal for cities above 130,000 population . . . When coupled with emerging industrial patterns in cities of different size, observed in the field study, this cost finding suggests that the search for opportunities for industrial agglomeration may start in cities around 130,000 to 300,000 . . . These conclusions confirm the importance of establishing a regional basis for industrial development efforts, identifying cities that are suitably located and can be efficiently equipped for different types of industries, and fostering effective complementarity among cities of different size.

[2] Generally, where must be to a point, line, or region (area). The middle city from the central government viewpoint may be seen as either a point or a region, depending upon scale and objective.

Things that the government may want to be located or go on in a certain areal array for development purposes include mainly capital and administration.[1] Also, however, the government in its development plan will have certain expectations of development activity. The plan may very well revolve around expectations of certain production, capital accumulation, employment, or other activity and its growth--over which the central government may have no direct control. Nevertheless, the pattern of the expectations will be a significant part of the areal logic of the development policy, and will, to a degree, be mappable.

Where things are wanted and put is determined in part by where things are believed to be, that is, on strategic intelligence available to a national government. Since generally the government is likely to have all the information available, it is difficult to do more with this segment of the logic than to identify inconsistencies and gaps in knowledge and to analyze the use to which areal intelligence is put.

The matter of where in the areal logic of development policy turns on areal concepts and administration. Policy flows to and through a middle city (diagrammed in Figure 1) are initially subject to filters of conceptual area (or the set of notions of areal units, types and dynamics in the minds of policymakers) and administrative area.[2]

Development policy is acted out according to an underlying set of assumptions about how things work in areas--the "development ecology" of areas. Such beliefs may stem from empiricist and theoretical literature--as with the center-periphery dichotomy in development,[3] or from an actual absence of technical

---

[1]Things that a government puts may be categorized thus: (1) money (government-owned or -controlled, including credit, (2) resources (real or potential production factors, usually investment, but including population), (3) channels of communication to the recipient system, (4) administrative authority, and (5) administrative responsibility. The determining characteristic of the first four categories is capital management and areal allocation of it, as, for example, to a middle city. When the areal patterns of development policy are analyzed in the area in policy chapters, it is investment under the development budget that is mapped. Administrative authority and responsibility likewise may be most readily defined in terms of control of capital resources and budgetary autonomy. This is feasible when a country separates its development from its routine budget, thereby facilitating the identification of the "development" intent of the central government.

[2]See Chapter III.

[3]See Friedmann, Regional Development Policy, and Stefan Robock, Brazil's Developing Northeast. Higgins et al., make the dubious but testable statement that, "both [peasant-handicraft-low productivity versus plantation-mining-high productivity] sectors are [in developing countries] usually distinct geograph-

guidance--as on the comparative efficiency of settlements of various sizes in
development. [1] Administrative Area in policy involves the location of administrative authority and responsibility[2] through a set of organizing units whose

---

ically . . . Sometimes they represent quite different regions. Nearly always
the two sectors appear in a contrast between one or a few large and growing
cities and the surrounding country-side--Djakarta, Surabaya and Indonesia . . .
Manila and the Philippines . . . " (C. Haar, B. Higgins, and L. Rodwin, "Economic and Physical Planning: Coordination in Developing Countries, " Journal
of the American Institute of Planners, XXIV [January, 1958], 169). The problem of significance here is that "big push" sectorally balanced growth strategies,
stressing complementarity of several sectors seem to be likely to yield sharp
differences in regional rates of growth (an implicit areal facet of policy) with a
bias--especially evident in the private sector, toward the more developed centers. (See W. F. Ilchman and R. C. Bhargava, "Balanced Thought and Economic Growth, " Economic Development and Cultural Change, XIV, No. 14 [July,
1966], 388).

[1]William Alonso ("Industrial Location and Regional Policy, " p. 34), Rodwin, and others have vaguely recommended creation of some pôles de crois-
sance, of course. (See Lloyd Rodwin, "Metropolitan Policy for Developing
Areas, " Regional Economic Planning: Techniques of Analysis, ed. Walter
Isard and J. H. Cumberland [Paris: O. E. C. D., 1960], p. 226.) And the Stanford Research Institute Case Study (op. cit.) makes strides in the direction of
specification for a region of India. Alonso comments elsewhere that "there are
good grounds for believing in increasing [economic development] returns to
urban size" ("Urban and Regional Imbalance, " loc. cit.).

[2]These may often be coincident, but the distinction is useful; for authority
involves the location of decision-making power, whoever's money is being spent,
and may involve "decentralization" of central power only; while responsibility
involves essentially the control of money for development, including its acquisition, and this certainly means a measure of "devolved" power. Maass discusses
this distinction in Area and Power, pp. 9-26. Thus, the central government
acts in two ways in distributing power: (1) negotiation with and assignment of
powers and sources of support among areal units (assignment of administrative
authority and responsibility through devolution); and (2) creation of its own executive administrative system having a specific areal form (decentralization).
Sometimes there is overlap of devolved and decentralized operations, as in the
state governments of Malaysia, where there are state and federal officers assigned to various development activities, and state and federal funds being dis-
pensed. In short, policy often is administered in constant conflict between central (national) and local interests and administrative units. William Alonso
comments: "it is therefore clear that the functions of regional planning, in contrast to that of sectoral planning, will be continually disrupted and enriched by
the introduction of local voices into the rumblings of processional technical dis-
course" (in "Industrial Location and Regional Policy in Economic Development, "
p. 10). He neglects the kind of competitiveness and conflict experienced among
departments or ministries of a central government whose functions yield particular sectoral development policy biases, for instance road versus rail transport,
or industrial versus agricultural capital development expenditure. See also
H. Franz Schurmann, Ideology and Organization in Communist China (Berkeley:
University of California Press, 1966), pp. 175-76; and cf. Bertram Gross, The
Administration of Economic Development Planning, p. 50, et passim.

areal nature may be very different from one another. It is the central ambition of this monograph, to explore whether area does, indeed, make any difference to development policy outcomes.

Development Policy in Area

Development policy is applied to and within area in the form of attention to points and lines--as when goal-achievement is intended through the simple act of location with no local administrative or policy activity requirements[1]-- and to several kinds of regions, conceptualized as having functional regionality, homogeneity, or some condition that differentiates an area from the rest of the national territory.[2] Having seen how various are the concepts of area in policy, however, the analysis of development policy in area must take a two-fold approach. First, a comparison is made of the intent to locate policy activity according to various areal concepts with the actual distribution of development policy activity, primarily development budget investments. This is done, for Malaysia, on a district basis, as well as among cities, with correlations to other district and city data.[3]

Second, in order to get at the ecology of development policy, i.e. the interaction of national development policy with the contents and structures of

---

[1]Examples might be financial assistance to private enterprises, or price controls.

[2]For example "rural" versus "urban" economic areas, which do not include plantation agriculture, but both of which might include traditional kampong areas within developing cities. Cf. Ginsburg, "The Regional Concept and Planning Regions," for the standard typology of regions in policy.

[3]Lloyd Rodwin (Nations and Cities, p. 13) has belatedly suggested that "development maps" showing locational patterns of past and future development policies be developed. The Policy in Area--National Patterns maps below go as far in this direction as it is possible to go for Malaysia, and may indicate possibilities for future work, although it could also be concluded, on examining them, that the exercise only graphically sets forth the obvious. Rodwin does not suggest this possibility. His other suggestion is that regional capital budgets be created. In Malaysia this is approached by a combination of the sum of federal development policy expenditures in combination with the State development budgets, and those, when apparent, of important local governments. It is interesting that governments have not been very interested in mapping even regional expenditure patterns, not to mention the more complicated overall areal structure of development activity that Rodwin suggests and I attempt below. (Cf. Bruce H. Herrick, Urban Migration and Economic Development in Chile [Cambridge: MIT Press, 1965], pp. 35-36, who comments that "In Chile the absence of regional accounting for government expenditures makes regional policy, even if clearly formulated and legislatively approved, difficult to carry out.")

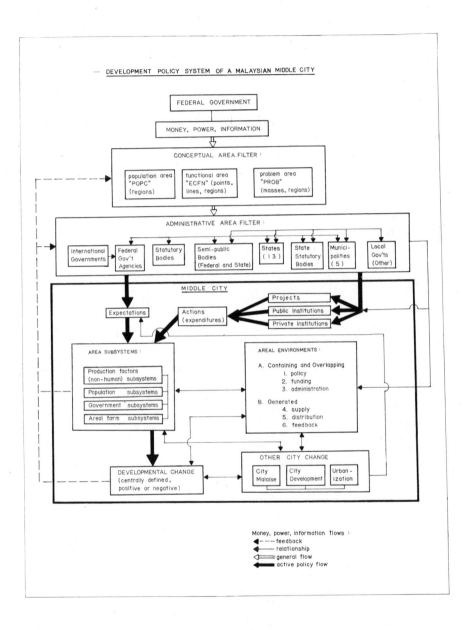

Fig. 1.--Development Policy System of a Malaysian Middle City

areas, certain places are examined. These are all Middle Cities, of several types. But a framework is needed in order to sort out the elements of applied areal development policy. So a model of the Development Policy System and its interaction with an area has been elaborated, in the form of a flow-chart (Figure 1).

This system contains the elements in a vertical array whereby development policy, and the money, power, and information that are its impulses, are moved through institutions to and through an areal unit of organization, a middle city. These development policy impulses may have been aimed at points, lines, this area or a conceptual area or mass of which the particular area is only a part. They are in any case, then, seen to interact with the institutions and sub-systems of the areal unit that are relevant to centrally defined development and with environments of the local area system that likewise seem relevant. Not all elements of centrally evolved development policy are included, only those involved in the policy area interaction at the local level. The model is conceived for the purpose of systematically identifying the elements important to the interaction and, in so far as possible, their interrelationships.

The development policy system of a Malaysian area, or Middle City, consists of a flow of money, power, and information through the conceptual area and administrative area filters to an area. Central government agencies, state agencies, semi-public institutions, and local governments all partake of development policy activity at the local level. There projects and public and private institutions receive the impulses. They interact with environments which contain and overlap them and which they themselves generate. Four subsystems of the area may be identified and seen to effect the success of the development policy activities: the production factor's sub-system, the population sub-system, the government sub-system, and the areal pattern sub-system. Developmental change is the goal and product of the system. It feeds back to policy-making and administering elements of the whole system.

The Study

This study treats Malaysia as a national unit. That has meant a concentration on the years after 1965. And it has necessitated a treatment of both Malaya and the Bornean States of Sabah and Sarawak as components of the same system even though in many senses, including that of statistical accounting by the national government, they are still very separate.

The strategy, followed sequentially in the chapters below has been first to briefly survey the development history of the territories that came to be Malaysia, including analysis of the development policies carried out in them. This was followed by examination of Malaysian development policy, the First and Second Malaysia Plans and concurrent policies, with reference to past development policies as a key to Area in Policy concerns, particularly of conceptual and administrative area.

The national patterns of Policy in Area were then set out in a series of maps and statistical analyses, with emphasis on change over time (from the pre-Malaysia period), and on changing proportions of development expenditures assigned to four and three conceptual areal types of projects. And these analyses, in turn, suggested a division of the set of Middle Cities into groups from which case studies were chosen and carried out.

Specifically, for the Malaysian area three time-periods of development policy were taken: 1950-1961, 1961-1965 (The Second Malaya Plan), and 1966-1968 (the first three, and only researchable years of The First Malaysia Plan). All areally definable development expenditures were mapped by district according to these four (and for Middle Cities the last three) conceptual categories: Urban (in town or city areas of >5,000 population), POPC (Population Coverage expenditures intended to follow population distribution), PROB (Problem Area expenditures destined for areas with special problems inherent in them), and ECFN (Economic-Functional expenditures whose locations are determined by the economic or development functions of their target areas or projects). This three-way classification of POPC, PROB, and ECFN is exhaustive and was intended to reflect the basic breakdown of concepts underlying location of development activity in Malaysia. Among these, appropriate correlation and cluster analyses were made on District, Middle City, and State data matrices. Factor analyses for districts and cities isolated independent patterns over the periods from among the development expenditures and other variables.

All of this national-scale policy in area material was then compared with preceding area in policy observations on the conceptual and administrative area content of Malaysian development policy. Finally, the development policy systems of nine Malaysian Middle Cities were examined (as well as possible, considering the paucity of city data) in order to isolate key functions and blockages in the overall system--by way of their development ecologies. Preceding analysis suggested the following sets of case study cities, covering, for Malaysia, a wide range of development experience: (1) three small cities--Alor Setar, Keluang, and Kota Baharu; (2) three singular cities--Ipoh, Sandakan, and

Kuching; and (3) the Penang Metropolitan Area--George Town, Butterworth-Prai (Province Wellesley Utara), and Ayer Itam Village. The results were uneven, but are not without value.

Malaysia is a well-documented country. The government produces tardy but highly reliable budgetary estimates and audits. The Department of Statistics supplies frequent surveys, censuses, and studies of economic indicators. For geographical investigation however, there have been drawbacks: (1) areal specificity rarely goes as far down as the district level in economic production and other tabulations; (2) the last complete population census publication was for 1957 and the 1970 census will not be fully available until 1973, although totals for districts are now available; and (3) in development-policy expenditure documents, areal specificity is uneven; it is mostly absent in the Development Estimates, and when sought through the relevant ministries is capricious as to form and availability even though government officials have the greatest desire to help and make great effort to provide information.

The history of Malaysia is well documented for the British period. For the study of the origins of the development policy of the central government, both official documents and the many excellent analytical histories have been of great value. Analysis of recent Area in Policy has proceeded through use of such documents, particularly those of the Economic Planning Unit and the Development Administration Unit and their forerunners, and the many fine scholarly studies of the 1950's and 1960's.

For Policy in Area, patterns of national development expenditures have been plotted and matrices filled for 111 districts, 28 Middle Cities (including the addition, for comparative purposes, of Kuala Lumpur), and the 13 states of Malaysia. Development expenditures or investment are the only major quantifiable measures of development policy activity.[1] No more than 63 per cent of development expenditures for any period has been plotted, however. Some expenditures, by their nature, such as purchase of capital equipment abroad could not be pinpointed, but are most likely destined for points already heavily invested in, such as electric power stations. In another case, the location pattern of expenditures for Federal Land Development Authority projects since 1963 inexplicably could not be obtained; although a large share is known to have

---

[1]There is some precedent for taking investment as the fundamental process in economic development and government investment as fundamental in government development policy. See Gayl Ness, Bureaucracy and Rural Development in Malaysia (Berkeley: University of California Press, 1967), p. 10.

gone to the Jengka Triangle, already heavily invested in as well. The sample of data that has been mapped for Chapter IV represents all the data available from central government authorities, but they should be accepted as only suggesting salient patterns.[1]

When Policy in Area was explored at the local level in the Middle Cities, an entirely different set of data and interpretive sources was sought. Here mathematical approaches seemed unlikely, except for a few statistical measures,[2] and it has been necessary to rely on depth interviews with officials and business men and on the scarcely comparable studies of the cities provided by government and private organizations over the years.[3] The case studies present as coherent a picture of policy system activity and impact as it has been possible to obtain in the absence of a large-scale survey approach. With the application of the Development Policy System model, the Middle City in national development rises in relief against the flow of national events, and as the components of its particular system are pieced together. The cities' rôles in national development are distinguishable from the phenomena of urbanization, the development of cities, and urban malaise, in their relationships to the development policy system. From the analysis come observations on the efficacy of locational, administrative, and perceptive procedures in national development planning and operation in modern Malaysia.

---

[1]No more than a suggestion is intended. See discussion of the fallacy of puristic induction in Oran R. Young, "Professor Russett: Industrious Tailor to a Naked Emperor," World Politics, XXI (April, 1969), 486-511, especially pp. 489-93; and Edward Shils, quoted in Robert K. Merton and Daniel Lerner, "Social Scientists and Research Policy," The Policy Sciences, ed. Lerner and Lasswell, p. 292. And for a discussion of the present limitation on the usefulness of mathematical models in the social sciences, see May Brodbeck, "Models, Meaning, and Theories," Readings in the Philosophy of the Social Sciences, ed. May Brodbeck (New York: Macmillan, 1968), pp. 579-601, especially, pp. 598-600.

[2]It has been said, in any case, that, "the importance of organizational and administrative dimensions calls for a relaxation of the arithmorphic slant of hypothesis testing . . . " As Georgescu-Peogen puts it: "qualitative change eludes arithmorphic schematization . . . " (T. N. Brewis and G. Paquet, "A Systematic View of Regional Development and Planning," Urban Studies, IV [January, 1967], p. 291).

[3]In Malaysia data are not collected by central agencies about cities except in a few special cases, for example registration and placement through employment-service offices by city. On the other hand most urban areas had some form of attention afforded them by the Town and Country Planning section of the Ministry of Local Government and Housing and/or the state government equivalent agencies.

CHAPTER II

MALAYSIAN AREA AND DEVELOPMENT TO 1966

This chapter identifies the elements that have shaped the changing contents of the territory of what has become Malaysia.[1] It concentrates on forces
of change in those aspects of Malaysian development which bear directly on
later development policy--the human and physical factors of production, the
administration of change, and the perceptions and motivations of the major
groups and organizations that have molded modern Malaysia and set the stage
for the First Malaysia Plan. Singapore is excluded from all but tangential discussion because it has no place in the First Malaysia Plan.

The pattern of natural phenomena and early human occupance in Malaysian territory is fragmented though not complex. The interior areas of the
Malay Peninsula and what became East Malaysia on the island of Borneo are
mountainous. Rivers fed by nearly year-round tropical rainfall bisect the
coastal plains and form great swamp areas. Population has historically been
associated with the river valleys and with the waterways--the major pre-British
routes of movements.[2] Fisher remarks:

> The outstanding geographical characteristic of the Malay Peninsula is
> its unity. Thanks to a basic structural homogeneity, a distinctive equa-
> torial climate and associated vegetation, and the fairly close correlation

---

[1] Malaysia in 1966 consisted of the States of Malaya, including the Straits
Settlements of Penang, Malacca and Labuan, but not Singapore, and, as additional states, Sarawak and Sabah. The latter two, the Borneo States (and
Labuan which is part of Sabah), are called East Malaysia, and the former,
taken together, West Malaysia. West Malaysia and Malaya are synonymous.

[2] The physical geography of Malaya is analyzed at length in Ooi Jin-bee,
Land, People, and Economy in Malaya (London: Longmans, 1963), pp. 3-86.
See pp. 103-25 for a discussion of the evolution of the Malayan population pat-
tern. For Sarawak, see James C. Jackson, Sarawak (London: University of
London Press, 1968), pp. 15-72; and Lee Yong-leng, Population and Settlement
in Sarawak (Singapore: Asia Pacific Press, 1970), pp. 2-37. For Sabah, see
Lee Yong-leng, North Borneo (Sabah): A Study in Settlement Geography (Singapore: Eastern University Press, 1965), pp. 1-27; and Godfrey A. Chatfield,
Sabah: A General Geography (London: University of London Press, 1965), pp.
11-73. See also Charles A. Fisher, South-East Asia (London: Methuen, 1964),
pp. 583-603, 662-72.

24

between the northern limits of these last and the religious-linguistic frontier separating Malays from Siamese [not corresponding to the international boundary established in 1909], Malaya would appear to be an almost perfect example of the hypothetical "geographical region."
The addition of the Borneo States to Malaya makes for a basic division of the Malaysian area; but the structural and early settlement patterns of Malay-stock people in the two areas are quite similar.[1]

Pre-British Activity

Malaya has been important in Asian history for a long time. East Malaysia never has. The importance of Malaya has lain in its position astride trade routes from the Indies and the China Sea westward to India, Arabia, and Europe, and astride migration and cultural dispersion routes east and west, north and south. Its central position has made it the object of repeated and differing forms of control and management from the outside. Malaya became important for its internal self only when tin and later rubber production were raised to high and then spectacular levels. The Borneo States were not economically significant until timber resources of Sabah attracted large-scale exploitation for overseas markets, primarily Japan. They received comparatively little migration of Chinese and Indians accordingly.

The several empires which treated Malaysia before the British had little effect on its internal development. Their perception of it was as an entrepôt, a source of small amounts of tribute and as a minor target of migration.[2] The Sri Vijaya and Majapahit empires of Indonesia and the Kingdom of Thailand, the latter under the wavering suzerainty of China, nominally controlled the Malaya Peninsula through the Fourteenth Century. Locally, small tribal states developed in both Malaya and Borneo, which owed vassalage to overseas empires. By the end of the Fifteenth Century Islam had spread to the Archipelago, with the growing Malacca Sultanate as its center. In 1500 the Malay Peninsula was weakly controlled by Malacca southward from Kedah and Patani.

Malacca, according to tradition, was founded by a disaffected Majapahit

---

[1] Moreover, Fisher observes that "despite its apparent arbitrariness, the 19th-Century division of Borneo into a British and Dutch sphere was geographically sound . . . the boundary between the two political spheres follows the main NW/SE water-parting or related uplands for most of its length" (South-East Asia, pp. 662-63).

[2] Pahang, however, exported increasing amounts of jungle aromatics and tin through the 14th Century. See Paul Wheatley, The Golden Khersonese (Kuala Lumpur: University of Malaya Press, 1961), p. 303.

vassal prince, after a period of residence in Tumasik (a Thai outpost, later Singapore). It developed in the Fifteenth Century into the preëminent trading city and toll-collecting point on the Straits of Malacca, and prospered, in part, because of its adoption of Islam, the religion of traders westward. Though inland or hinterland development was minimal, one notes:

> It is with the founding and growth of the empire of Malacca that the cornerstone of modern Malayan history appears. With Malacca, Malaya becomes an historical, political, cultural, and geographical entity, rather than a peripheral and shadowy appendix to the histories of other cultures. [1]

In 1511 Malacca fell to the Portuguese. The Portuguese had two reasons to covet Malacca: (1) to control the Indian trade, for which reason Goa was captured the year before; and (2) to hinder the spread of Islam. [2] Thus was opened the way for the later four-part imperial struggle in Southeast Asia among the Portuguese, the Spanish, the Dutch, and the British--with added harassment of the Malacca trade monopoly by Achinese and other pirates and agents of rival ports. The Dutch and British trading empires expanded in the Seventeenth Century, finally ceasing to tolerate Portuguese control of Malacca. The Dutch, while trading directly with Java for spices collected throughout the Indies, found it necessary to capture Malacca to solidify their power in the region in 1641. Being unimportant to the spice trade, Malacca became a backwater notwithstanding a Dutch interest in Malayan tin, which was brought to Malacca by Indian, British, and other traders. The Dutch sought exclusive power to trade in it at Malacca, and forced treaties to that effect on the rulers of Perak and Kedah during this time.

Meanwhile, the several Malay states not only fought a great deal among themselves, they also traded and resisted expansion of Dutch economic power. The Sultan of Johore had aided the Dutch in taking Malacca from the Portuguese: but from then on was a serious trading rival, despite occasional treaties. Likewise Perak, whose tin the Dutch sought, struggled for independence of action, especially in trade. With Kedah, Perak suffered a Dutch blockade but still managed to trade with outsiders, notably the Achinese and Portuguese. The Dutch,

---

[1] Preceding paragraphs adapted and this quotation taken from Norton Ginsburg and Chester F. Roberts Jr., Malaya (Seattle: University of Washington Press, 1958), pp. 16-26; quotation, p. 26. See also R. I. Windstedt, A History of Malaya (Singapore: Marican and Sons, 1962), pp. 29-64; and John Bastin and Robin W. Winks, eds., Malaysia: Selected Historical Readings (London: Oxford University Press, 1966), pp. 1-32.

[2] See D. G. E. Hall, A History of South-East Asia (New York: St. Martin's Press, 1965), pp. 215-47.

in short, coped unevenly with the internal politics of often hostile princely states and with the trading interests of outside powers, including the Bugis.[1]

The British Approach 1786-1895

During the Seventeenth Century Great Britain was concerned to manage and protect her interests in India, and increase her Eastern trade generally, for example with establishment of several short-lived factories in the Malay Archipelago that succumbed to Dutch competition and force. Her first lasting approach to Malaya was for purposes of naval strategy (primarily directed at the French but also with the Dutch in mind)[2] in the Indian Ocean. A repair and supply depot was needed on the eastern side of the Bay of Bengal.[3] Possibilities were examined in Burma and the Andaman Islands. The island of Penang was chosen by Captain Francis Light who, with difficulty, persuaded the East India Company of its worth. He established a settlement there named George Town in 1786, made possible through a generous agreement with the Sultan of Kedah.[4]

From 1786 to 1805 the island was a dependency of Bengal. In 1805 Penang became an Indian Presidency, accompanying what came to be seen as excessive optimism as to Penang's worth as a trading center and her effectiveness as a naval base. In fact, the establishment of the naval base was a major factor in the elevation of Penang's status. So it was especially unhappy that by 1807 the scheme had to be abandoned because of labor and materials, as well as financial shortages. Meanwhile, in 1800 piracy caused the Penang authorities to expand onto the mainland so that the harbor could be fully protected.[5] In

---

[1] Sea people from Macassar who had designs on Western Malaya that were not checked until the end of the 18th Century.

[2] See B. K. Basselt, "European Influence in the Malay Peninsula," Journal of the Malayan Branch of the Royal Asiatic Society, XXXIII, pt. 3 (1960), 31.

[3] In winter the East India squadron took shelter at Bombay, leaving the Coromandel Coast open to French attack from Mauritius in the absence of a southeastern base.

[4] The Sultan was to receive $30,000 a year "in respect of the Sultan's former profit from his monopoly of tin, opium, and rattan at the mouths of the rivers nearest to Penang, the Muda, the Prai, and the Krian," and of defensive assistance (K. G. Tregonning, The British in Malaya: The First Forty Years [Tucson: University of Arizona Press, 1965], p. 75).

[5] Another reason may have been Penang's desire for independence in food supply. (See L. A. Mills, British Malaya 1824-6 [Singapore: Journal of the Malayan Branch of the Royal Asiatic Society, XXXIII, pt. 3 (1960) (originally published in 1924)], p. 49.)

1800 a three-mile wide strip of land between the Muda and Krian Rivers, Province Wellesley, was ceded to the British by the Sultan of Kedah at an annual cost of $4,000.[1]

By 1811 Britain was paramount in the Indian Ocean and the original need for Penang was permanently removed. Its second purpose, trade, was given little chance to fulfill itself. The British took over Malacca in 1795 (returning it briefly to the Dutch in 1818 and retrieving it again in 1824 under the terms of the Treaty of London which separated British and Dutch spheres of influence in the Indies once and for all), but also failed to significantly increase her trade. In 1819 Sir Stamford Raffles established Singapore. Superior in every way as an entrepôt, Singapore was to gradually eclipse Penang as the major trade center:

> Penang to some extent remained the center for the trade of Siam, Burma, Achin, and the western states of the Peninsula, but its position rendered it unsuitable, as compared to Singapore, for the commerce of the Archipelago and of China. Malacca, hampered by the silting up of its harbor, retained a small trade with Sumatra and its Malay hinterland.[2]

Penang's agriculture was a disappointment also, except for sugar, which was grown by Chinese cultivators who had a monopoly on sugar-planting from before 1800. The Chinese were already a potent economic force in Penang at the turn of the Century, as they were to become in Singapore soon after.[3]

In 1826 British powers sought to consolidate their holdings in Malaya and placed Singapore and Malacca under the control of Penang. In 1830 the three were made, together, the Residency of the Straits Settlements under the authority of Bengal, which was a reduction in status from Presidency. From 1824 to 1867 Singapore grew rapidly in population trade and power in the region. In 1832 it was made capital of the Straits Settlements. Penang enjoyed modest development, and Malacca stagnated. Chinese migration to Malaya, especially to Penang and Singapore, proceeded rapidly in this period, due to general "push" factors in Southern China and the moderately welcoming policy of the British administrators. The Chinese population of Penang, for example, rose

---

[1]Throughout the manuscript dollars, unless otherwise noted are Straits or Malaysian dollars, whose value in 1968 was 3M$ = 1US$.

[2]Rupert Emerson, Malaysia: A Study in Direct and Indirect Rule (Kuala Lumpur: University of Malaya Press, 1964; first published in 1937), p. 94.

[3]See Victor Purcell, The Chinese in Malaya (London: Oxford University Press, 1948), pp. 46-48, et passim.

from 7, 558 (out of a total population of 26, 107) in 1812, to 67, 354 in 1881 (out of a total 188, 245). [1]

Through the mid-Nineteenth Century tin-mining likewise grew apace. Discovery of new very rich deposits in the Larut Valley of Perak led to the first "tin rush," which disrupted the Malaya power structure immensely. The Malay chiefs arranged with Chinese financiers in the Straits Settlements to exploit the mineral through the use of Chinese miners there and in the Kinta Valley of Perak and the Kelang Valley of Selangor. "The resultant tax revenues were so large as to multiply many-fold the rewards of governing such a district."[2] Thus, the general situation is described by Mills as follows:

> During the whole period between 1786 and 1867 the Malay States of the Peninsula were hard at work committing political "hara-kiri." The process had begun at a much earlier date; but during the 19th Century it became greatly accelerated. There were constant wars between the different Sultans, and the states were also weakened by frequent civil wars between rival claimants to the throne. The power of the Sultans decayed until even petty rajas were able to set themselves up as independent local rulers, free to plunder and fight pretty much at will. Piracy flourished, and trade declined. [3]

To 1867, then, there was political anarchy of the mainland, accompanied by increasing Chinese economic exploitation of tin and even some spices (in Johore). Singapore was the center of British commerce in the East Indies; and Penang was reduced to the status of a local trading center. Meanwhile, British attention to Borneo revived. In 1838 James Brooke, an adventurer set sail to trade in Marudu Bay of North Borneo. By the end of 1841, he was assigned the government of Sarawak and its dependencies by Hasim, the regent and uncle of the Sultan of Brunei, "in return for a small annual payment of the Sultan of Brunei and a promise to respect the laws and religion of the country."[4] Brooke was proclaimed Rajah and Governor of Sarawak, primarily because he promised to settle its tribal unrest and political chaos, both of which were similar to Malaya's despite the absence of tin. Expansion of the State eastward signaled the continuing success of the Brooke regime of Kuching in winning support of the

---

[1] See. L. F. Comber, Chinese Secret Societies in Malaya (New York: J. J. Augustin, 1959), p. 36.

[2] S. M. Gullick, Malaya (London: Ernest Benn, 1963), p. 33.

[3] L. A. Mills, British Malaya 1824-1867, pp. 203-4.

[4] Steven Runciman, The White Rajahs: A History of Sarawak from 1841 to 1946 (Cambridge: Cambridge University Press, 1960), p. 67.

native peoples and bringing elements of order, especially vis à vis the Chinese communities and the pirates. Sarawak's total external trade trebled, between 1858 and 1864, following the temporary interruption by an Achinese revolt earlier. This was, with the exception of antimony, a free trade, carried on as in Malaya to a large extent by Chinese merchants and by British trading houses.[1]

By contrast to that of Rajah Brooke, the policy of the British government, as represented by India, toward the States of Malaya was one of strict non-intervention. It was feared that alliances would lead to intercession in unending and profitless internecine wars, and to trade competitiveness. This view was supported by the British conception of the Straits Settlements as just centers of trade, and the Malay Peninsula as having only commercial importance, tangential at that, to British Far Eastern activity.[2]

This policy was continued briefly when in 1867 the Colonial Office took control of the Straits Settlements. But in the 1860's the political situation in the Peninsula was worsening. Armed controversies among and between Chinese and Malay factions in various states, especially Perak and Selangor,[3] sometimes supported from the Straits Settlements, were causing great losses, not least to the Straits merchants, who lobbied incessantly for some form of intervention by the British authorities. In 1873 a complete reversal of policy occurred. Oddly, the decision to intervene is seen to have been necessitated "not by conditions in the Peninsula nor by any consideration of British economic interests there, but by fear of foreign intervention,"[4] meaning European, possibly German.[5] It was followed by 85 years of direct British impress on the economy, administration, self-view, and developmental potential of Malaysia.

The new policy meant intervention to eliminate hostilities and the intro-

---

[1] See James C. Jackson, Sarawak: A Geographical Survey of a Developing State, pp. 176-77.

[2] See Mills, op. cit., pp. 202-3, and C. D. Cowan, Nineteenth Century Malaya (London: Oxford University Press, 1961), pp. 1-27, et passim.

[3] The wars of succession in Pahang, Perak, and Selangor of the time are likened by Victor Pucell to local Wars of the Roses. (The Memories of a Malayan Official [London: Cassell, 1965,] p. 287.)

[4] Cowan, op. cit., p. 169.

[5] See also Gullick, op. cit., pp. 34-35. Thai claims to Kedah (and Perlis), Kelantan, and Trengganu, and occasional incursions southward are not to be discounted, nor is a British tendency to intervene short of force. See Nicholas Tarling, "Intervention and Non-Intervention in Malaya," Journal of Asian Studies, XXI (December, 1962), 523-27.

duction of British administrators into the State governments of Malaya. This began in 1874 with settlement of the Larut war and placement of a British Resident and an Assistant Resident in the government of Perak; similar assignments went to Sungai Ujong and Selangor. Such growth of British protection of the Peninsula--the Forward Movement--was piecemeal. The states of Negri Sembilan (after Sungai Ujong), Jelebu in 1883, and Remnau in 1887 followed. Pahang came under protection in 1888; and, as will be seen below, Johore followed in 1914, and Kedah, through agreement with the Thais in 1909, accompanied by Kelantan, Trengganu, and Perlis. By 1895 the four states to whose governments Residents had been attached were fairly peaceful. The stage was set for further centralization.

Malaysia under Britain to 1942

Between 1895 and 1942 the forces of change in Malaya and British Borneo consisted of increasing British domination of the administration of the country, and their creation of economic and social infrastructure. There was gradual development of a Western-oriented and -educated elite, and ease of primarily British and Chinese commercial exploitation of the country supported by immigration of Indian and Chinese laborers, and enhanced by a well-managed and growing foreign trade. With the centralizing of British management in the peninsula the Malay rulers found their positions increasingly weakened; although the British are said to have "done their best to enhance the rulers' prestige by carefully staying in the background and by trying to get their way by means of tactful persuasion rather than by giving commands."[1]

An exceptionally complicated administrative framework emerged as the result of the British Forward Movement. The States of Perak, Selangor, Negri Sembilan, and Pahang were joined, at British insistence, into the Federated Malay States (F.M.S.) in 1896, with Frank Swettenham as Resident General ruling from Kuala Lumpur.

This administrative union greatly strengthened British control over these states. Federal executive power was in the hands of a Resident General (from 1909 known as Chief Secretary), and the heads of several federal departments. There was no Federal Executive Council, but there was a strong tendency towards greater centralization. It actually led to

---

[1]The words of Sumitro Djojohadikusumo, an Indonesian scholar not known for apologia of the imperialists, in his Trade and Aid in South-East Asia (Melbourne: F. W. Cheshire, 1968), p. 8. This situation held particularly in the case of Sarawak, where Brooke family rule is blamed now for benignly neglecting social and economic development of the territory.

the controlling of the day-to-day policies by officials in the federal sphere and to gradual curtailing of the powers of the four state governments. [1]

The Straits Settlements were administrated directly by the British and ruled by a Governor. Johore adamantly stayed out of the Federation, becoming the first Unfederated Malay State, joined later by Kelantan, Trengganu, Perlis, and Kedah, following their release from Thai Suzerainty in 1909 as part of the Anglo-Siamese Treaty of that year. [2] In 1909 Kelantan accepted a British Adviser to replace her Thai one, and, under British protection, the Sultan of Kelantan created a State Council to help him govern in the manner of the F. M. S. The Sultan of Trengganu was more independent and did not accept a British Adviser (having been content with an Agent) until 1919. Johore finally accepted a British Adviser in 1914, "after seeing that the rapid development of Johore, with the new plantations of rubber, was making government of the state too complicated." [3]

For the F. M. S., and gradually the Unfederated States, there came to be not so much a federation in the normal sense of the meaning, but, as Fisher points out, "the superimposition of an entirely new centralized and British administered state on the old order." [4] After 1914, Fisher adds, the problem of Malayan unity took a new form--one which abides today: "bringing the various territories concerned into closer relationship to one another." [5] This replaced the earlier goal of unification, and presents one of the underlying themes of Malaysian developmental history.

For British Borneo there was no question of unity with the Malay Peninsula until much later; but British imperial strategy still affected the approach to and control of the Borneo states. The East India Company was prevented from

---

[1] Ibid.

[2] In return Siam received a loan of £4 millions for completion of her portion of the railway between Bangkok and Singapore, and Britain relinquished certain rights of her traders living in Siam.

[3] Horace Stone, From Malacca to Malaysia (London: Harrap, 1966), p. 155. Stone remarks that "the British had always taken the view that Johore was an independent state allied to them. These arrangements worked so well that no further changes were made up to 1914." (Ibid.)

[4] C. A. Fisher, "The Problem of Malayan Unity in its Geographical Setting," Geographical Essays on British Tropical Lands, ed. R. W. Steel and C. A. Fisher (London: George Philip and Son, 1956), p. 297.

[5] "The Problem," p. 309.

agreeing to Dutch exclusive control of Borneo between 1818 and 1824. And strategy in the words of Graham Irwin,

provided James Brooke and Henry Wise [Brooke's sometime London agent] with their strongest arguments for the creation of a British naval base and harbour refuge at Labuan in 1846, induced Her Majesty's Government to grant a Royal charter to the North Borneo Company in 1881 and led, finally, to the declaration of British Protectorates over North Borneo, Brunei, and Sarawak in 1888.[1]

Labuan had been ceded by the Sultan of Brunei to Great Britain in 1846, becoming a Crown Colony in 1848 (and part of the Straits Settlements in 1907). Beyond strategic value, the port was hoped to have commercial potential with respect to inter-island trade. This never developed.

Meanwhile, following an abortive private American attempt to operate a trading settlement in North Borneo at Kimanis in the 1860's,[2] British traders acquired grants of territory from the Sultan of Brunei and other rulers in 1877 and 1878. These coastal areas stretched 300 miles around North Borneo and came in return for annual payments. The Brookes who coveted North Borneo, were out-manoeuvered. The newly formed North Borneo Company posted agents to Sandakan, Tempasuk, and Papar, and after receipt of the Royal Charter, established headquarters first at Labuan and then at Kudat, North Borneo's first capital. Like Labuan, this failed as an entrepôt, and in 1883 the capital of the Chartered Company, which had become a purely administrative operation in 1882, was moved to already thriving Sandakan. In the late Nineteenth Century and later, North Borneo was administered by a professional civil service. It was divided first between the East and West Coast Residencies which contained, then, various provinces with District Officer administration. Heads of Departments were in Sandakan, as was the Resident of the East Coast, the Governor and, after 1883, an Advisory Council.[3]

Sarawak came formally under British protection in 1888, having enjoyed a somewhat precarious independence prior to that. Like North Borneo, a small British civil service tended to administration and what social services and eco-

---

[1]Graham Irwin, Nineteenth-Century Borneo: A Study in Diplomatic Rivalry (Singapore: Donald Moore, 1955), p. 217.

[2]See K. G. Tregonning, "American Activity in North Borneo, 1865-81," The Pacific Historical Review, XXIII (November, 1954), 357-72; and, for a brief review, Lee Long-leng, North Borneo, pp. 21-24.

[3]K. G. Tregonning, A History of Modern Sabah (Singapore: University of Malaya Press, 1965), pp. 49-51.

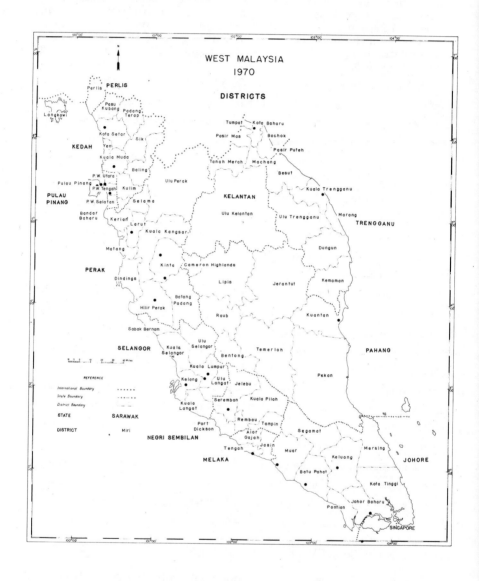

Fig. 2.--Malaysia: District Names

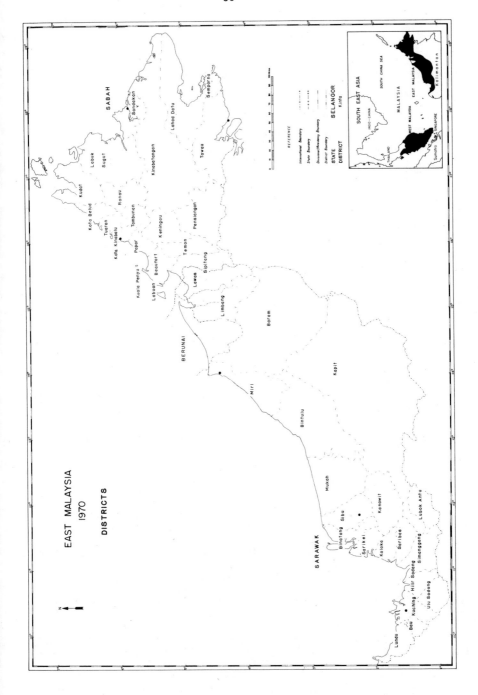

EAST MALAYSIA
1970

DISTRICTS

nomic infrastructure were forthcoming. The geographical divisions, eventually five in number, were administered by Residents under whom District Officers worked,[1] especially after 1917.[2] Gradually central government departments appeared in Kuching, the Capital, in a similar fashion to that of North Borneo. A cash economy was introduced gradually.[3] Unlike North Borneo, large economic stimulation ventures were not undertaken.

Thus evolved in North Borneo, Sarawak, and Malaya, alike, an administrative system suited to the British needs and perceptions of the area. Key to administration was the District Officer known alternatively as District Magistrate: "He was in intimate contact with the people of his area and represented the government to them in almost every one of its manifestations."[4] In the developing urban areas of Malaya, i. e., the Straits Settlements, a measure of local government was provided, with Municipal committees established in 1848 with five Councillors each in George Town, Malacca, and Singapore by 1856. Elsewhere Sanitary Boards were established as Government Departments under the authority of the respective Residents.[5]

The Resident system was thus designed primarily as a means of imposing law and order in Malaya and British Borneo, though differing in details of organization between the FMS, the Unfederated States, and the Borneo States. The forces of economic, as well as social and administrative development follow a consistent pattern over the years there. For Malaya, including Singapore, that depended upon:

> a favorable ratio of population to resources, a natural environment particularly suited to rubber cultivation, rich and abundant deposits of tin and an advantageous location as an entrepôt center. On these bases, Malaya has built an active economy concentrated to a large extent on the production of

---

[1] See R. S. Milne, Government and Politics in Malaysia (Boston: Houghton-Mifflin, 1967), pp. 56-59; and The White Rajahs, pp. 202-4.

[2] This to some degree replicated the Sultan of Brunei's former administrative system.

[3] Above observations adapted from J. M. Reinhardt, "Administrative Policy and Practice in Sarawak: Continuity and Change under the Brookes," Journal of Asian Studies, XXIX (August, 1970), 851-62.

[4] Rupert Emerson, Malaysia: A Study in Direct and Indirect Rule, p. 158. See also Sir Frank Swettenham, British Malaya (London: Allan and Unwin, 1948), p. 242 et passim.

[5] Including ones in North Borneo at the turn of the Century. (See M. H. Baker, Sabah: The First Ten Years as a Colony, Singapore Studies on Malaysia, No. 1 [Singapore: Department of History, University of Singapore, 1965], p. 50.)

rubber and tin for export, on the output of a variety of foodstuffs and secondary manufactures mainly for domestic consumption, and on commercial and financial services for the domestic markets and for the large entrepôt trade with the rest of Southeast Asia. The role of foreign capital and enterprise (particularly European and Chinese) and of foreign labor (particularly Chinese and Indian) has been of special significance in the economic development of Malaya and accounts for the heterogeneous character of the population.[1]

The development of rubber and tin production and export and the mobility of population and general flexibility of the economy were enhanced from the beginning by governmental emphasis on infrastructure development. This included roads and the railway, but also post and telegraph services and encouragement of intra-national and inter-island shipping services in both Malaya and Borneo.

The present settlement pattern of Malaya and British Borneo evolved as population grew and arable land was found to be available only along river valleys and some coastal plains. Heavy concentration of population followed opening up of the Perak tin deposits and followed in what became the Kuala Lumpur capital area. Chinese businessmen created commercial networks connecting the settlement areas. The produce of the country, rubber coming from estates and private holdings, the former worked by Indian immigrants, was funnelled through Penang and Singapore which grew in size and complexity accordingly.[2]

Indians and Chinese together came to outnumber the Malays in Malaya (including Singapore). Their numbers were not proportionally so important in Borneo; though their commercial role was similar. Immigration of Chinese and Indian laborers was permitted and encouraged by the British in Malaya and North Borneo for practical economic reasons, as noted above. In Sarawak, the Brookes actually discouraged rapid economic development, partly from a desire to protect the indigenous way of life. This, and an awareness of "the extreme sparseness and backwardness of the population" led to active encouragement of Chinese settlement, which was viewed as a stimulus to dynamism in the society.[3] North Borneo likewise sought to attract Chinese settlers, offering financial incentives to migration after the early 1880's. In Malaya, considerable numbers

---

[1]International Bank for Reconstruction and Development, The Economic Development of Malaya (Baltimore: Johns Hopkins Press, 1955), p. 14.

[2]In the late 1800's Port Weld, too, was a leading Peninsula port, being The chief outlet for Larut and Northern Perak and serving Kinta as well, until its impracticalities outweighted the advantage and the railway north reduced its advantage. (See K. G. Tregonning, Home Port Singapore Singapore: Oxford University Press, 1967, p. 26.)

[3]C. A. Fisher, South-East Asia, p. 672.

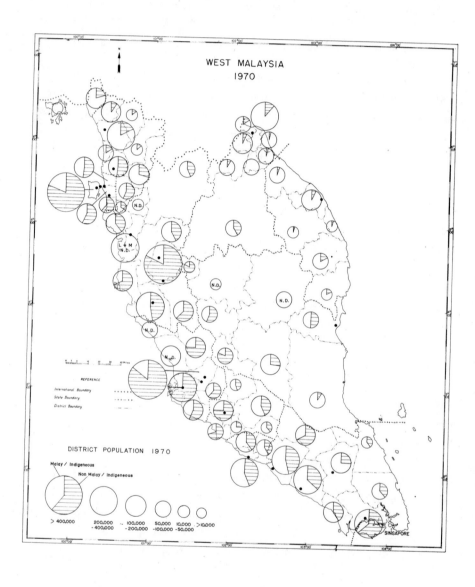

Fig. 3.--Malaysia: District Population 1970

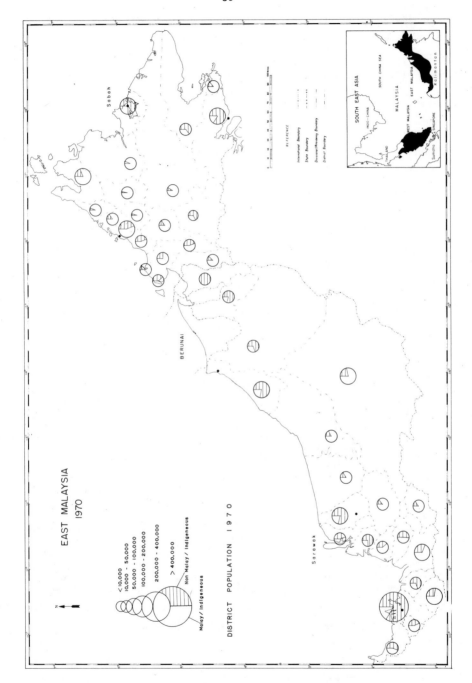

EAST MALAYSIA
1970

DISTRICT POPULATION 1970

<10,000
10,000 - 50,000
50,000 - 100,000
100,000 - 200,000
200,000 - 400,000
> 400,000

Malay / Indigeneous

Non Malay / Indigeneous

of Chinese had settled in the Straits Settlements by 1850; and this growth, along with that of Indian population, accelerated from then on. In 1881 Malays in Penang were outnumbered by Chinese and Indians together. Later Nineteenth Century growth of rubber and tin production accompanied immigration in numbers to Kedah, Perak, Selangor, Negeri Sembilan, and Johore. [1]

Immigration to Malaya was unrestricted until the depression; although Chinese were treated basically as resident aliens until World War II. [2] At the beginning of the Twentieth Century tin was second to rubber as an attracting force. By 1911, 60 per cent of the estate population in the FMS was Indian, and 25 per cent Chinese. Chinese population in Malaya grew from 104, 615, or 34 per cent in 1871 to 2, 418, 615 or 44 per cent in 1941. Correspondingly, Indian population grew from 33, 390 or 11 per cent in 1871 to 767, 693 or 14 per cent in 1941. [3] Yet, despite all the changes brought by the British in administration and the migrations and development of the export economy,

> the rural Malays were, until recently, carefully shielded from the realities of the 20th-Century world. Protected by British paternalism, they were encouraged to carry on winning their livelihood as nearly as possible in their traditional unhurried manner, while the more hard-headed immigrants transformed at least the western third of Malaya from a tangle of jungle into one of the most intensively exploited regions in the whole of South-East Asia. [4]

The overall economic/demographic and administrative pattern of the country, then, was set in the late Nineteenth Century and early Twentieth Century. Allen and Donnithorne observe that:

> The new economy was built up on the initiative of private entrepreneurs, and the transformation of the country's life came about through the response of individuals--Malays, Chinese and Europeans--to the appeal of self-interest. The government had no direct part in the economic activity. It provided an arena in which private enterprise could work unhampered (or

---

[1] Ginsburg and Roberts write: "By 1880 the development of the west coast was under way. Perak experienced huge influxes of both Chinese and Indians between 1891 and 1900. There apparently was a continuing movement of Indians into Perak, Selangor, Negeri Sembilan, Johore, and Kedah from 1910 to 1931. Pahang has had much less immigration, and the east-coast states and Perlis have had very little." (See Norton Ginsburg and Chester Roberts, eds., Malaya, p. 64.)

[2] See Gordon P. Means, Malaysian Politics (New York: New York University Press, 1970), pp. 26-28.

[3] Statistics are for the Straits Settlements only in 1871, and for Malaya as a whole in 1941, from Ooi Jin-Bee, Land, People and Economy in Malaya, pp. 111-17.

[4] Fisher, op. cit., p. 638.

unassisted) by official direction and guidance. Yet to conclude that the
government's function was merely that of keeping order and setting a legal
framework for private economic activity would be erroneous. A primitive
country which embarks on a career of rapid development calls for basic
equipment and services, and these the public authority must usually provide. It is true that in Malaya some of the activities which elsewhere are
normally carried out by public authorities were undertaken by large European companies; this applies, for example, to housing and health services.
Nevertheless, a contribution by the government was indispensable. The
State took the lead in building railways in Malaya and the extensive system
which it created during the present century was operated as a national
undertaking. The State was also in part responsible for the construction
of an admirable road system. The first roads were intended to serve the
tin-mines and the populations around them; that is to say, they were mainly
on the west coast. When the rubber planters arrived, the location of their
estates was determined to a large extent by the existing road system. For
this reason the west coast was the scene of the outstanding economic developments after the turn of the century and attracted most of the immigrants,
Chinese, and Indian. In contrast, the States of Pahang, Kelantan and Trengganu remained economically backward as compared with other parts of the
country. In those regions Malays predominated, and Chinese, European
and Indian influences were relatively slight.

The government was active during the present century in providing various other forms of public overhead capital and institutions needed by a modern community. Although the authorities in Malaya, unlike those of the
Netherlands East Indies, were never large estate owners, they had a powerful influence on agricultural development. For example, rubber-growing
was introduced on official initiative; the Department of Agriculture, established in 1905, operated research and experimental stations and undertook
settlement and irrigation schemes; and village agricultural schools were
instrumental in diffusing knowledge of improved agricultural methods. The
Mines Department, from early in the Century, helped to provide a framework for the economical development of the country's mineral resources.[1]

Thus Swettenham notes:

The introduction of a great agricultural industry, necessitating the
expenditure of something approaching one hundred millions sterling, changed
the face of the country, and forced the Government into the rapid extension
of practically all public services--railways, roads, post, telephones, tele-
graphs, water supplies, hospitals, and many other conveniences--and those
responsible for directing affairs--for the idea of advising native rulers had
long been abandoned--decided upon a general policy . . . dictated . . . by
the wish of Europeans to introduce into the Malay States the same sort of
civilization as they had been accustomed to in the countries of their origin.[2]

Such activity was financed through the very large input of the tin tax,
which early was the largest element in the combined revenues of the states.[3]

[1]G. C. Allen and Audrey Donnithorne, Western Enterprise in Indonesia
and Malaya (London: George Allen and Unwin, 1954), pp. 43-44.

[2]British Malaya (London: Allen and Unwin, 1948), p. 50.

[3]See Emily Sadka, The Protected Malay States 1874-1895 (Singapore:
University of Malaya Press, 1968), p. 332.

The Federation's revenues increased from $8,434,083 in 1896 to $105,404,458 in 1927.[1] An example of the provision of development facilities thus financed is that of electricity, which began to have large importance in Malaya in the 1920's. Through the Electricity Departments of the FMS and Unfederated States, the Municipality of Penang, the Perak River Hydro-Electric Power Company, and private Companies in Malacca and Kedah, electricity supplies were installed in almost all the medium and large towns in Malaya by the Second World War. Moreover, about half the tin-mining in Perak and Selangor was conducted by electrical means.[2]

Figure 7 shows the major roads and railways in Malaysia. The Malayan Railway was opened in 1884 with 8 miles laid between Port Weld and Taiping for the transport of tin. In 1901 the Federated Malay States' Railway was created as a system combining the railway lines of various states. In 1909 the continuous line from Johore Baharu to Bukit Mertajam was completed, and in 1913 the Singapore Government Railway was purchased, with the causeway connecting Singapore and the mainland built in 1923. By 1918 the link between Bukit Mertajam and the Thai Border was finished; but it was not until 1931 that the East Coast line from Gemas to Kota Baharu was completed. By 1932 the maximum route mileage was attained. Between 1896 and 1905 the North Borneo railroad was built connecting Weston, Beaufort, and Jesselton.[3]

Railway development by the states of Perak and Selangor and then the Federated Malay States Railways are credited with opening up the west-central Johore rubber belt through their construction and operation of the Johore States Railway. FMS competition with the Straits Settlements resulted in a push for a port competitive with Penang and Singapore at Port Swettenham-- to which a railway line was extended in 1899.[4] Here was an example especially as the depression of the 1930's hit Malaya, of the need for a supra-Malay state authority to coordinate important economic functions of the Peninsula as a whole. Such a notion was put forth then, amidst great controversy and little success, by Sir Cecil Clementi who had become Governor and High Commissioner in 1930. Simandjuntak writes, "reduced to its simplest form, the political strategy

---

[1] Emerson, op. cit., p. 186.   [2] Lembaga Lestrik Negara.

[3] See Robert Nathan Associates, Transport Development in Malaysia, Vol. III, Annex C (Kuala Lumpur: Robert Nathan, 1968), pp. 1-3, 183.

[4] C. A. Fisher, "The Railway Geography of British Malaya," The Scottish Geographical Magazine, LXIV (1948), 127.

of what was to become the Malayan Union Proposal was to defederate in order
to refederate."[1] Opposition to greater union came from all sides, particularly
the Unfederated States which sought to maintain their Malay independence, and
from the Colony, on the one hand, and the FMS hierarchy on the other, who
each feared the other's eventual takeover of their affairs in the Peninsula.[2]
Nothing came of this union idea before the war; although aspects of the decentralization of powers in the FMS were effected, particularly the returning of
revenues of State Councils by the Federation Government. So "on the eve of the
fall of Malaya into the hands of the Japanese, British dependencies in Southern
Asia were as fragmented as fifty years previously, in spite of the painstaking
efforts of British Colonists to unite and rule."[3]

Malaysia under Britain 1945-1957

The Japanese occupied Malaysia for three and one half years during the
Second World War, from the late winter of 1942. Their impact was purely
destructive. When the British returned in 1945 their tasks were to reconstruct
the mining and estate agricultural industries, to repair the vastly ruined infrastructure, to reëstablish food distribution systems, to reorganize the administration of Malaya, and, then, to meet the threat of Communist insurgency
spawned by remnants of the British-supported anti-Japanese guerrilla units of
the War. Large commercial-scale tin miners had the problem of reconstruct-
ing destroyed equipment, especially dredges. Smaller scale Chinese mines
recovered quicker. Rubber made a fast recovery, as well. So by 1948 rubber

---

[1]State Councils were to receive responsibilities in the FMS that had been
held by the Federation government. And then Clementi "envisaged as part of
this Malayan Union scheme, a pan-Malayan economic community based on the
concept of a customs union that would remove all internal tariff barriers so as
to allow a free flow of inter-state trade within the walls of a common external
tariff." Then, in the expanded form a political union of the FMS, Unfederated
Malay States, and the Straits Settlement Colony would be formed with all advisory powers centralized in Kuala Lumpur. B. Simandjuntak, Malayan Federalism 1945-1963 (London: Oxford University Press, 1969), pp. 29-30.

[2]See Rupert Emerson, op. cit., 312-77, especially p. 340: "The strengthening of the State administrations has taken the dual form of extending the
degree of State control over the departmental officers serving in the State and in
enlarging and modernizing the State services and State Councils." In the budget
of 1935 the Federal Council allocated to each of the States lump sums, amounting
in all to less than half the Federal estimated revenue, leaving allocation to de
partments of these sums to the discretion of the various States.

[3]Simandjuntak, p. 35.

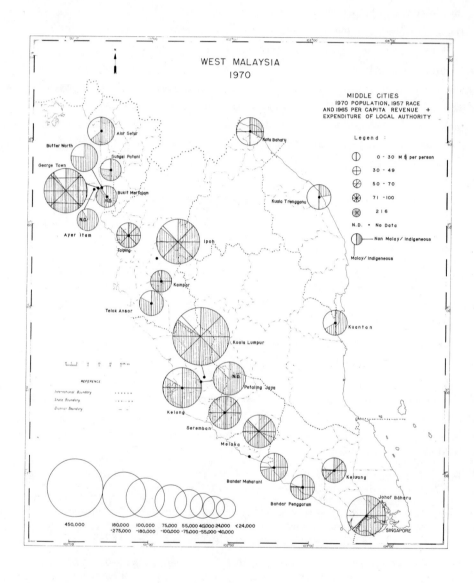

Fig. 4. --Malaysia: Middle Cities' Population and Local Authorities Finance

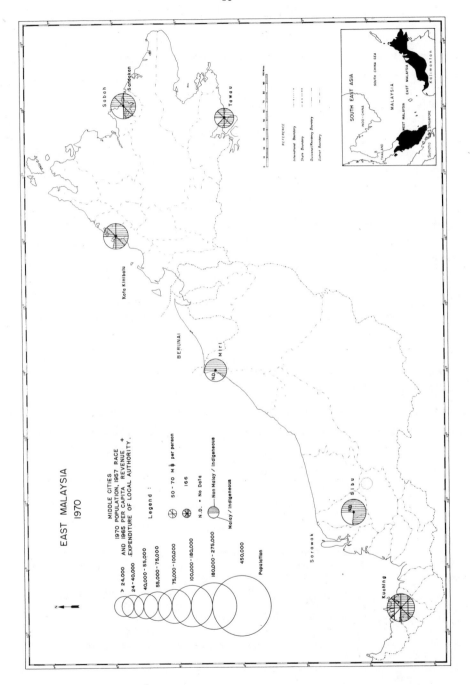

EAST MALAYSIA
1970

MIDDLE CITIES

1970 POPULATION, 1957 RACE
AND 1965 PER CAPITA REVENUE +
EXPENDITURE OF LOCAL AUTHORITY.

Legend :

> 24,000
24 - 40,000
40,000 - 55,000
55,000 - 75,000
75,000 - 100,000
100,000 - 180,000
180,000 - 275,000

450,000

Population

50 - 70 M $ per person

166

N.D. = No Data

Non Malay / Indigeneous

Malay / Indigeneous

REFERENCE

International Boundary
State Boundary
Division/Revenue Boundary
District Boundary

SOUTH EAST ASIA

had reached its pre-war production level. By 1950 tin production had surpassed the pre-war production level. [1]

In 1948, a compromise Malayan Union was proposed in the Federation of Malaya Order in Council:

> The old distinction between the FMS· and the Unfederated Malay States was at last resolved. The federation plan gave the central government of Malaya nearly all the wider powers needed for a strong and efficient administration conferred by the Malayan Union plan, and yet it respected the personality of the States as distinct federal units. The novelty of the system was that the British government would still rule supreme over a unified Malaya through the 'adviser' system and the executive powers of the High Commissioner. [2]

Significant victory had been won by the Malays, in retention of their state and Sultan systems in an advantageous Federal citizenship system. [3] The financial supremacy of the central government, however, was preserved through maintenance of the colonial system of "unified finance." [4]

In June 1948, special emergency regulations were enforced throughout the Federation, for the purpose of meeting the Communist terrorists' threat. They mobilized military, civil administrative, and economic forces on a country-wide basis. And this had a strong centralizing effect in the next ten years of Emergency. [5] Another result of the Emergency measures was the creation of at least 480 "new villages," whose purpose was to cut off the insurgents' support from Chinese squatters. Most of these were provided with local councils; and, with nearly 10 per cent of the country's population thus moved or otherwise affected, 70 towns with populations exceeding 2,000 were created--not all of them by any means stable as to economic or social form and status. Eighty per

---

[1] D. G. E. Hall, A History of South-East Asia (London: Methuen, 1964), pp. 832-33.

[2] Simandjuntak, op. cit., p. 47.

[3] An earlier proposal for Malayan union, not including Singapore, but uniting the rest of the Peninsula had been energetically promoted by the British, but resisted and finally killed by a combination of opposing forces in Malaya. Although it was intended as preliminary to possible independence, the move was most heavily resisted by the Malay leaders in Malaya, who opposed inclusion of the Straits Chinese and Indians--who would then, together, outnumber them. Likewise the Penang traders opposed the Union concept because it was felt to jeopardize Penang's economic advantages, especially its free port status, an issue that abides today.

[4] Simandjuntak, pp. 55-56.

[5] See Simandjuntak, op. cit., pp. 56-60.

cent of the new villages were in Western Malaya, and nearly half of them in Perak and Johore. [1]

The 1950's were years in which local government in Malaysia took on greater importance. In Sarawak Municipal Boards had been provided for in 1921. [2] The Kuching Municipal Ordinance of 1952 established the Kuching Municipal Council in place of the old Kuching Municipal Board. [3] In North Borneo, Sanitary Boards had been in force since 1931; in 1953 the Municipal and Urban Authorities Ordinance was passed providing for three types of urban local government: township authorities, town boards, and municipal councils. No town there at the time or since has been judged ready for a municipal council. On July 1, 1954, Sandakan and Jesselton became Town Boards. [4] In Malaya the Emergency delayed democratization of local governments until 1951, when Malacca, Penang and Kuala Lumpur held elections for the first time. Kota Baharu, Muar, and Batu Pahat held their first elections in 1952. In all these the local government bodies are subordinate to the State governments, especially as to budget approval. The aim of their establishment was to unify the diverse, particularly racial and cultural, elements of the plural society. [5]

By 1950 Malaya was enabled by her rapid recovery from the war to turn to economic expansion and away from reconstruction. In the early 1950's the pre-war economic pattern was again manifested: exports of domestic produce constituted over a third of the GNP; while almost a third of gross domestic expenditure went for imports, primarily of consumer items. [6] Likewise:

---

[1] See Hamzah Sendut, "Patterns of Urbanization in Malaya, " Journal of Tropical Geography, XVI (October, 1962), 116; and Kernial Singh Sandhu, "Emergency Resettlement in Malaya, " Journal of Tropical Geography, XVIII (August, 1964), 164.

[2] Malaysia, Report of the Royal Commission of Enquiry to Investigate into the Workings of Local Authorities in West Malaysia (Nahappan Report) (Kuala Lumpur: Department of Local Government and Housing, 1968), pp. 32-36; and Gerald Hawkins, "First Steps in Malaya Local Government, " Pacific Affairs, XXVI (July, 1953), 155.

[3] See Hugh Hicklin, Sarawak and Its Government (Kuching: Government Printing Office, 1954), pp. 34-35.

[4] See M. H. Baker, Sabah: The First Ten Years as a Colony (Singapore: Department of History, University of Singapore, 1965), pp. 49-52.

[5] T. H. Silcock, The Commonwealth Economy of South-East Asia (London: Cambridge University Press, 1959), p. 110.

[6] IBRD, The Economic Development of Malaya (Baltimore: Johns Hopkins Press, 1955), p. 22.

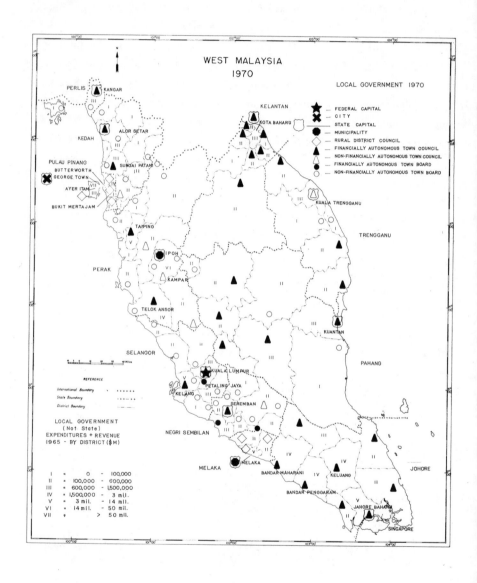

Fig. 5. --Malaysia: Local Government

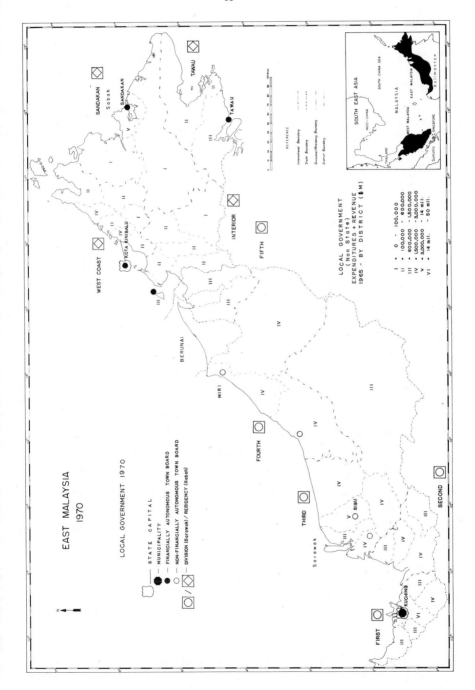

EAST MALAYSIA
1970

LOCAL GOVERNMENT 1970

STATE CAPITAL
MUNICIPALITY
FINANCIALLY AUTONOMOUS TOWN BOARD
NON-FINANCIALLY AUTONOMOUS TOWN BOARD
DIVISION (Sarawak) / RESIDENCY (Sabah)

LOCAL GOVERNMENT
(Non State)
EXPENDITURES + REVENUE
1965 - BY DISTRICT ($M)

I   0 - 100,000
II   100,000 - 600,000
III   600,000 - 1,500,000
IV   1,500,000 - 3,000,000
V   3,000,000 - 14 mil.
VI   14 mil. - 50 mil.

REFERENCE

International Boundary
State Boundary
Divisional/Residency Boundary
District Boundary

SOUTH EAST ASIA

By Asian standards, the Malayan economy has reached a relatively
advanced state, not only in the level of per capita income, but also in
structure: it is a more varied and complex economy than is characteristic
of most underdeveloped countries. Power, transport, communications
and other basic facilities are reasonably well developed; a considerable
foundation of secondary industry has been established; there is a substantial nucleus of skills and enterprise; standards of public administration
are high; and institutional habits and patterns of commerce and finance
are correspondingly advanced. Industrial, commercial, professional and
governmental activities outside the fields of primary industry now probably
account for nearly half the national income. [1]

With this heavy dependence on rubber and tin world markets, Malaya's economic

prosperity, of course, fluctuated in the 1950's and since, according to world

levels of economic activity. For example, a decline in prosperity was felt in

Malaya following the end of the Korean war. [2]

In 1955 the first real general election of Malaya took place; that is the

Legislative Council was accorded an elected majority. On August 31, full inde-

pendence, merdeka, was achieved for the Federation of Malaya, following on

the Federation of Malaya Agreement of 1948. [3] Sarawak and North Borneo

retained the Crown Colony status acquired in 1946. The new Federation of

Malaya Agreement of 1957 replaced the agreement of 1948 and contained as

schedules the new Federal Constitution and the Constitutions of Penang and

Malacca. Various acts ensued, and in the Federation the Federal Constitution

Ordinance, 1957 was enacted by the Federal Legislative Council. In each of the

Malay States, State Enactments were passed. The Alliance Party represented

political agreements between leading figures in the three racial/communal

groups of Malaya: Malays, Chinese, and Indians--by and large consisting of

progressive, Western-oriented nationalist leaders. Their compromise con-

sisted, in effect, of providing Malaya with the accoutrements of nationhood on a

Malay format, continuing the British practice of support for the hereditary rul-

ers and Malay cultural predominance in public forms, while leaving the economy

completely "capitalist, conservative, and open"[4]--and therefore amenable to

---

[1]Ibid., p. 20.

[2]Ibid. And see general discussion of the Malaysia economy in Sumitro
Djojohadikusumo, Trade and Aid in South-East Asia: Malaysia and Singapore,
pp. 22-43.

[3]See R. H. Hisckling, An Introduction to the Federal Constitution, in
Malaysia: Selected Historical Readings, ed. John Bastin and Robin W. Winks,
p. 380.

[4]T. H. Silcock's phrase, in "General Review of Economic Policy," The
Political Economy of Independent Malaya, ed. Silcock and E. K. Fisk (Singapore:
Eastern Universities Press, 1963, p. 251.

and supporting Chinese and Indian urban business practice.

During the post war pre-independence period the British-managed governments of Malaya and the Colonies of Sarawak and North Borneo continued their policies of gradual economic development concentrating on the export sectors. For Malaya, the rubber Smallholders' Replanting Scheme emerged as a "critical factor in the future of that important sector of the nation's greatest industry";[1] while problems of competition from synthetics were watched closely. A national policy for Malayan education emerged in the early 50's, requiring changes in the Draft Development Plan of that period.

Development planning in Malaysia, on a coordinated basis and related to specific periods of time, began in 1945 when the United Kingdom Colonial Development and Welfare Act of that year was passed. This provided £120 million for development and welfare schemes in Colonial and dependent territories for a ten-year period. Malaya, North Borneo, and Sarawak responded with plans. The Malayan Union Government's draft development plan was divided into four parts, concerning possible sources of finance, and the development of (a) social services, (b) national resources, and utilities, and (c) trade and industry. It proposed the expenditure of Colonial Development and Welfare Funds of $M214,643,000 on capital works and raising recurrent expenditures to a maximum of $M28,584,000. Of these combined Federal, State, and Settlement expenditures approximately, $M35 million were allocated to education, $M67 million to public works, $M29 million to telecommunications, and $M29 million for drainage and irrigation. Such direct public expenditure did not include some projects included in Colombo Plan documents, which were to be financed from loans and/or were to be undertaken by public authorities with their own sources of capital, such as the Planter Loans Board and the Central Electricity Board-- estimated at $M211.5 million for the period 1951-57.[2]

Despite the organized approach thus set out, this was not development planning in the modern sense: it was unintegrated even at the conceptualization level, and did not set wide economic or social goals. More important, as the 1953 Progress Report makes clear, the basic assumptions on which it was based invalidated it. Primarily, it was supposed that the anti-communist Emergency would progressively abate. Instead it lasted until 1958 and made "development"

---

[1]Federation of Malaya, Progress Report on the Development Plan of the Federation of Malaya 1950-1952 (Kuala Lumpur: Government Printer, 1953), p. v.

[2]Ibid., p. 2. Hereafter $ refers to Straits or Malaysian dollars, US$1 = M$3, approximately.

a peculiar thing in the pre-independence period. On the positive side, assumptions as to exports value and export prices were exceedingly low. [1]

At this time, however, many of the basic characteristics of Malayan development policy were set, including (1) central capital expenditure planning conceived and implemented through functional departmental hierarchies (e.g. Drainage and Irrigation), (2) specific attention to foreign resource inputs to public sector development activity; and (3) the planned use of existing and new special governmental or semi-governmental institutions, such as the Central Electricity Board on the one hand, and the newly established Housing Trust ($10 million capital in 1951) and the Federal Land Development Authority (1955) on the other.

The Colony of North Borneo published in 1948 a Reconstruction and Development Plan 1948-1955. [2] The greatest development needs in that period arose from war-time destruction, including complete rebuilding of Sandakan and Labuan, which had been leveled, and reclamation in commercial areas there and in Jesselton (now Kota Kinabalu). Rebuilding extended to electricity facilities in Sandakan, assistance to housing construction, and pushing of road development outward from the cities, particularly to the Kudat Peninsula. This Plan, then, had an urban (re-) development emphasis new in what were to become Malaysian areas. In later years this gave way to more general (and rural) development policies; but, as we shall see in the case of Sandakan, the North Borneo cities so affected still benefit from a comparatively great modernity in their central commercial areas.

Sarawak approved a Development Plan in 1950, which covered the period 1947/48 to 1955/56. It was revised in 1952 to extend to 1957. [3] The revision occurred because, like Malaya, Sarawak found in the early fifties that it had far higher revenues than had earlier been expected. Thus planned expenditures rose from $23.7 million to $75.3 million, adding emphasis on roads, electricity supplies, government buildings and technical education. [4]

---

[1] From an average annual export (including reëxport) figure of $41 million for 1947-49 exports moved up and then down, settling at $2.134 million for 1952. (Ibid., p. 6.)

[2] Jesselton: Government Printer, 1948, see pp. 1-3, 114-19.

[3] See Sarawak, Revised Development Plan (Kuching: Government Printing Office, 1952), pp. 1-3, et passim.

[4] Approximately $18 million were to be provided in Colonial Development and Welfare Funds. (See Sarawak, Sarawak Development Plan 1959-1963 [Kuching: Government Printer, 1959], p. 1.)

The Independence Period of 1957-1966

On 31 August 1957 the Federation of Malaya became an independent nation-state and member of the British Commonwealth; Sarawak and North Borneo, Crown Colonies since 1946, remained so. In 1959 Singapore became a dependent self-governing city state. While economic growth and development policy proceeded into the sixties as seen above and below, the stage was set for a political/administrative reorganization of the various territories.

Early Development Policy

The General Plan for Development of Malaya 1956-60 was approved in October, 1956, and contained a series of provisional allocations among ministries and new recurrent expenditures of about $90 million per year. Sixty per cent of capital expenditures were allocated to the economic sector, 30 per cent to the social sector (or what this study calls Population-Coverage), and 10 per cent to Government, including government housing. Highest importance was assigned rubber replanting, general agricultural development to reduce dependence on inputs, mining, industrial development, land development, and the development of Port Swettenham. Education, health, and water facilities as a group ranked second, housing and communications third.[1]

Although there was a 15 per cent shortfall in actual, over planned, investment, Malayan public investment for the 1956-60 period was nearly double that of the preceding five years. Of $971.7 million spent, 15.8 per cent ($153.4 million) went to rubber replanting, and another 4 per cent to drainage and irrigation. Despite the indicated priorities, 24.6 per cent was spent on utilities (of which 14.6 per cent to electricity); and 21.2 per cent went to transport.[2]

---

[1] See Federation of Malaya, Report on Economic Planning in the Federation of Malaya 1956 (Kuala Lumpur: Government Printer, 1957), p. 3.

[2] In this policy period the pioneer industry incentives system was inaugurated (1958) through which more than 50 firms with a called up capital of about $27 million and producing 238 products were awarded pioneer status, 35 having begun production (Second Five Year Plan, p. 4). During the plan period the Federal Land Development Authority, cooperating with state Governments, started 22 schemes but fell far short of physical targets, as was the case with irrigation plans where financial investment targets were even undermet by 36 per cent. Road construction was 36 per cent underspent and included such crucial developments as a river bridge at Kelang, completion of the Temerloh-Marin Road, and surfacing and general improvement of the East Coast Route (ibid., pp. 6-10). (See also Government of Malaya, Interim Review of Development in Malaya under the Second Five Year Plan Kuala Lumpur: Government Printer, 1963, pp. 22-23, and Federation of Malaya, Second Five Year Plan 1961-1965 Kuala Lumpur: Government Printer, 1961, pp. 1-2, 4, 6.)

Development policies in North Borneo and Sarawak during the 1950's were subject to yearly adjustment, and until 1954 had no real overall conceptualization. Both initiated 1959-64 plans which will be considered together with the Second Malaya Plan 1960-65 below. In the case of Sarawak this overlapped the 1955-60 plan by two years. Likewise in North Borneo the 1959-63 plan carried on from planning in the 1956-58 interim. Percentage expenditure on development in North Borneo and Sarawak in the 1955-60 period shows heavy emphasis on transport and government. Sarawak spent proportionally more on social services and agriculture, less on government and utilities.

From Financial Statements for the period from 1949 to 1960 an overall pattern of development expenditure and its emphasis in Malaysia can be discerned. This shows, for East and West Malaysian areas a total calculable development expenditure of $1,416.5 million, of which the highest budget line items were Ministry of Commerce and Industry $244 million (including electricity and rubber replanting), $126.7 million to railways, $101.8 million to roads and bridges, $93.3 million for water supplies, $91.5 million for education, $67.7 million for government buildings, and $54.7 million for the Royal Malaysia Police.[1] Expenditure that could clearly be identified as urban, such as for housing and ports totalled $382.6 million, and clearly rural expenditures (including agriculture and land development) totalled $154.6 million. Expenditures over population coverage were $388.5 million, for problem areas $129.6 million, and for Economic Development Functions $785 million. Thus the modern sector of the economy definitely received the greater attention; and the rural areas, apart from those contributing to the export economy, were not receiving large capital inputs. Only the gradual spread of schools, feeder roads, and health clinics can be said to have been benefitting the kampong (village) sector.

In a mappable sample of these expenditures of 31 per cent, which could include neither rubber replanting (greatest in west and central Johore, Negeri Sembilan, Eastern Selangor and Southern Kedah) nor railway expenditures (a large part of which were for equipment), this urban/modern bias is shown by the fact that 63 per cent of the mapped expenditures went to the Districts of Kuala Lumpur, Penang, Kuching, Kelang, Semanggang, Kota Kinabalu, Sibu, Sandakan, and Miri, in that order, with 20 per cent going to Kuala Lumpur, 11 per cent to Penang, and 9 per cent and 8 per cent respectively to Kuching and Kelang. Population coverage expenditures (POPC: for social welfare and edu-

---

[1] See Appendix I.

cational needs--with a correlation coefficient of .652 with 67/60 population) went most to, Kuala Lumpur ($26 million), Kelang ($23 million), Penang ($13.5 million), Kuching ($12.7 million) and Sandakan, ($6.3 million). Problem area expenditure (PROB: for special problem areas, like land development and housing target areas--correlation of .685 with population) went most to Kuala Lumpur ($38.8 million), Penang ($28 million), dropping very low, then, to Sibu, third, with $2.1 million. Economic functional expenditures (ECFN: correlation to population of .442) went highest to Kuala Lumpur ($25 million), but next to Kuching, Semanggang following with $8 million.[1] (See Table 1.)

Thus the rough areal patterns of development expenditures of the 1950's indicate heavy rubber replanting and transport investment, and predominance of Kuala Lumpur, Penang, and Kuching. Development of the Kuala Lumpur-Kelang corridor was encouraged by water projects and port development near Kelang though not in Kelang itself. There was moderate correlation, over districts, among the three conceptual types of expenditures, with 67/60 estimated population (67/60 POPN, used for purposes of later comparisons), and with Revenues plus expenditures of local authorities (65 R+ELA). These patterns will assume more meaning when considered in conjunction with later ones below.

On September 16, 1963, the Federation of Malaysia was proclaimed, incorporating the Crown Colonies of Sarawak and North Borneo, Singapore, and the Federation of Malaya. In 1961 the Malayan government had reversed its long held opposition to political union with her neighbors. A major reason for this was perhaps political instability in Singapore--a state which would be granted its independence in 1963.[2] The Malaysia agreement created a House of Representatives containing 159 elected members (104 from Malaya, 16 Sabah, 24 Sarawak, 15 Singapore).

Special grants were set which took into consideration the Borneo States' relatively greater financial needs.[3] Sabah and Sarawak were granted additional sources of revenue including export duties on timber and forest produce and excise duty on petroleum products. In special grants, Sarawak received $5.8 million per year plus an escalating increment for five years reaching $21 million in the last year. This was meant to offset loss of revenue and increased state

---

[1] See Figure 16.

[2] See Gordon P. Means, Malaysian Politics (New York: New York University Press, 1970), pp. 292-96.

[3] That is lower living standards and greater relative development expenditure needs.

TABLE 1

DEVELOPMENT EXPENDITURES TO 1961:
PEARSON PRODUCT MOMENT CORRELATION COEFFICIENTS

	TO61 POPC	TO61 PROB	TO61 ECFN	TO61 URBN	TO61 TOTL	6760 POPN	65R+ ELA
	DISTRICTS						
TO61POPC (to 1961 Population Coverage)	---	.722	.741	.848	.918	.652	.643
TO61PROB (Problem Area)	.786	---	.598	.932	.886	.685	.843
TO61ECFN (Economic-functional)	.879	.471	---	.785	.963	.442	.618
TO61URBN (Urban)				---	.967	.697	.850
TO61TOTL (Total)	.957	.909	.880		---	.674	.800
6760POPN (1967 Estimated West Malaysia and 1960 East Malaysia Population)	.818	.876	.611		.857	---	.655
65R+ELA[a] (1965 Revenues + Expenditures of Local Authorities)	.601	.950	.308		.803	.892	---
65R+EPP[b] (Revenue + Expenditures of Local Authorities per person)	.834	.752	.706		.924	.694	.828
	CITIES						

[a]1965 Revenue plus Expenditure of Local authorities.

[b]1965 Revenue plus Expenditure of Local authorities per person--for cities only.

Source: See Appendix II.

services costs especially for improved state government departments; but it was also a tacit recognition first by the Cobbold Commission and then by the Governments involved that only special developmental assistance for the Borneo States would be an acceptable condition of their entry.[1] In addition the Malaya Govern-

---

[1]See Malaysia, Report of the Inter-Governmental Committee 1962 (Kuala Lumpur: Government Printer, 1963), pp. 13-17, and "Malaysia Agreement Concluded between the United Kingdom of Great Britain and Northern Ireland, the Federation of Malaya, North Borneo, Sarawak and Singapore" (London: Her Majesty's Stationery Office, Command Paper 2094, July, 1963), pp. 33, 76.

ment agreed on base figures of $300 million for Sarawak and $200 million for Sabah for development expenditure in those states in the first five years of Malaysia. The Inter-Governmental Committee emphasized the need for financial aid from outside of Borneo and outside Malaysia (i.e. from Britain) to meet these commitments.[1] Some assistance for Borneo came from Singapore in the form of a 15-year loan of $150 million on liberal terms.[2]

Singapore split from Malaysia on August 9, 1965, on mutual agreement of the Federal and State Governments. The reasons were mutually unreconcilable differences and power conflicts among leaders and factions. It is ironic that Malaysia was left with the Borneo States and without Singapore, when the objective of the union had been to link Malaysia with Singapore, her developed commercial and communications center, once and for all. The London Times concluded that Lee Kuan-Yew and Singapore were evicted.[3] And Malaysia in 1965 was not without internal instability. Although the Cobbold Commission strongly urged union with the Borneo states, concluding that only one third of the affected Borneo population opposed federation, anti-federation and autonomy feelings have been evident in Sabah and Sarawak since August 1965.[4] A net transfer to East Malaysia of about $200 million in 1964, and $230 million in 1965, about two thirds going to Sarawak, mostly from federal government accounts, can be construed as the "price Malaya must pay" for continuation in the Federation.[5]

Later Development Policy

The Federation of Malaya began to implement its Second Five Year Plan in 1961. This was considered to be a "big push" effort by the central govern-

---

[1] Report of the Inter-Governmental Committee, pp. 16-17. The actual expenditure for five years, 1964-1968, appears to be approximately $270 million for Sarawak and $185 million for Sabah.

[2] The Malayan government, however, had sought a grant; see Milton E. Osborne, "Singapore and Malaysia," Data Paper 53, Southeast Asia Program, Department of Area Studies, Cornell University (July, 1964), p. 84.

[3] 10 August 1965, quoted in Bastin and Winks, op. cit., p. 446.

[4] Report of the Commission of Enquiry, North Borneo and Sarawak (Cobbold Commission) (Kuala Lumpur: Government Printer, 1962), p. 50, et passim.

[5] See Donald Snodgrass, "Some Development Implications of Political Integration and Disintegration in Malaysia," in Government and Economic Development, ed. Gustav Ranis (New Haven: Yale University Press, 1971), pp. 30-47, especially pp. 41-42.

ment, bringing together its development programs with those of the states, local authorities, and public enterprises for the first time in a coordinated fashion clearly directed toward development.

In the preceding five-year period the Malayan population was estimated to have been growing at the very high rate of 3.3 per cent per annum. But estimated total output of goods and resources grew at a yearly rate of 4 per cent; so there was some cause for optimism. Total gross investment amounted to about $3 billion or 12 per cent of total income, three-fifths of it being in the private sector.[1] Output growth was concentrated in food stuffs (tin being affected by a world trade recession in 1957-58), and private intestment in manufacturing. Illustrative of the development policy thrusts were the creation of the Petaling Jaya industrial estate outside of Kuala Lumpur, enormous rubber replanting schemes, increased electricity production capacity and, in 1958, inauguration of the Pioneer Industry Policy, which gave tax incentives to qualified enterprises.

Apart from population expansion, the main problems of Malaya in 1960 were seen as economic depression, land hunger of rural individuals, and, as before, excessive national economic dependence on rubber and tin exports, especially rubber. Therefore the objectives of the Plan stressed provision of facilities which would improve conditions for broadening the national economic base. Expanded social services were projected. It was assumed that a stable monetary and financial climate would, as in the recent past, prevail, and that political instability was over.[2]

The greatest change in development financing was to come in the increase of public sector investment, more than doubling that of the First Malaya Plan period, a fair measure of the expansionist attitude of the planners in 1960.[3] It

---

[1] Federation of Malaya, Second Five-Year Plan 1961-1965 (Kuala Lumpur: Government Printer, 1961), p. 123.

[2] See Second Five-Year Plan, pp. 14-16.

[3] In the First Five Year Plan period (1956-60), $964 million was spent for non-security development. The Second Plan period envisaged $2,150 and it was estimated afterward to have cost $2,344.4 million. (See Sumitro, Trade and Aid, p. 243.) However, calculations for Malaysia based on the 1965 Federation of Malaya Financial Statements and similar accounts for Sabah and Sarawak, give a total of $1,706, and $636, respectively. The main discrepancy is in the commerce and industry budget line, where electricity, especially, and also rubber replanting are over-valued by the EPU. Water supply and drainage and irrigation and also development expenditures of public authorities are particularly difficult to handle for development expenditure computation. See Appendix I.

began to stretch Malaysia's resources. As much as 84 per cent was to be borrowed or externally granted, as compared to 52 per cent in the 1956-60 period. Private investment was expected to increase by 40 per cent. (In fact it rose by approximately 85 per cent.)[1]

The greatest changes in emphasis from the First to the Second Malaya Plans were in increased land development expenditures (from approximately $16.7 million to a planned level of $191 million and an actual level of $130 million), and growth in social services (mainly health and education), from 14 per cent in 1956-1960 to a planned proportion of 24.5 per cent, actually 20 per cent. [2] Significant divergences in actual versus planned expenditures show that the planned change in priorities, from "urban" and custodial, to more "rural" and developmental[3] was more illusive than expected. (See Tables 2 and 3.) Even health targets (especially reflecting rural health services needs) were 30 per cent under-fulfilled.

The Colony of North Borneo created a rather conservative development plan for the period, 1959-1964. It assumed initially that $78 million would be available. Subsequently this was increased, so that for the period 1960-65 the final expenditure was approximately $203 million for non-security capital development. The emphasis was on transport, especially road development; Sabah was seen as vastly rich but underserved by communications and access. General government needs and social services came next in importance. As the sixties progressed, however, a shift in balance emerged, reflecting perhaps a new "developmental" bias parallel to that of Malaya: agriculture, utilities, and social services all increased in relation to transport and government which declined in relative importance in the increased development expenditure. Isolated points continued to absorb the major development policy attention, especially Tawau, Jesselton, Sandakan, Semporna, and Labuan. When Malaysia was created, Sabah merged its plan with that of Malaya, functionally operating on a yearly basis until the 1966-1970 First Malaysia Plan.

Sarawak also launched a 1959-1963 Development Plan, an extension of

---

[1] Malaysia, First Malaysia Plan 1966-1970 (Kuala Lumpur: Government Printer, 1965), p. 25.

[2] Sumitro, loc. cit.; Second Five Year Plan, p. 28; Appendix I.

[3] Cf. Gayl Ness, Bureaucracy and Rural Development in Malaysia (Berkeley: University of California Press, 1967), p. 89, et passim; and William Hughes, "Social Benefits through Improved Transport in Malaysia, " in Transport and National Goals, ed. Edwin T. Hoefle (Washington: Brookings, 1969), pp. 105-7.

TABLE 2

SELECTED PLANNED AND ACTUAL SECOND
FIVE-YEAR PLAN SECTORAL EXPENDITURES

	Planned (Mil M$)	Approx. Actual (Mil M$)
"Rural"		
Rubber Replanting	165	130.9
Drainage & Irrigation	100	28.1
Land Development[a]	191	157.3 (1298 Land development alone)
"Urban"		
Roads & Bridges[b]	190	353.4
Civil Aviation	32	63.7
Telecommunications	50	102.2
Broadcasting	5	26.8
Railroads	65	17.7

[a] Includes some rural roads.

[b] Includes expenditures listed elsewhere as going to certain urban areas and believed to be overstated in these sources.

Source: See Appendix II.

the 1955-1960 Plan, with an initial estimated expenditure of about $107.1 million. The goals were said to be unchanged from the past: development of the economy and improvement of social services with emphasis on agriculture and some infrastructure. Social services took a planned and actual 20 per cent of development expenditures. This was regarded by the planners as a fair balance (agriculture and transport, mainly roads, together adding up to 62 per cent. See Table 3.) or compromise between Sarawak's development needs, perhaps newly perceived by the people, and the more general desire for increasing services.

Kuching continued to dominate development policy in Sarawak, especially in population coverage expenditures, i.e. social services. Roads were spread and improved through the First and Second Divisions, particularly those emanating from Simanggang and Sarikei. Eleven per cent of expenditures went to education, which did not include local authorities' expenditures--where there is a basic responsibility for primary education with up to a quarter of the cost there born.[1] But by 1963 it was felt that the tempo of Sarawak's development had to

[1] Accounting in the past for the exceptional high level generally of Sarawak authorities' budgets.

TABLE 3

MALAYSIA PROPORTIONAL PLANNED AND ACTUAL SECTORAL DEVELOPMENT EXPENDITURES 1955-1965

	Malaya			Sabah			Sarawak			Malaysia	
	1955-60 Actual	1960-65 Planned	Est. 1960-65 Actual	1955-60 Actual	1959-63 Planned	1960-65 Actual	1955-60 Actual	1959-63 Planned	Est. 1960-65 Actual	1964-68 Planned	Est. 1960-65 Actual
Initially estimated total (M$000)	884	2090	2,344.7	1093	78	203	147.2	115	250[a]	343	2797[a]
Agriculture %	07	26	20	5[e]	5	8	10	27.4	18	31.7	17
Transport %	13[b]	17	22.4	33[b]	41[b]	33[b]	29[e]	34.8	35[b]	32.2	26[b]
PWD Plant %	--	03	2.7	--	--	--	--	1.1	--	5.8	--
Communications %	6	04	4.8	--	3	4	--	2.2	3	1.9	4
Utilities %	25[d]	19	22.8	0	5[c]	14	0[f]	10.2	13	5.6	21
Industry %	24	01	2.5	50	3[c]	2	39[f]	.2	2	0.2	2
Government & General %	17	06	7.1		31	16		3.6	7	8.1	6
Social Services %	8	24	17.6	12	12	25	22	20.5	20	20	25

Note: Columns do not necessarily add, due to rounding.

[a] This estimate by the EPU is certainly too high, possibly by as much as 50%.

[b] N.D. absorbed in General and Government, utilities, and social services.

[c] Includes credit facilities.

[d] Called civil works.

[e] Includes communications.

[f] Includes utilities.

Source: See Appendix II.

be increased "if the standard of living [was] to be maintained and the economy made secure for the future. "[1] Sarawak was heavily dependent on exports which comprised 40 per cent of the output of the economy and concentrated in rubber (49 per cent), but 81 per cent of the population was in agriculture (64 per cent in rice, with a net [value-added] output per head of $130[2]). There was a clear need for diversification and increased agricultural efficiency. Unlike Sabah, whose timber and prawn exports could serve increasing financing demands, Sarawak at its very low level of development, had large competitive and survival problems--hence, the grants to it associated with the Malaysia agreement. Thus the 1964-1968 Plan, which is subtitled "to be absorbed into the First Malaysian Development Plan 1966-1970 with such revision as may then appear desireable, " was clearly meant as a means of staking out ground for special development strategy and adequate levels of investment in Sarawak (not to be reduced because no one had planned how to spend funds) when Malaysia was viewed as a developmental whole, for the first time, in 1965.

The goals of the 1964-1968 Sarawak Plan were as usual: improved rural standard of living, higher employment and per capita output of the economy, widening of the production base, and expanded social services. The strategy was to increase government and its services and to further emphasize agricultural technological development with rubber replanting research, training and extension, rural credit, and oil-palm and coconut planting. Likewise feeder roads were pushed (36 per cent of planned transport expenditure). Commercial oil-palm estate development was the most important single objective of the plan because it seemed to offer proved potential for agricultural diversification and efficient management in the manner of Malaya and Sabah.

Between 1961 and 1965 projects over $900,000 each in Malaysia concentrated like everything else along the West Coast of Malaya and the few centers of East Malaysia. This will be best seen in the discussion below (Chapter IV) where Policy in Area under the Malaysia Plans is compared to that in this period. Briefly, however, we see that water supply projects concentrated around Kuala Lumpur, Seremban, Penang, Sandakan, and Malacca, as did other population coverage or welfare expenditures (POPC) whose proportion was 35 per cent of total expenditures. Land development schemes were spread from Kedah throughout the Peninsula, but were concentrated in southern Kedah and northern Perak,

---

[1]See Sarawak, Development Plan 1964-1968 (Kuching: Government Printer, 1963), pp. 6-9, 29-34, 56-57, et passim.

[2]Ibid.

TABLE 4

DEVELOPMENT EXPENDITURES 1961-1965:
PEARSON PRODUCT MOMENT CORRELATION COEFFICIENTS

	6165 POPC	6165 PROB	6165 ECFN	6165 URBN	6165 TOTL	6760 POPN	65R+ ELA
			DISTRICTS				
6165POPC (1961-1965 Population Coverage)	---	.610	.862	.968	.954	.766	.963
6165PROB (Problem Area)	.961	---	.527	.607	.704	.533	.623
6165ECFN (Economic-functional)	.929	.922	---	.919	.952	.626	.853
6165URBN (Urban)	---	---	---	---	.969	.695	.971
6165TOTL (Total)	.978	.967	.984	---	---	.725	.937
6760POPN (1967 Estimated West Malaysia & East Malaysia Population)	.865	.914	.808	---	.861	---	.655
65R+ELA (1965 Revenue + Expenditure of Local Authorities)	.726	.946	.145	---	.804	.892	---
65R+EPP (Revenue + Expenditure of Local Authorities per person)	.764	.745	.305	---	.320	.694	.828
			CITIES				

Source: See Appendix II.

western Selangor, eastern Negri Sembilan, central Johore, western Pahang, and eastern Trengganu, and were notably important in Sabah. Problem-area expenditures (PROB: ones to areas with perceived special needs), totalled 12 per cent of expenditures; and expenditures whose locations were (theoretically) determined by economic-functional consideration (ECFN) closely followed urban and transportation patterns along both coasts of Malaya and to the capitals of East Malaysia, constituting 53 per cent of Plan expenditures. Development expenditures that were identifiably purely rural in locational characteristics were $552, 805, 448. Those urban (not counting government buildings at $41, 876, 485) were $236, 062, 384. Patterns of expenditures distributions across districts were correlated rather highly, as indicated in Table 4. Problem-area expenditures showed the least inclination to follow population or the two other expenditure types; and population coverage expenditures as might be expected, followed population, local authority activity, and economic-functional expenditures the most.

Areal Patterns Reconsidered

Malaya, Sabah, and Sarawak, as large units, show striking dissimilarities within a large similarity. They are all tropical, dependent on primary production, administered in British style, comparatively stable and with ethnic patterns that show Chinese and Indians in manufacturing, services, and primary production for export, and Malays and other indigenes in subsistence agriculture and the lowest service jobs. Beyond these elements of commonality, as Snodgrass' table (Table 5) illustrates, variation is wide; and with Singapore in Malaysia there was considerable complementarity.

Malaya in 1963 was a relatively rich, highly specialized exporter of tropical products to the world market, somewhat overpopulated relative to developed land but also with considerable quantities of uncultivated land remaining for future development. Its main development problem was the fact that its two dominant exports, rubber and tin, both had poor future prospects as earners of foreign exchange. Malayan development plans therefore stressed diversification into new lines of production, both agricultural and industrial. . . . Sarawak emerges as the poorest component of the new federation, underpopulated and totally dependent on agriculture and natural resource extraction. Sarawak's economic potential appears to be low; it is hard to conceive any strategy by which it might achieve substantial development, short of really massive applications of capital. Sabah is seen in Table [5] to be underpopulated as well, but it is richer and appears to have a high potential for growth based on plantation and extractive industries, provided (especially in the case of the plantations) that an adequate labor supply is somehow made available. [1]

The areal patterns of population, land use, production, and circulation are well understood. Malaysian policy planners benefit from frequent statistical surveys of Malaya and somewhat similar though so far not usually immediately comparable data from Sabah and Sarawak. Figures Three through Seven show

---

[1] Snodgrass, loc. cit.

TABLE 5

EAST AND WEST MALAYSIA STATISTICS, 1964

	Malaya	Sabah	Sarawak	Malaysia
Population (000)	7,810	507	820	9,137
Malays	3,905 (50%)	---	144 (17.5%)	4,099 (44%)
Chinese	2,890 (37%)	118 (23%)	255 (31.1%)	3,263 (36%)
Indians/Pakistanis	859 (11%)	---	---	859 (9%)
Other Indigenous	4	340 (67%)	412 (50%)	756 (8%)
Other Non-Indigenous	152 (2%)	48 (10%)	9 (1.1%)	209 (2%)
Area (mi^2)	50,700	48,342	29,388	128,430
Density (p/mi^2)	153	17	17	71
GDP (Mil M$) per capita	897	674	809	871
GDP by Sector (%)				
Primary Production	37	54	48	39
Rubber planting	15	8	12	14
Other agi/forestry	14	46	28	17
Mining	9	--	7	8
Industry	17	11	12	13
Services	46	34	40	47
Exports by commodity (Mil M$)	2,781	260	401	3,397
Rubber	1,303	32	60	1,396
Tin	728	---	---	728
Timber	87	149	62	295
Others	663	79	279	978
Exports/Imports by Destination/Source (Mil M$)	2,781/2,521	260/298	401/448	3,397/3,227
West Malaysia	x	1/12	16/9	x
East Malaysia	14/16	4/3	9/1	x
Singapore	569/248	31/37	170/43	770/328
Rest of world	2,198/2,257	224/246	206/396	2,627/2,899

Note: Some columns' elements do not add because of rounding and source discrepancies.

Sources: See Appendix II.

concentrations of human occupance on the west side of Malaya and the south, and in isolated points on the Malayan East Coast and river valleys, and the coasts and riverine areas of Sabah and Sarawak--intermittently connected by roads and generally by air and shipping services.

Land use in Malaysia is sharply determined by physical boundaries and, additionally, by lack of demand for new land. Forest, jungle and swamp areas cover three-quarters of West Malaysia and a high proportion of East Malaysia--

much of central and east Malaya, central and south Sabah, and central and east Sarawak. Shifting cultivation extends through northern Sabah and central Sarawak at the fringes of rice and small-holder rubber plantings, so that only 2-3 per cent of the land is cultivated at one time. Intense padi production in Malaya concentrates in the alluvial valleys of Kedah, Kelantan, and Trengganu, and in riverine areas throughout West Malaya. Tin-mining dominates Perak's Kinta and Larut Valleys and is heavy in Selangor, scattered in Trengganu and Pahang. Some iron is mined in Kedah, Pahang, and Trengganu; and antimony is mined in Sarawak.

Malaysia's total population was estimated in mid-1967 to be 10, 071, 000, with 3 per cent per annum growth rate. In 1970 the Census showed 10, 421, 865 (West Malaysia, 8, 791, 690; Sabah, 655, 295; Sarawak, 974, 880). [1] Population is heavily concentrated on Malaya's West Coast, as can be seen in Figure 4, where the non-Malay population also predominates. The First and Second Divisions of Sarawak and the East and West Coastal areas of Sabah have the larger populations in these states, although density is much lower ($17/mi^2$ in East Malaysia; $153/mi^2$ in West Malaysia).

The West Coast of Malaya is comparatively heavily urbanized, but the urban population, measured as a proportion of district population (the smallest unit at which anything is measured nationally by the government), shows a localized and dispersed pattern. The highest urban percentages are found in Penang, Kuala Lumpur, Kelang, Bentong, Kinta, Seremban, Johore Baharu, Kuantan, and Dungun in Malaya, and Sandakan and Kota Kinabalu in East Malaysia. Racial distribution patterns follow this urban one to a large degree (see Figure 4, cf. Figures 13-15). [2] Chinese and Indian-Pakistani comprise approximately 48 per cent of Malaysia's total population. Chinese live mainly in towns and industrial areas (including a large tin-mining population in Perak and Selangor). Indians[3] are for the most part either town dwellers or rubber estate workers. Malays predominate in East and South Coast States, living mainly in rural and agricultural areas, although there has been an increasing migration to urban areas since the 1950's. Figure 4 shows, nevertheless, a large number of Malays in

---

[1] Malaysia, Department of Statistics, 1971 Population and Housing Census of Malaysia, Field Count Summary (Kuala Lumpur: Department of Statistics, 1971), pp. 22-24, 65-66.

[2] As Racial data are only available for 1957 at this time, correlations and other machine calculations on them seem pointless.

[3] That term will henceforth designate the communal groups originating in the Indian Sub-continent.

all Middle Cities (George Town, Bukit Mertajam, and Kampar having the lowest proportion of Malays, and Kuala Trengganu the highest). East Malaysian ethnic patterns involve non-Malay indigenous peoples, who, for broad economic comparative purposes have been categorized as Malays.[1] Thus in Sabah only four of twenty districts (Sandakan, Lahad Datu, Tawau and Pensiangan) have less than 50 per cent Malay/Indigenes. This is seemingly not correlated with urban population of the districts, but can be explained functionally: timber-exporting and general trading (to the archipelago) cities attract Chinese; administrative and agricultural centers do not in the same degree. Sarawak has a different pattern: Chinese predominate in river port districts (Kuching, Sibu, and Sarikei) and, oddly, in the four eastern districts, where reduced native population, and overseas trading may be the attractions.

In 1967, approximately half the economically active population of West Malaysia was employed in agriculture (more than half of those in rubber).[2] Hence, according to the 1957/60 censuses, about 42 per cent of Malaysia's total population resided in 450 towns and villages with populations exceeding 1,000. Twenty-seven per cent of the population of Malaya was in towns greater than 5,000 in population in West Malaysia and 3,000 or greater in East Malaysia. Penang and Selangor, naturally, possessed the highest proportions of urban population. (See Table 8.) Selangor received a gigantic in-migration of 299,900 new residents between 1956 and 1967; while Kedah, Negeri Sembilan, and Sabah. all exceeded Penang's 16,900.[3]

Cities with the highest growth rate between 1947 and 1967 were Kuala Lumpur (220 per cent), Petaling Jaya (more than 264 per cent), Ipoh (186 per cent), Kota Baharu (162 per cent), and Johore Baharu (137 per cent). Keluang, Miri, Kota Kinabalu, Tawau also had spurts in the 1957-1967 decade. Only Johore Baharu had significantly slower growth then, among the fast-growing centers. (See Table 13.) Notwithstanding government-inspired growth in Kuala Lumpur and the spectacular development of its satellite Petaling Jaya in the

---

[1]They are similarly rural and agricultural, though are not to be supposed adherent to Malay political power structures necessarily.

[2]IBRD-IDA, Current Economic Position and Prospects of Malaysia, I (Kuala Lumpur: IBRD, 1968), 4-5.

[3]See Table 7. Except where land development occurs, primarily in Pahang (which has negative migration indices anyway), it can be assumed from the meager literature that migration is to urban areas.

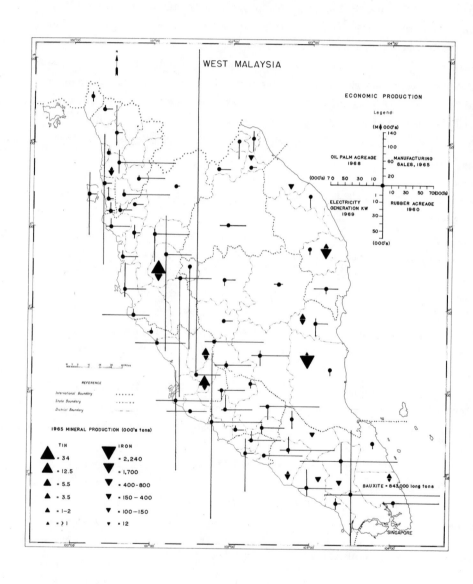

Fig. 6.--Malaysia: Economic Production

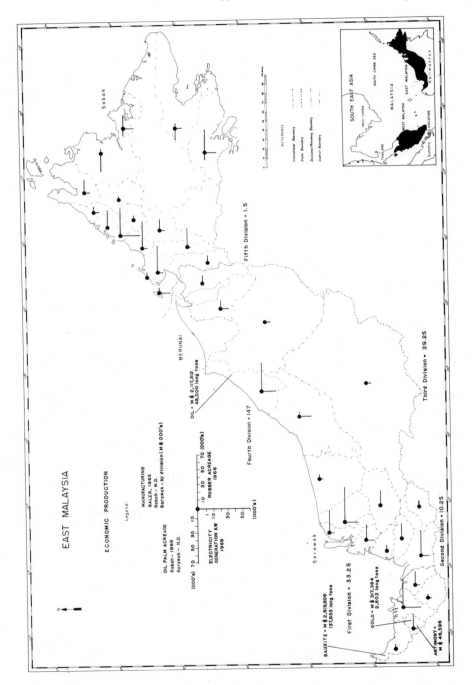

period,[1] this pattern suggests at least a demographic inclination to a multi-centered urban system in modern Malaysia. Hamzah has also observed a significant increase in the number of small towns (2,000-10,000), at least between 1947 and 1957, whose rôles as modernizers may have hastened migrants on their way to larger settlements.[2] Penang's comparative stagnation is notable.

Unemployment in Malaysia naturally has been affected by city-ward migration. With a national unemployment rate of 6 per cent in 1962 and 6.8 per cent in 1967/68, the corresponding metropolitan figures were 9.6 and 10.1; unemployment in smaller urban areas was 8.1 and 9.7 respectively; and in rural areas it was 5.0 and 5.4. The urban labor force in 1967/68 showed ethnic variation, however: Indians had a 12.6 per cent active unemployment rate, Malays 11.7 per cent, and Chinese only 8.5 per cent. This suggests higher unemployment among recent migrants as, to a degree, does the breakdown by type of jobs sought: highest percentages were among seekers of clerical jobs (24.7 per cent) and craftsmen and production processes personnel (20.9 per cent). Professional and technical (11.3 per cent) and sales jobs (5.1 per cent) had a correspondingly lower number of unsuccessful applicants, with labor and services (14.4 per cent and 14.6 per cent) in between.[3]

The demographic pattern described above is reflected in voting behavior in Malaysia and follows or has led administrative forms and quirks as well. Malaysia's Alliance Party dominates most areas and consists of fairly conservative representation of the three significant communal groups. Its leaders were instrumental in setting the British-inspired compromise by which, until May 1969, the centrifugal forces of racial enmity and mistrust were successfully contained. This consisted of constitutionally establishing Malay traditional rulers, language, and symbols as the national artifacts, while leaving, as they would most wish, the Chinese and Indians to do business unhindered in a free enterprise economy.[4] Two Malay-directed manifestations have been the continuation of large Malay and indigenous peoples' reservation areas, that is, land to

---

[1] See Hamzah Sendut, "Statistical Distribution of Cities in Malaysia," Kajian Ekonomi Malaysia, II (December, 1965), 60-61.

[2] See Hamzah Sendut, "Pattern of Urbanization in Malaya," pp. 118-19.

[3] See Department of Statistics, Socio-Economic Survey of Households-- West Malaysia (Kuala Lumpur: Department of Statistics, 1970), pp. 130-39.

[4] This has changed with the New Economic Policy of the Second Malaysia Plan. See Chapter III.

be owned (and for the most part used) only by them, [1] and the setting of voting constituency boundaries to encourage a rural Malay domination of Federal and State Houses of Parliament. [2]

More aggressive and unsatisfied elements break down primarily between Malay and non-Malay opposition parties. This effect may be seen areally. Three patterns emerge from the Federal Parliamentary and State Assembly elections of 1959, 1964, 1969: (1) the Pan Malayan Islamic Party, a rural-based Moslem group, has dominated in Kelantan and somewhat less so in Trengganu; whereas (2) Sabah has been strongly gripped by the Alliance, and Sarawak, which like Sabah had its first election since entering Malaysia in 1970, has splintered into a set of anti-Kuala Lumpur but co-optable voting blocs which are unpredictable; [3] and (3) urban areas generally tend to have strong opposition to the party predominant in their state (the Alliance in all but Kelantan and Trengganu). Thus George Town, Ipoh, Kuala Lumpur, Melaka, and Johore Baharu have supported Chinese community leaders, and Kota Baharu, in 1969, voted in Alliance candidates. Likewise, George Town, Ipoh, Melaka, and Kota Baharu have had opposition party city governments. Some inconsistency, as pointed out by McGee, arises from the heavy across-the-board win of the Alliance in 1964. This makes the 1950 and 1969 patterns more nearly similar, and the 1964 outcome, which was probably related both to fear of Confrontation with Indonesia and satisfaction with Malaysia, odd. [4] Such political behavior will be seen as a complicating factor in the Area in Policy and Policy in Area discussions below.

The administration of Malaysia follows a federal system whose major constituents are the 13 states. This is far from an artificial structure, as all are very distinct in tradition and to a fair degree form and function. This situation is reflected in Table 8 and most of the figures. States hold power over land and local government, and various forms of local taxation, services, and

---

[1] These cover most of habitable Kelantan, Perlis, and Kedah, the Perak and Pahang River Valleys, central Negeri Sembilan, and large parts of interior Sarawak and Sabah.

[2] In West Malaysia. T. G. McGee states that through 1969 this "basic inequality" has not been corrected. See "Down but Not Out," Far Eastern Economic Review (June, 1969), pp. 566-68.

[3] See Bob Reece, "Alliance Troubles," Far Eastern Economic Review (18 June 1970), pp. 7-8.

[4] McGee, "Down but Not Out," loc. cit.

Muslim and native laws, cadastral surveys, and the North Borneo Railway. Concurrently, the State and Federal governments are responsible for amusement regulation, pest control, and agricultural and forestry research. Sabah and Sarawak retained additional powers because of their developed and historically important specialized departments. They have concurrent authority over public health and sanitation, drainage and irrigation, education, and, to a degree, town and country planning and immigration.[1]

The states have vastly varying revenues and expenditures. These have had a low negative correlation with Malay population on a state basis (.187) and a low positive correlation with 1961 (.240) and 1969 (.278) federal grants, 1965 Gross state domestic product (.151), and 1967 estimated population (.253). (See Table 9.) Federal grants have correlated higher with Chinese state populations than with Malay (1961, .902 versus .730; 1969, .501 with Chinese and .098 with Malay population).[2] These consist of road grants, capitation grants, and grants in lieu of rates. They plainly benefit the higher developed states; although the distribution is far more even than might have been expected. It became even more so, as among states, in 1969 when the East Coast states increased spectacularly in proportional allotments.[3]

The states have constitutional responsibility for local government and in the 1960's took over many of the significant local government bodies, which were either ineffectual or financially insolvent, following the national suspension of local elections since 1962. (See Chapter III.) Figure 5 shows the distribution of administration. Kuala Lumpur is the Federal Capital, and has been administered by a Commissioner under the authority of the Ministry of Local Government and Housing, acting in the role of a State under the Federal Capital Act of 1960, and the Municipal Ordinance and Town Boards Enactment. It is functionally a Municipality, as is George Town, (whose official designation, by grace of the Queen in 1957 is "City"). The remaining Municipalities are Ipoh, Melaka, and Kuching. These Municipalities (all state capitals) have a history of

---

[1]See Chapter III below, and Malaysia, Report of the Inter-Governmental Committee, pp. 31-45. This breakdown should not be confused with the location in state departments of federal officers, especially in West Malaysia, where the Federal Departments they represent hold the authority and responsibility, and the states provide assistance and office space.

[2]The discrepancy between 1961 and 1969 can be accounted for by the addition of Sabah and Sarawak and their disproportionally large Federal inputs.

[3]Kelangan, 67 per cent; Trengganu, 156 per cent; Pahang, 24 per cent; versus Selangor, 57 per cent; Penang, 20 per cent; and Johore, 60 per cent.

greater budgetary virtuosity (though no greater powers than financially autonomous Town Councils), and higher levels of public service, in contrast, for
example, to Johore Baharu and Seremban. City government revenues plus
expenditures per capita in 1965 were significantly higher in the Municipalities.
This accounts for the comparatively low correlation (.694) of this variable
(65R+EPP) with 1967 estimated city populations (see Figure 4). Of Municipalities, only Ipoh and Kuching have functioning elected Councils; George Town and
Melaka were taken over in 1967 by their respective State Governments.[1]

Of Town Councils, the next lower category, Seremban was taken over in
1965, for, like George Town, alleged malpractices, and Johore Baharu in 1966
for the same reason. Functioning Town Councils can and do act fairly independently, however, and have the financial difficulties that accrue thereby.[2] They,
like Town Boards, may be either financially autonomous (from their States) or
not. The 37 Town Councils have a total estimated 1967 population of 1,086,516,
and an average of 29,365. They are widely dispersed in the settled areas and
serve a variety of functions. Of the 27 Middle Cities treated here, 14 are Town
Councils.

They are paralleled in size and importance by certain Town Boards and
District Councils to which administrative happenstance has denied Town Council
status. Such are the governments of Butterworth and Bukit Mertajam which, as
in the case of Melaka, also govern a district containing them, for historical
reasons, as District Councils. Similarly, in Sarawak, every part of the country is governed by an elected local authority. Sabah has a like coverage, though
not democracy of authority.[3] Sibu and Miri, like Kota Kinabalu and Sandakan,
are Town Boards. Petaling Jaya, anomalously, is also a Town Board, but with
a State Government Branch Office.[4]

---

[1] Ipoh's and Kuching's and the other remaining elected local governments
in Malaysia may cease to exist soon as well. See Chapter III.

[2] Much of local revenue for such governments derives from a general
assessment rate, which is made difficult by antique and inadequate property
assessing. Only 3 per cent of all national revenue accrues to local authorities,
and 90 per cent goes to municipalities in West Malaysia, not counting transfers.
(Source: Ministry of Housing and Local Government, 1970.)

[3] Its 1962 Local Government (District Councils) Ordinance established
local authorities in rural areas, achieving total areal coverage by 1964.

[4] With publication and, at least, limited acceptance of the Nahappan Royal
Commission report on local government, it is hoped that the distribution of local
authority will be rationalized. (See Chapter III.)

74

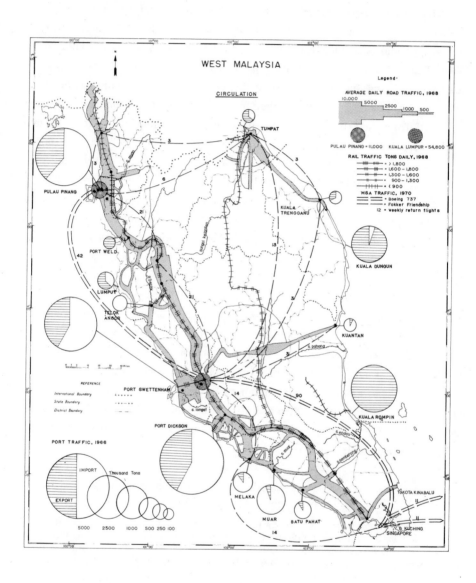

Fig. 7.--Malaysia: Circulation

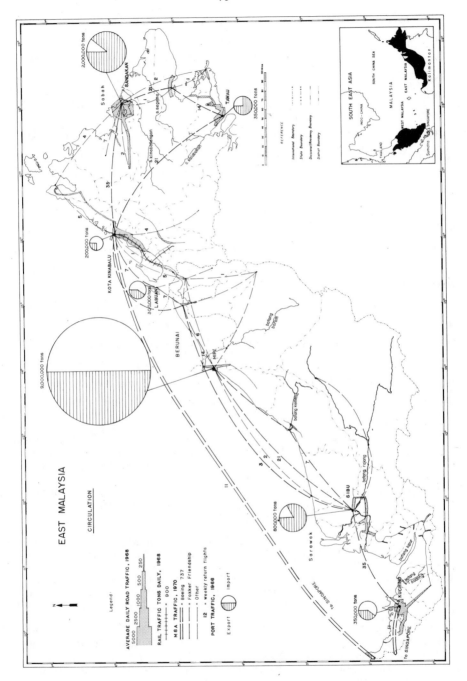

EAST MALAYSIA

CIRCULATION

Naturally, patterns of economic production in Malaysia are highly associated with settlement patterns. In West Malaysia and to a far lesser degree in
East Malaysia a dual economy has developed. The export economy has always
employed and sometimes been operated by Chinese in the case of tin, and Tamils,
mostly, in the case of plantation rubber. Processing, what limited manufacturing there is, and services are practically monopolized by non-Malays, and all
of this modern economic activity, with the exception of logging, is associated
with the non-Malay population on the West and South Coast of Malaya and centered on medium- and (comparatively) large-sized cities there and on the coast
of East Malaysia. Until recently expatriate management has predominated.[1]

All together agriculture accounted for 31 per cent of Malaysia's Gross
Domestic Product in 1964, with rubber taking 14 per cent.[2] Mining was second
to agricultural production in export importance in 1964. (But note the importance of services in the GDP.) Tin and iron export values both rose in the
early sixties.[3]

Manufacturing follows the modern sector pattern most closely. As much
as 53 per cent of the manufacturing industry's market is believed to be within a
50-mile radius of Kuala Lumpur, reflecting both population potentials and especially buying-power concentrated there.[4] Kuala Lumpur had 383 per cent greater sales of its own manufacturing goods in 1967 than its nearest competitor,
the Penang Metropolitan Area (George Town, Butterworth, Prai, Ayer Itam).

---

[1] Plantation agriculture is spread throughout west and south Malaya. Rubber is particularly concentrated in southern Kedah, western Perak, Selangor,
Negeri Sembilan, and Johore, as well as the First and Second Divisions of Sarawak and the west coast of Sabah. Oil palm has been recently introduced at a
large scale and can be grown on land formerly accommodating rubber; but in
1968 oil palm acreage was concentrated in lower Perak, western Selangor,
south-central Johore, and in a large development west of Sandakan.

[2] Despite 6.2 per cent growth from 1960 to 1965 in the export value due to
declining prices. (See Malaysia, First Malaysia Plan [Kuala Lumpur: Government Printer, 1965], p. 123.) Endless decline of rubber prices is not to be
taken for granted, however: after falls in 1970 and 1971, the price in 1972 was
up over 50 per cent. And the plantation firms have diversified not only into oil
palm but outside the industry as well. (See Economist, January 27, 1973, p. 84.)

[3] Tin deposits are found primarily in Kinta, and Kuala and Ulu Selangor.
Iron is mined in quantity in these districts, as well as in Kuala Muda, west and
central Johore, and in scattered locations along the Malay East Coast. Antimony, bauxite, oil and gold are all produced in moderate, though commercial
amounts in Sarawak. (See Figure 6.)

[4] EPU, "Some Data on the Distribution of Economic Activity in West Malaysia," n.d., fugitive, p. 4.

Close behind Penang were Port Dickson (petroleum primarily), Johore Baharu, and Ipoh. In fact Kuala Lumpur dominates all manufacturing except that of primary agricultural products (rubber milling, coconut oil and palm oil milling and rubber products manufacturing), and tin smelting.[1] In 1965 Selangor accounted for 39.1 per cent of full-time industrial employment. But there, as in Penang, Ipoh, Melaka, and Kelang, unemployment was very high--said to be about 10 per cent in such towns in 1968, versus a maximum figure of 5.4 per cent in the rural areas of West Malaysia.[2]

Circulation[3] in Malaysia understandably is oriented to moving export products out, to transporting mass consumption articles and people between population centers, and to connecting the East and West divisions of the country. In terms of cargo values, the port of Penang is only slightly larger now than Port Swettenham, with about the same moderate overbalance, in tons, of imports.[4] In West Malaysia the gigantic presence of Singapore is especially felt through the circulation pattern: Singapore's hinterland extends, especially by rail, as far north as Kota Baharu on the East, and beyond Melaka on the West.[5] Road and air traffic patterns appear to follow population distributions. Electricity is moved by a north-south, west-coast network to major use centers from Butterworth, Cameron Highlands, Batang Padang, Kelang, Port Dickson, and Johore Baharu, as well as numerous smaller generators.

---

[1] Among Middle Cities, Ipoh, Johore Baharu, Butterworth, Kelang, George Town, and Melaka, in that order, predominate. Ipoh appears to rank highest in industrial machinery, Johore Baharu in rubber products, and Penang in publishing, among larger-scale manufacturing activities. (1965, establishments with gross sales greater than $100,000. See Survey of the Manufacturing Industry in West Malaysia [Kuala Lumpur: Department of Statistics, 1965], passim.) In West Malaysia industrial value-added by subsectors in 1965 was as follows: food, etc., 21 per cent; textiles, etc. 1.6 per cent; wood, paper, printing, 15.1 per cent; rubber processing and products, 23 per cent; minerals, 6 per cent; chemicals and petroleum products, 16 per cent; and metals and machinery, 15 per cent. Thus rubber is the biggest industry, and food processing and textiles are seen to be relatively underdeveloped for Southeast Asia. (See Current Economic Position and Prospects of Malaysia, p. 7.)

[2] Kuala Lumpur, Ipoh, Johore Baharu, George Town, Butterworth, Alor Setar, and Melaka, in that order had the highest registered unemployment (employment applicants) in January, 1970. This (unreliable) indicator was exceptionally low for East Malaysian cities. (See Table 13.) (Tun Razak, Budget Address [Kuala Lumpur: Government Printer, 1970], p. 8.)

[3] See Figure 7.

[4] Port Dickson and Miri specialize in petroleum, and Bandar Maharani, Batu Pahat, Melaka, Kuching, and Kota Kinabalu in general imports. Sandakan, Tawau, and Sibu primarily export primary exports.

[5] Robert Nathan, Malaysia Transportation Survey, p. 91, and Figure 11.

CHAPTER III

AREA IN POLICY

The Malaysia Plans

On 25 November 1965, the First Malaysia Plan was promulgated. Its duration was to be five years, through 1970. It was the first development plan to treat East and West Malaysia together; but the states of Sabah and Sarawak were given even more attention than their low levels of development might have merited. The recent expulsion of Singapore also complicated matters. In June, 1971 the Second Malaysia Plan was made public, a year and a half late. Also a five-year plan, it continued many of the policies of the First Plan, while incorporating new or strengthening former goals and strategy directed at correcting economic imbalances among groups.

This chapter analyzes the areal content of the two plans, that is, area in policy. Because the policy in area chapters that follow must deal primarily with the years 1966-68, for which expenditure data in detail have been available, emphasis is placed in this monograph on the First Malaysia Plan, which includes those years, except where striking changes in areal conception or administration is contemplated in the Second Plan.

The First Malaysia Plan (FMP) specified four main socio-economic problems facing Malaysia: (1) overdependence on rubber and tin export; (2) high rates of population increase; (3) uneven distribution of income as between rural and urban populations and between West and East Malaysia; and (4) a low level of human resource development, yielding shortages of skills.[1] Added to these were the problems of (5) a poor areal distribution of manpower;[2] and (6) urban unemployment. Resources for financing development policy were not regarded as a serious problem; nor were gross poverty, disease, communications, physical malaise, or will to develop. Malaysia, in short, was a comparatively rich

---

[1] Malaysia, The First Malaysia Plan (Kuala Lumpur: Government Printer, 1965), p. 1.

[2] Ibid., p. 79.

country whose development problems were somewhat esoteric by Third World
standards.

These problems persisted into the period of the Second Malaysia Plan,
just as they had existed in earlier planning periods. Of the six problems, economic disparities has greatest prominence in the Second Malaysia Plan (SMP),
followed by unemployment. In the language of the "New Economic Policy" of
1971, eradication of poverty became the greatest need.[1]

Hence the goals of the FMP, in order of mention, were (1) to promote
integration of the peoples and states of Malaysia; (2) to provide steady increases
in levels of income and consumption per capita; (3) to increase the well-being of
rural and low income groups; (4) to generate increasing employment opportunities; (5) to stimulate new economic activities which would lessen dependence on
rubber and tin exports; (6) to educate and train the population for increased
development; (7) to institute an effective family-planning program; (8) to open
new land for agricultural development; (9) to provide more infrastructure; and
(10) to progress with health and social welfare development.[2]

The Second Malaysia Plan refined these into two prongs of policy. Its
goals are (1) "to reduce and eventually eradicate poverty by raising income
levels and increasing employment opportunities for all Malaysians, irrespective
of race"; and (2) to accelerate "the process of restructuring Malaysian society
to correct economic imbalance, so as to reduce and eventually eliminate the
identification of race with economic function. This process involves the modernization of rural life, a rapid and balanced growth of urban activities and the creation of a Malay commercial and industrial community in all categories . . . "[3]

The order of objectives of the plans differs somewhat when planned expenditures are seen. In the First Malaysia Plan the order of expenditures priorities was: electricity, education, roads, land development, drainage and irrigation, agriculture, water supply, health, housing, telecommunications, ports
and so on. In the Second Malaysia Plan the order for slightly broader categories
is: agriculture and rural development, transport, utilities, commerce and
industry, education and training, communications, social and community services, health and family planning, etc. (See Table 6.)

The strategy of Malaysian development policy depends heavily on free
and encouraged private sector dynamism, especially new investments. The

---

[1]Malaysia, Second Malaysia Plan (Kuala Lumpur: Government Printer,
1971), pp. 4-5.

[2]First Malaysia Plan, p. 2.   [3]Second Malaysia Plan, p. 1.

TABLE 6

MALAYSIA: SECTORAL ALLOCATION OF PUBLIC DEVELOPMENT EXPENDITURES 1966-1975: PART I
($ millions)

Sectors	Plan Target 1966-70	Estimated Expenditure 1966-68	Achievement %	Revised Plan Target 1966-70	Balance to Complete 1969-70	Consolidated[a] Current Expenditure of Federal and State Governments 1966-68	Capital Expenditure of Federal and States Governments and Public Authorities 1966-68
Agriculture & Rural Development	1,086.6	556.0	51.2	1,177.9	621.9	169	551.5
Agriculture	267.5	158.7	59.3	342.7	184.0		
Animal Husbandry	33.8	11.5	34.0	29.0	17.5		
Fisheries	22.3	4.7	21.1	21.7	17.0		
Forestry	12.4	8.1	65.3	21.4	13.3		
Drainage & Irrigation	332.7	185.6	55.8	349.9	164.3	138	189.2
Land Development	375.9	172.5	45.9	393.0	220.5		187.1
Others	42.0	14.9	35.5	20.2	5.3		
Mining	1.3	.4	30.8	.8	.4	66	
Mines	.5	-	-	-	-		
Geological Survey	.8	.4	50.0	.8	.4		104.2
Industrial Development	114.5	90.4	79.0	133.9	43.5	16	
MIDF	16.0	16.0	100.0	16.0	-		
Industrial Estates	14.0	18.0	128.6	22.6	4.6		
NISIR	5.0	.3	6.0	2.3	2.0		
FIDA[b]	5.0	2.2	44.0	6.0	3.8		
MARA[b]	70.0	48.0	68.6	78.4	30.4		
Borneo Development Corp. Ltd.	4.2	2.4	57.1	4.0	1.6		

Others	.3	3.5	1,166.7	4.6	1.1		349.5
Transport	546.0	332.5	60.9	705.7	373.2	60	196.3
Roads & Bridges	389.5	192.1	49.3	430.9	238.8		
Railways	21.3	35.5	166.7	65.3	29.8		
Civil Aviation	21.5	41.5	193.0	64.3	22.8		
Ports	113.7	63.4	55.8	145.2	81.8		
Communications	205.4	103.2	50.2	236.9	133.7		106
Telecommunications	142.5	74.4	52.2	173.0	98.6		
Broadcasting	53.0	25.8	48.7	52.6	26.8	98	
Meteorological Service	.3	.6	200.0	1.6	1.0		
Posts	9.6	2.4	25.0	9.7	7.3		
Utilities	786.3	453.6	57.7	793.5	339.9		462
Electricity	584.3	359.0	61.4	548.9	189.9	639	360
Water Supplies	202.0	94.6	46.8	244.6	150.0		102
Education & Training	440.8	191.1	43.4	391.5	200.4	1,179	182.6
Health & Family Planning	189.5	106.5	56.2	178.9	72.4	454	108.8
Social & Community Services	315.1	175.8	55.8	323.8	148.0	66	162.2
Housing	188.1	103.5	55.0	203.5	100.0		
Major Sewerage Schemes	21.6	1.0	4.6	5.0	4.0		
Others	105.4	71.3	67.6	115.3	44.0		
Genl. Administration	126.2	87.7	69.5	205.2	117.5	1,772	117.7
Subtotal (Nonsecurity)	3,811.7	2,097.2	55.0	4,148.1	2,050.9	4,657	2,144.5
Defense	600.0	345.4	57.6	555.3	209.9	729	382.4
Internal Security	139.0	66.5	47.8	135.5	69.0	467	68.6
Subtotal (Security)	739.0	411.9	55.7	690.8	278.9	1,196	451.0
Total	4,550.7	2,509.1	55.1	4,838.9c	2,329.8	5,853	2,595.5

[a] Excluding public authorities.
[b] Excludes capital cost of MARA Institute of Technology, which is included under Education and Training.
[c] Allowing for shortfalls, the revised Plan target is $4,477 million.

Note: Discrepancies occur because of revisions by governments.
Source: See Appendix II.

TABLE 6

MALAYSIA: SECTORAL ALLOCATION OF PUBLIC DEVELOPMENT EXPENDITURES 1966-1975: PART II
($ million)

Sectors	1966-70 (Estimated)					1971-75 (Allocation)				
	West Malaysia[a]	Sabah[b]	Sarawak[c]	Total	%	West Malaysia[d]	Sabah[e]	Sarawak[f]	Total	%
Economic	2,210.8	278.3	196.3	2,685.4	63.3	3,898.76	555.55	416.66	4,870.97	67.2
Agriculture & Rural Development	911.2	116.2	86.7	1,114.1	26.3	1,570.86	198.40	151.60	1,920.86	26.5
Agriculture	61.0	23.0	12.8	96.8	2.3	108.70	8.48	32.03	149.21	2.1
Rubber Replanting	116.3	10.0	42.6	168.9	4.0	210.40	8.25	50.43	269.08	3.7
Land Development (FLDA, FELCRA, Youth Land Schemes, Public Estates)	309.7	47.0	6.9	363.6	8.6	795.14	102.55	10.96	908.65	12.5
Drainage & Irrigation	328.5	8.4	5.7	342.6	8.1	228.17	15.39	12.93	256.49	3.5
Forestry	11.9	1.7	1.3	14.9	0.4	8.67	7.21	2.35	18.23	0.3
Animal Husbandry	13.9	2.7	1.9	18.5	0.4	37.01	3.83	3.26	44.10	0.6
Fisheries	5.3	2.1	1.6	9.0	0.2	39.79	2.18	3.87	45.84	0.6
Agricultural Credit & Marketing (Bank Pertanian, FAMA, Cooperatives, Padi Board & Rural Credit)	13.8	9.3	6.5	29.6	0.7	97.25	29.25	28.60	155.10	2.1
Agricultural Research (MARDI & Division of Food Technology)	8.8	3.0	1.2	13.0	0.3	34.03	13.26	2.92	50.21	0.7
Others	42.0	9.0	6.2	57.2	1.3	11.70	8.00	4.25	23.95	0.3

Mineral Resources Development	0.4	0.3	---	0.7	---	0.50	0.18	---	0.68	---
Mines Department	---	---	---	---	---	---	---	---	---	---
Geological Survey	0.4	0.3	---	0.7	---	0.50	0.18	---	0.68	---
Commerce & Industry	137.0	1.9	2.4	141.3	3.3	564.53	12.75	6.32	583.60	8.0
National Corporation (PERNAS)	10.0	---	---	10.0	0.2	100.00	---	---	100.00	1.4
Majlis Amanah Ra'ayat (MARA)	50.9	---	---	50.9	1.2	73.00	---	---	73.00	1.0
State Economic Development Corporations (SEDC's)	---	---	---	---	---	45.60	---	---	45.60	0.6
Industrial Estates	19.3	1.9	2.4	23.6	0.6	4.40	12.75	6.32	23.47	0.3
Urban Development Authority (UDA)g	---	---	---	---	---	100.00	---	---	100.00	1.4
Malaysian Industrial Development Finance Bhd. (MIDF)	16.0	---	---	16.0	0.4	100.00	---	---	100.00	1.4
Malaysian Rubber Development Corporation (MRD)	2.6	---	---	2.6	0.1	35.00	---	---	35.00	0.5
Malaysian International Shipping Corporation (MISC)	10.1	---	---	10.1	0.2	46.00	---	---	46.00	0.6
Other investment in economic enterprises (including a new Development Bankh)	7.3	---	---	7.3	0.2	45.05	---	---	45.05	0.6
Tourism	0.4	---	---	0.4	---	10.00	---	---	10.00	0.2
NISIR, SIM, NPC	0.3	---	---	0.3	---	5.48	---	---	5.48	0.1

TABLE 6--Continued

Sectors	1966-70 (Estimated)					1971-75 (Allocation)				
	West Malaysia [a]	Sabah [b]	Sarawak [c]	Total	%	West Malaysia [d]	Sabah [e]	Sarawak [f]	Total	%
Federal Industrial Development Authority (FIDA)	3.4	---	---	3.4	0.1	(10)[h]	---	---	(10)[h]	---
Others	16.7	---	---	16.7	0.4	---	---	---	---	---
Feasibility Studies	---	---	---	---	---	23.26	0.10	7.00	30.36	0.4
Transport	355.9	108.5	80.5	544.9	12.8	794.50	243.30	150.56	1,188.36	16.4
Roads & Bridges	161.3	79.8	68.2	309.3	7.3	505.10	123.67	64.79	693.56	9.6
Railways	47.0	3.9	---	50.9	1.2	85.70	8.02	---	93.72	1.3
Civil Aviation	40.3	14.3	6.5	61.1	1.4	49.76	46.60	12.40	108.76	1.6
Ports & Marine	82.9	5.8	4.3	93.0	2.2	122.94	60.26	46.59	229.79	3.2
PWD Plant & Equipment	24.4	4.7	1.5	30.6	0.7	31.00	4.75	26.78	62.53	0.5
Communications	159.5	25.1	18.4	203.0	4.8	287.31	65.54	47.17	400.02	5.5
Telecommunications	118.7	13.8	13.7	146.2	3.4	222.95	38.44	37.00	298.39	4.1
Broadcasting	35.2	11.2	4.6	51.0	1.2	45.70	25.60	7.85	79.15	1.1
Postal	4.4	0.1	0.1	4.6	0.1	15.16	1.50	2.32	18.98	0.3
Meteorological Services	1.2	---	---	1.2	---	3.50	---	---	3.50	---
Utilities	646.8	26.3	8.3	681.4	16.1	657.80	35.28	54.01	747.09	10.3
Electricity	494.6	9.3	2.7	506.6	11.9	480.80	17.38	40.34	538.52	7.4
Rural Electrification	23.0	1.0	---	24.0	0.6	20.00	3.32	1.50	24.82	0.3
Water	129.2	16.0	5.6	150.8	3.6	157.00	14.58	12.17	183.75	2.5
Social	644.7	54.0	53.4	752.1	17.7	836.02	123.93	107.43	1,067.38	14.7
Education & Training	286.9	16.5	26.0	329.4	7.8	458.89	36.00	42.37	537.26	7.4
Ministry of Education	213.1	16.5	26.0	255.6	6.0	370.11	36.00	42.37	448.48	6.2

Industrial Training									
MARA (Institute of Technology, Scholarships & Training)	73.0	---	---	73.0	1.7	85.08	---	---	85.08	1.2
Health & Family Planning	114.2	13.0	19.4	146.6	3.5	171.08	25.00	17.57	213.65	2.9
Social & Community Services	243.6	24.5	8.0	276.1	6.5	206.05	62.93	47.49	316.47	4.4
Housing	181.1	13.0	3.1	197.2	4.6	136.16	23.23	12.50	171.89	2.4
Sewerage	6.8	2.4	0.4	9.6	0.2	13.60	10.37	---	23.97	0.3
Culture, Youth & Sports	4.6	---	---	4.6	0.1	5.00	1.23	1.00	7.23	0.1
Community Services	42.8	9.1	4.5	56.4	1.3	32.98	26.04	33.51	92.53	1.3
Welfare	3.4	---	---	3.4	0.1	10.93	2.06	0.48	13.47	0.2
Aborigines	4.9	---	---	4.9	0.1	7.38	---	---	7.38	0.1
General Administration	109.0	19.1	10.0	138.1	3.3	139.27	39.72	32.59	211.58	2.9
Security	645.7	7.3	13.8	666.8	15.7	994.07	54.60	51.40	1,100.07	15.2
Defense	532.4	---	---	532.4	12.5	813.07	24.60	12.40	850.07	11.7
Accommodation	130.0	---	---	130.0	3.1	173.57	24.60	12.40	210.57	2.9
Equipment	402.4	---	---	402.4	9.5	639.50	---	---	639.50	8.8
Internal Security	113.3	7.3	13.8	134.4	3.2	181.00	30.00	39.00	250.00	3.4
Accommodation	83.4	7.3	13.8	104.5	2.5	140.20	30.00	39.00	209.20	2.9
Equipment	29.9	---	---	29.9	0.7	40.80	---	---	40.80	0.6
Total	3,610.2	358.7	273.5	4,242.4	100.0	5,868.12	773.80	608.08	7,250.00	100.0

a Includes development expenditure of Statutory Authorities ($504.9 million) and States of West Malaysia ($267.2 million).

b Includes Federal expenditure of $151.8 million.

c Includes Federal expenditure of $254.7 million.

d Includes development allocations of $518.6 million and $242.8 million from internal resources of Public Authorities and States of West Malaysia, respectively.

e Includes Federal allocation of $383.4 million.

f Includes Federal allocation of $383.1 million.

g The allocation of $100 million for UDA will cover building of business complexes and commercial centers incorporating housing units. The division of this allocation between commercial and business complexes and housing incorporated therein has not yet been determined. The percentage in the Social sector will be proportionately adjusted to the extent of the allocation made for housing units, when finalized.

h Token provision, pending the formulation of projects.

Source: See Appendix II.

target of expectation for private expenditure in the First Malaysia Plan was M$5, 950 million, versus M$4, 550 in the public sector. In the Second Malaysia Plan it is $7, 843, versus $7, 250 public sector investment. For the period 1966-68, private investment increased by 6.3 per cent annually, only slightly short of the Plan projection; but gross investment expanded only at a rate of 3.1 per cent annually, as compared to the target of 4.2 per cent. The considerable weakness between 1967 and 1969 was eliminated thereafter, when in 1970 private investment jumped more than 30 per cent over the 1969 level. Output volume increased unexpectedly fast in the 1966-68 period (7.6 per cent per annum or more than five times the projection), while production for domestic use grew by only 5.8 per cent (as compared to the Plan projection of 7 per cent). Planners observe that they had underestimated the growth potentials of palm oil, timber, and tin. [1]

In the public sector, the strategy of the First Malaysia Plan was, as suggested above, to concentrate expenditures as usual on infrastructure, but with increasing attention to land development and training enterprises. [2] It was realized, however, that there were only limited development possibilities in the traditional sectors of the Malaysian economy:

> As the agricultural resources of the country become more fully exploited, growth in secondary industry will have to be relied upon to produce progressive increases in income and employment for a growing population. If national income and employment are to rise over the next twenty years . . . , considerable structural changes in the economy will have to occur, with industry accounting for an increasing share of the total . . . [3]

A key emphasis of the government's development program, then, was to be on projects which were designed to "increase productivity and investment in a

---

[1] In terms of receipts at current prices, indeed, exports increased by only 1.4 per cent a year (tin, rubber, and palm-oil prices being especially depressed); whereas the current value of production for domestic use grew as planned at about 8 per cent annually. Average annual growth of total private investment from 1966 to 1970, then, was 9.7 per cent. (See First Malaysia Plan, pp. 46-47; Malaysia, Mid-Term Review of the First Malaysia Plan [Kuala Lumpur: Government Printer,] 1969 , pp. 4-7; and Second Malaysia Plan, pp. 82-84.)

[2] For example the Water Supply Branch wrote during the period: "It is the aim of the government to make treated pipe water available to as large a proportion of the population as possible . . . and to devise means to enable rural people to have water connections to their homes" (undated memorandum, PWD); and "Government planners see highway developments as the most effective way in bridging the gap between the developed West Coast and the lesser-developed East Coast." (George Tan, Malay Mail [Kuala Lumpur], May 14, 1970, p. 7.)

[3] First Malaysia Plan, p. 23.

widening range of primary and secondary industries, particularly labor intensive, or those utilizing natural products or markets."[1] This meant the promotion of industrial activities primarily through special government bodies, whose
functions are described in the discussion of "Administrative Area" below.

Overall strategy took a turn, seemingly, with the New Economic Policy,
and the Second Malaysia Plan. "Greater participation by Malays and other
indigenous people in manufacturing and commercial activities is a fundamental
objective of the Plan."[2] The government has decided to intervene in the private
enterprise economy, including its urban sector, on behalf of the Malays and
indigenes,[3] meaning institutional changes, as well as adjustments in expenditure
patterns. A distinction is made between two types of poverty: rural and urban.
Both of them are to be eradicated. And their identification has led the way to
the beginning of an urban policy. Two striking strategic aspects of the Second
Malaysia Plan are: (1) that employment is such a severe problem that even with
all that the public sector can do, the goal will be simply to avoid an increase in
unemployment in the next five years;[4] and (2) that transport allocations will
increase (to nearly one-fifth of the total non-security expenditure). That is surprising in light of the high expenditures of the past and the feeling then that these
would taper off in the future. The rationale is that a modern economy needs
improved main routes, dispersal of industrial activities, and the development
of new growth centers.[5]

There are two remaining generally important aspects of development
planning in Malaysia which have areal significance: (1) there has been and con-
tinues to be a distinct project orientation. This has meant that when planning is
rushed, as usually is the case, choice of projects and their aggregation into sectoral plans can be less than optimal.[6] And integrated regional planning is diffi-

---

[1] Ibid., p. 67; and see Mid-Term Review, pp. 73-74.

[2] Emphasis in text, Second Malaysia Plan, p. 158.

[3] The target has 30 per cent of total commercial industrial ownership and
management activities to be in indigenous or Malay hands in two developments;
Second Malaysia Plan, p. 158.

[4] The goal has to hold the rate at no more than 7.3 per cent a year, i.e.
to create 3 per cent more jobs each year. (Ibid., p. 5.)

[5] Ibid., p. 73.

[6] The Economic Planning Unit of the Prime Minister's Office (EPU) reports in an undated paper: "The preparation of the First Malaysia Plan, in as
far as the Ministry of Works, Posts and Telecommunications was concerned

cult to conceive. (2) Some ministries and operating agencies are more efficient than others at fulfilling their tasks. Land development has been a laggard;[1] the public works department has been far behind in building schools, water supply systems, and some transportation facilities. On the other hand, where purchase of equipment from abroad (airplanes, generators) is the major expenditure, development can proceed apace. Thus, certain sectors (like road-building, in the past) can keep going on their momentum, eating up funds, and later denying resources to slower activities or departments because of the flexibility of the yearly budget system and the finiteness of the total plan expenditure.[2]

It is interesting that in the Second Malaysia Plan the problem of shortfalls in performance of departments, which totalled 32 per cent overall for the First Malaysia Plan, has been handled by a laissez-faire approach: each department has been allocated more money than it is expected to be able to spend-- all for specific projects. The Second Malaysia Plan itself really contains two budgets for the 1971-75 period. One has a total of M$7,250 million for the public sector which is the figure to which the departmental segments add. But the Plan then notes: "Out of this targeted allocation, the actual public development expenditure will be at least $6,000 million."[3] Although the Prime Minister has said, in effect, that money will be no problem during this plan period (whereas the Treasury was rather tight at the beginning of the First Malaysia Plan), departments are still expected in toto to be unable to exceed the approximately M$6,000 million figure. Ones which can spend all of the larger amount allocated to them are invited to. Those who cannot spend their maximum or even their minimum will find the funds transferred to departments which can.

---

was done in a hurry with a note of urgency . . . in the case of water supplies schemes, especially, the requests were compiled by the State Engineers and forwarded to the PWD Headquarters. The Headquarters had no means of determining the viability and feasibility of such projects . . . " The apparent downplaying of East Malaysia in the Second Malaysia Plan may be accounted for, as well, by an absence of data and poor coordination in preparing projects for the Second Malaysia Plan. Lesser mention of Sabah and Sarawak may not mean less attention as the plan proceeds, however.

[1] Especially prior to the First Malaysia Plan, and in agencies other than the Federal Land Development Authority (FLDA) in the First Malaysia Plan.

[2] See Albert Waterston, Development Planning: Lessons of Experience (Baltimore: Johns Hopkins Press, 1965), p. 203. He points out that in Malaysia the annual budget substitutes for an annual plan smoothly. See also Second Malaysia Plan, p. 181.

[3] See Development Administration Unit of the Prime Minister's Office (DAU), "The Problem of Shortfalls," 1969, fugitive (mimeographed). And see Table 10, 1966-68 percentage of fulfillment, and Second Malaysia Plan, p. 116.

The past shortfalls and the present policy tend to favor development policy implementation in urban and central areas, where equipment purchased overseas for the most part goes and where road and other government construction in likely to be the most efficient. Unlike during the First Malaysia Plan, which started distinctly slowly, the budget for 1971, the first year of the Second Malaysia Plan, was higher than the planned average for the five-year period. This was explained as the result of "certain building up of expenditures, in 1971 particularly for completion of major projects during the year" and to cover still-unfinished First Malaysia Plan commitments.[1] Thus certain discrepancies between planned and actual areal disposition of development policy activity are built into Malaysian Plans and in the SMP period will be felt immediately.

What have been the results of Malaysian development programs? One agrees first of all with the conclusions that, "among mixed economy countries, Malaya probably has the most effective comprehensive system for planning at [federal,] state, district and local levels,"[2] and likewise that in Southeast Asia, "only in Malaysia has [plan execution] been thorough and sustained."[3] Progress of the national economy during the First Malaysia Plan period was very impressive: GNP in constant prices rose an average of 6 per cent per year, exceeding the target rate of 4.9 per cent, moving from $8,637 million in 1965 to $11,821 in 1970 at current market prices; per capita real income rose 5.3 per cent per year, or from M$8,637 million to $11,190, i.e. $747 per capita in 1965 to $805 in 1970.[4] Public investment was planned for 1966-70 to be maintained at approximately the 1965 level of about $705 million, per year. Total public investment in this period was short of the plan target, by slightly more than 11 per cent; although a more narrowly defined development expenditure sum (eliminating defense, land purchase, and transfers to the private sector) found the shortfall amounting to only about 7 per cent.[5]

---

[1] Malaysia, "Treasury Memorandum on the Development Estimates of the Government of Malaysia, 1971" (Kuala Lumpur: Treasury, 1971), p. 2.

[2] Albert Waterston, op. cit., p. 548.

[3] Clair Wilcox, quoted in University of Wisconsin-AID Research Project, Economic Interdependence in Southeast Asia (Washington: AID, 1970), pp. 159-60.

[4] Second Malaysia Plan, pp. 18-19.

[5] In the first two years, as the Second Malaysia Plan puts it, "public investment was well below this level due in large part to difficulties in obtaining foreign financing . . . In the latter part of the Plan period, the increase in public investment was constrained more by implementation difficulties than by financing." (Ibid., p. 29.)

Progress in the economy in the 1966 to 1968 period, which is analyzed for <u>Policy in Area</u> below, was as follows: exports grew by 7.6 per cent per annum; GNP at constant prices rose by 6.7 per cent per year; "infrastructure development in East Malaysia proceeded apace."[1] Increases in employment were not so good as planned; although job creation in manufacturing increased perhaps by as much as 5 per cent per year in this small sector.[2] Increased amounts of public sector development expenditure went to rural, especially land development. Of this, a large part went into the beginning of the Muda and Kemubu drainage and irrigation schemes and the Jengka Triangle project. Aggregate agricultural production grew at an annual average rate of 6.4 per cent in 1966 and 1967, while output for export and domestic use expanded at 6.2 per cent and 7 per cent per year respectively.[3]

Manufacturing output in West Malaysia grew in 1966 and 1967 with an average net annual increase at current rates of 9.8 per cent, as compared with an annual growth rate of 9.2 per cent from 1960 to 1965.[4] Public transportation development in West Malaysia was quite delayed; while the capital investment program of the National Electricity Board (NEB) was unusually large in the 1966-68 period.[5] Hospital construction proceeded on schedule; but housing programs got off to a "slow start" in 1966-67.[6] In short, the years 1966 to 1968 were good but not spectacular ones for Malaysian development. They illustrated the major problems of implementation inherent in the new Malaysian development policy system and in the old line agencies.

In the Second Malaysia Plan planned expenditures (at the higher level) differ proportionally from those executed in the First Malaysia Plan mainly in allocations for "national and rural development," which double, drainage and irrigation which are reduced by almost 40 per cent, telecoms which practically

---

[1] <u>Mid-Year Review</u>, pp. 4-7.   [2] Ibid., p. 16.

[3] That was in spite of the fact that the pace of new land development in 1966-68 seems to have slowed from that of the 1962-1965 period, reflecting, perhaps, a consolidation of programs operating in the earlier period which was "necessary to ensure sound planning and eventual success of these efforts." (Ibid., pp. 45 and 48.)

[4] Ibid., p. 62. The plan target was 10 per cent per year.

[5] Such was not the case, however, of the Sarawak Electricity Supply Corporation (SESCO) and the Sabah Electricity Board (SEB) which experienced delays in their programs due to financing difficulties. (Ibid., pp. 113-15.)

[6] Ibid., pp. 120-21.

double, railways which increase their allocation by 5.5 times, and in urban development allocations.

In general, the pattern of planned expenditure is similar to past ones, however. The concepts of development in Malaysia have not changed markedly, except that redistribution of income within a growing economy has assumed far greater importance in the Second Malaysia Plan. National stability and integration are also taken very seriously. However aggregate national growth targets still take precedence, whereas the location of investments to disperse benefits is only mentioned.

Conceptual Area

To Malaysian development policy-makers "area" was largely a subconscious concern under the First Malaysia Plan. This was practical in a country that was small and with a large element of private uncontrolled activity. During preparation of the First Malaysia Plan, there may even have been a deliberate ignoring of the question of "where" and a focus on national aggregate targets, so that local political considerations would not arise.[1] This did not mean, however, that areal concepts were absent in the planning documents. Owing to the prevailing project orientation (although there were fewer projects put up than would have been convenient[2]) which was furthered by the large project bias of external assisting organizations like the World Bank, particular points and regions in Malaysia assumed large importance. In the Second Malaysia Plan there is a far clearer areal conceptualization of policy needs and implementation goals, with broadened emphasis on regions and unbounded special conceptual areas (especially those called "urban" or "rural," which may be termed "masses.")[3]

---

[1]Professor Warren Hunsberger, former Harvard Development Advisory Service economic advisor to the Economic Planning Unit, private communication, 10 March 1971.

[2]Hunsberger, loc. cit.

[3]This change in emphasis is reflected, to a degree, in the loan and technical assistance program of the Asian Development Bank (ADB) in Malaysia in recent years. The eight projects approved in 1970-1972 have a projected cost (in US$ millions) of 61.5, of which the largest amount (15.0) goes to the Malaysia Industrial Development Finance Berhad, to meet medium and long-term credit requirements of private industries--presumably largely Malay urban ones. The Kuala Lumpur-Karak Highway (13.4), Penang Airport (10.9), and the Sibu Port extension (3.5), all regional transportation undertakings comprise almost half the total ADB investments. (See ADB, Quarterly Newsletter January, 1973, p. 10.)

Area pointal concern in the First Malaysia Plan is seen in the mention of power plant sites in South Malaya, port development in Butterworth, Sandakan (lighterage), and Kuching, industrial estates in Penang, Perak, and Selangor, and higher educational institutions in Kuala Lumpur. Likewise electricity distribution, air corridor, and telecommunications lines were specified. Industrial estates and port development were the major ways in which the government intended to influence industrial and commercial development. Industrial estates were planned at Tampoi and Larkin (Johore Baharu), Tasek (Ipoh), Mak Mandin (Butterworth), Senawang (Seremban), and Tupai (Taiping) (see Figure 8). Broadcasting expenditures were intended for the Pantai Valley Center and for transmitters in Johore Baharu, Kajang, Kuantan, and Ipoh. Electricity expansion was planned for Kota Kinabalu. Sewerage systems were supposed to be improved in the four municipalities in West Malaysia (nothing for sewerage was done in Ipoh). Major water supply projects were planned for many middle cities, including Melaka, Kota Baharu, Alor Setar, Kuching, and Kota Kinabalu and other centers in East Malaysia, as well as Kuala Lumpur. Hospitals were planned for Kuala Lumpur, Seremban, Petaling Jaya (Teaching Hospital), Dungun, Tanjong Karang, and Changkat Melintang. Numerous Court House improvements or construction were mentioned in the Plan.[1]

Under the Second Malaysia Plan points and lines of development continue to be prominent; although regions take on greater importance.[2] Point and line

---

[1]First Malaysia Plan, pp. 126, 146, 160, 177, 183, 187-88.

[2]Tourism projects assume greater potential importance, with such expenditures specified for Maxwell Hill, Pangkor Island, Kuala Lumpur, Pahang and Johore. Penang is not mentioned for federal government tourism expenditure; although it is entitled the "Western Gateway" to Malaysia. (Kota Kinabalu is the "Eastern Gateway.") The University of Penang, however, receives specific important mention, along with the Science Education Center in Kuala Lumpur and the MARA Institute of Technology there, and the Universities of Malaya and Kebangsaan. Most important for future transportation patterns and Penang's development, the northern East-West Highway is planned for completion during the Second Malaysia Plan period, and: "to meet the long-term requirements of both passenger and vehicular traffic between the mainland and Penang Island, some sort of fixed linkage will be constructed. A full scale detailed engineering and economic study will be undertaken at the beginning of the Second Malaysia Plan to determine the most suitable form of fixed linkage. In the meantime, the present ferry services will be expanded to meet traffic requirements until such time as the fixed linkage is put in place and becomes operational." Improvement to the minor ports of Kuantan and Kuala Trengganu is planned to meet the "increased tempo of land development activities in the East Coast States." Rubber and oil-palm processing facilities are planned for rural Selangor, Johore, and Pahang. For power circulation, the Port Dickson Third Stage, and the Temanga hydro project (the second in West Malaysia) are planned; and the

expenditures were and continue to be urban-related and located. In the "Press Kit" put out by the Federal Industrial Development Authority (FIDA) in 1970, the important points for development were Port Dickson ($133.3 million) and the Upper Perak River electricity ($460 million) schemes, the Butterworth Deep Water wharves ($57 million) (since completed), and the Kuching ($12 million), Sibu ($12 million), Kota Kinabalu ($22.5 million), and Sandakan ($30.5 million--for deep water wharves at a new site) port projects. The important lines for development were the northern East-West Highway ($112 million) and the distribution system of the above generating projects. Concern for "region" in the First Malaysia Plan began with East versus West Malaysia. That is, in fact, what the First Malaysia Plan meant by "geographical distribution"--whereby about $3,110 million were allocated for Malaya, and $300 million and $400 million respectively for Sabah and Sarawak. The First Malaysia Plan allows that:

a number of factors were taken into account in the determination of this distribution among the three main parts of the country. These factors include their populations, development potential, needs for economic and social infrastructure investment, financial capacities and their respective abilities to implement expanded development programmes without inflationary consequences.
The overall economic and social development expenditure target for Malaya is 32 per cent more than the amount expended during 1961-65, while the targets for Sabah and Sarawak represent respectively increases of 47 per cent and 57 per cent over the expenditure achievement of the last five years. The substantial expenditure increases which are planned for the Borneo States are clearly indicative of the government's determination to ensure that as large an allocation is provided as can be expected to be achieved within the technical and administrative capacities of these states.[1]

The other current (already financed) projects noted by Federal Industrial Development Authority were all functional-regional ones, such as the Muda ($204 million) and Kemubu ($53 million)[2] rice double-cropping projects, and also the Jengka Triangle land development scheme ($240 million).

---

national grid is to be extended to Central West Malaysia, with its first interconnection with the East Coast (in 1974) planned to Kuantan. Thirty per cent of the Federal road system and 45 per cent of the state road system is regarded as deficient in quality. In addition to the northern highway, the extension of Route III from Kuantan to Segamat is planned as a major factor in Pahang Tenggara regional development. High priority, not surprisingly, is accorded to improvements of Routes I and II around Butterworth, Ipoh, and in and out of Kuala Lumpur. (Second Malaysia Plan, pp. 128, 168, 190, 211-12, 235, 238.)

[1] Author's emphasis; First Malaysia Plan, p. 71.

[2] Every time this project is mentioned it has a different price tag, ranging from $40 to $78 million.

94

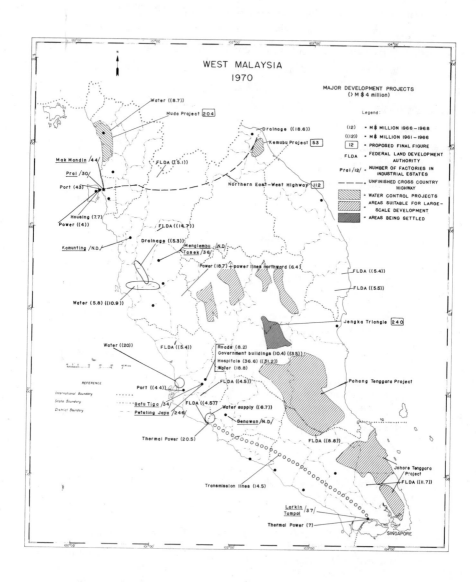

Fig. 8.--Malaysia: Major Development Projects

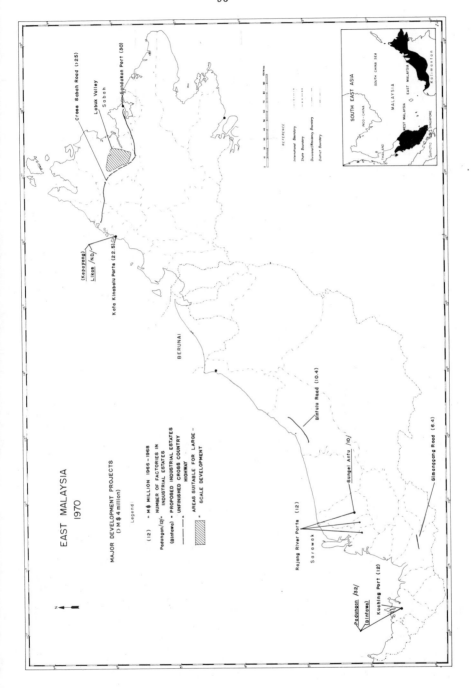

EAST MALAYSIA
1970

MAJOR DEVELOPMENT PROJECTS
(> M $ 4 million)

Legend

(12) = M$ MILLION 1966 - 1968
NUMBER OF FACTORIES IN
INDUSTRIAL ESTATES
Padungan /32/- PROPOSED INDUSTRIAL ESTATES
(Bintawa) = UNFINISHED CROSS COUNTRY
HIGHWAY
AREAS SUITABLE FOR LARGE -
SCALE DEVELOPMENT

Another manifestation of concern for the region is the Jayadiri concept.
Fourteen small areas, plus the Muda region, were targeted for concentrated
development, the number reaching 23 by 1971. They supposedly possess the
necessary infrastructure, including credit facilities and "readiness of the farmers themselves and the community to move towards greater development," and
have enjoyed the introduction of diversified crops such as rice, coconuts, maize,
and tapioca.[1] This may have limited usefulness, but oddly, although Article 42
of the National Land Code provides for declaration of a given area as a "development area" (and East Malaysia and the East Coast of Malaya are sometimes
referred to as that), the Development Administration Unit has practically no
record of this potentially better and more extensive means of area development
and development administration being used, even to get around sticky states'
prerogatives.[2]

As a large region East Malaysia was treated, then, somewhat separately
and as an area with special development needs (extra money) and toward which
the central government had a special responsibility. Significantly, the East
Coast of Malaya, which is as depressed and with less potential than Sabah, was
hardly mentioned as such.[3]

In the Second Malaysia Plan there is less emphasis on East Malaysia;
although tables, including those of the Development Estimates 1971 still break
down figures for Malaya, Sabah, and Sarawak, as well as aggregating all of
them. One reason for this may be that the major problems facing Malaysia at
this juncture are not amenable to macro-regional discussion. Additionally,
information for detailed planning is not so readily available interregionally.[4]
Economic Planning Unit sources report, however, that Sabah and Sarawak,
which fight very hard for what they want from the Federal Government in devel-

---

[1] It will be interesting to see what becomes of this approach of the Ministry of Rural and National Development. In 1969 the Research Unit of that Ministry was still collecting "benchmark data" for the program. (See Mid-Term
Review of the First Malaysia Plan, p. 47; Malaysia, The Expenditure Budget of
the Federal Government, 1971 [Kuala Lumpur: Government Printer, 1971], p.
227; and Malaysia, Budget Summary of Federal Government Expenditure, 1969
[Kuala Lumpur: Government Printer, 1969], p. 245.)

[2] Fugitive memorandum, 1970.

[3] Political opposition in Kelantan was certainly a factor; although similar
opposition (similar in unsympathy, not racial tone) in cities like George Town
and Ipoh did not prevent them from receiving explicit attention.

[4] Interviews in the Economic Planning Unit: Snodgrass, T. Kandasami,
4 October and 15 October 1971.

opment projects, get practically all they asked for in the Second Malaysia Plan; whereas traditionally the West Malaysian States (perhaps excepting Penang) do not place so much emphasis on acquiring central government development largesse, per se, and have been somewhat disappointed accordingly.[1] An East versus West Malaysia discrepancy thus persists, though it may be downgraded.

In the Second Malaysia Plan, too, regional concern means planning of rural development projects, mainly integrated land development in areas hitherto unused. The Regional Planning Division of the Economic Planning Unit prepares or supervises planning for agricultural development, natural resources appraisal, and regional master planning for both estate and small-holder agriculture, particularly in connection with the Jengka Triangle, and Johore Tenggara, and the Pahang Tenggara Master Plans. The latter two were in preparation in 1971.[2] A Trangganu regional plan, of limited usefulness, was prepared during the First Malaysia Plan, and one is in the works for Sarawak. The most elaborate Master plan has been that for Penang State.

The Jengka Triangle and Pahang and Johore Tenggara projects are planned to make "important contributions to regional [meaning interregional] balance" as will, presumably, the East-West North Highway, and what comes from the regional studies for Kelantan and the Fourth Division of Sarawak, including flood control in the former. And:

> the establishment of manufacturing activities in the less developed areas of the country represents an important dimension of the industrialization programme of the Plan. It is also an important part of the strategy to modernize the less developed areas in both East and West Malaysia, and to foster the development of new growth centers and new townships . . . The government itself will actively promote the dispersal of new industrial activities by directly participating in the establishment of new enterprises and by providing special incentives and facilities for the location of new economic ventures in such areas. The development of industries in new growth centers will diversify job opportunities in areas now dependent upon agricultural activities and facilitate greater participation by Malays and other indigenous people in the manufacturing sector and in other modern economic activities, thus speeding up the process of modernization of the rural areas.[3]

It remains to be seen what of this is in fact done significantly. Similar though far less specific sentiments were a part of past plans but to no great avail.

With the exceptions, then, of the Penang Master Plan, and diminishing East versus West Malaysia considerations, "regional" concern has come to

---

[1] Idem. [2] 1971 Expenditure Budget, p. 19.

[3] Author's emphasis; Second Malaysia Plan, p. 154.

mean "rural" concern, isolated in specific functional regions.[1] Rural electrification and health facilities for the whole rural sector were emphasized in the First Malaysia Plan, and are again in the Second Malaysia Plan. In the Second Malaysia Plan, modernization of the whole rural sector (or mass), however, is a goal, to be achieved through increased technological, land, and infrastructural inputs and the introduction of new secondary schools emphasizing science and technology.[2]

Thus, we find in the Second Malaysia Plan major mention of coordinated wide-ranging "rural" programs (aimed at an areal mass), and of urban development programs (aimed only at Kuala Lumpur, a point). This follows the realization that new land development projects cannot absorb all the ambitious and dissatisfied rural dwellers, many of whom are equally or more attracted to the urban scene anyway. In the First Malaysia Plan some urban housing and infrastructure projects were pushed; but there was nothing like a coordinated urban development policy. In the Second Malaysia Plan there still is not; but certain urban problems are accorded far greater emphasis than ever before, and the meaning of urbanization for national development is more fully appreciated:

> The urban centers are an important focus of [social and community services] programs. While these centers are in the forefront of modernizing Malaysian society, their very growth creates economic and social problems. The growth of industries and services in these areas has attracted large numbers of young people from the rural areas and smaller towns. This in turn has led to problems of congestion and unemployment. . . . Housing, utilities and community services have not been able to keep pace with urban growth. The rapid growth of urban centers has also accentuated the general imbalance in the racial participation in modern sector activities.
> In the Second Malaysia Plan period, greater attention will be paid to resolving these problems. Programmes of urban development, including slum and squatter clearance, the construction of housing schemes, improvement of water supply and sewerage systems and the provision of other public amenities are important aspects of the Plan.[3]

The most interesting and a related shift in form of areal concepts in the Second Malaysia Plan has been the implicit notion of "urbanizing" the rural areas (as well as Malayanizing, if not "ruralizing" an existing urban area). The Plan states:

---

[1] Distribution of Federal Land Development Authority schemes had a policy change in 1968/69 from being "scattered all over Malaysia," to "a new concept of land schemes based [each] on a single large area." (Budget Summary, 1969, p. 250.)

[2] This may or may not be a significant areal conceptual change. Mention of general welfare improvements in Malaya has been a constant theme, though an unrealized policy goal, throughout Malayan planning history. (Ibid., p. 44.)

[3] Ibid., p. 256.

The introduction of modern industries in rural areas and the development of new growth centres in new areas and the migration of rural inhabitants to urban areas are essential to economic balance between the urban and rural areas, and elimination of the identification of race with vocation as well as location. Policies will be designed and measures undertaken to foster the development of modern commercial and industrial activities in rural areas generally and in selected new growth centers in present rural areas in particular. This will speed up the exposure of rural inhabitants, particularly Malays and other indigenous people, to the influences of an urban environment. Industrialization in existing areas will be further developed so that migrants, particularly Malays and other indigenous people, as well as persons already living in the areas, will play an increasing role in this development both in terms of ownership and control and in terms of employment levels.

The Plan includes a number of projects concerned directly with increasing the participation of Malays and other indigenous people in urban-type activities in existing towns and new growth centers. Included are projects that will provide business premises, finance, technical and marketing advice, training and business contacts to aid such persons in starting their own commercial ventures . . .

. . . Greater geographic dispersal of industries will relieve dependence of employment on a few activities, in addition to widening contacts with modern and new approaches to economic activity and facilitating the spread of urbanization. [1]

Significantly, the Plan mentions no new growth centers by name; nor is it clear how urban business will be provided to rural Malays. Specific measures for improvement of urban conditions in Kuala Lumpur, however, are detailed; greater funds are set aside for Ipoh, including, again, its sewerage system; and there is considerable emphasis on urban job creation.

In terms of areal form, then, the First Malaysia Plan, like the development documents it succeeded, did not seek to organize Malaysia areally. The Second Malaysia Plan does. The First Malaysia Plan identified and concentrated on basically isolated and functionally limited and specific points, lines, and small regions via projects--still the major expenditure plan pattern of the Second Malaysia Plan, as suggested by the Development Estimates. The First Malaysia Plan was vague on the larger conceptual matters of where to put complex programmatic efforts, as for rectifying economic imbalance; whereas the Second Malaysia Plan is far less vague and is even heroic on behalf of the rural poor, even though a project approach and a "law of the jungle" system will prevail in the distribution of expenditure among sectors and ministries.

Expenditures allocated for economic-functional purposes (ECFN) constituted 61 per cent, 53 per cent, and 49 per cent respectively of the development expenditures in the periods 1950-60, 1961-65, and 1966-68. Expenditures for

---

[1] Author's emphasis; ibid., p. 45.

providing services to people (POPC) were fairly stable at 27 per cent, 35 per cent, 31 per cent for the three periods. The high point of POPC during the Second Malaysia Plan indicates the change at that time away from economic infrastructure but not yet fully into large housing projects and land development schemes. Such problem-area expenditures (PROB) showed the greatest change over the years: from 11 per cent and 12 per cent in the first two periods, to 21 per cent of expenditures in 1966-68. The planned proportions of development expenditures for the Second Malaysia Plan period are ECFN = 55 per cent, POPC = 25 per cent, and PROB = 20 per cent. This allocation resembles the 1966-68 pattern, with population coverage expenditures relatively down, economic-functional expenditures relatively up, each by 6 per cent, and PROB expenditures staying the same.

This is a policy change, and not one caused by significantly better knowledge. In fact, planning documents indicate that Malaysian policy makers have had a fairly good idea of where things of development relevance are. The Land Capability Classification project of the Economic Planning Unit has produced sound data on land use, which has been perhaps the least well understood matter. The Development Administration Unit remarks:

> There is an uneven distribution of land suitable and ready to be exploited among the various states. For instance most of the land suitable for exploitation for agricultural development is located in the states of Pahang (Pahang Tenggara Project), Johore (Southeast Johore Project), and Perak (East/West Highway). So if doubling the rate of new land development for the whole country is desired, there is an implication that for particular states, that the rate of new land development may have to be accelerated up to as much as 3 or 4 times that being achieved at present.[1]

However, that statement neglects to mention Sabah and was contradicted later by the Minister of National and Rural Development, who declared in 1970 that land for big rural development projects in Perak has been exhausted. Then, as an alternative he did not mention Johore,[2] thus clouding the question of the location of later rural development projects, and indicating that although information can be good, perceptions can still differ.[3]

---

[1] Untitled advisory paper, 1969.

[2] Hadji Abdul Ghafar bin Baba, quoted in the Straits Times (Kuala Lumpur), August 21, 1970, p. 8.

[3] Projects are now desired to be, in any case, in large enough units to permit large-scale development of a multitude of activities, including logging and tourism; and there are still millions of acres of adequate, productive land. (See Malaysia, A New Industrial Development Strategy [booklet; Kuala Lumpur: Government Printer,] 1969, p. 4.)

The planners know well where the manufacturing and commercial activities of the country are located at least; although data for East Malaysia are of a much lower quality than those for Malaya. In past planning eras, lip service alone was paid to dispersal to less developed regions of modern economic activities; and no service was paid to urban areas beyond for obvious physical needs, mostly in the Municipalities.

In so far as balanced regional development was desired in the past it was not achieved. In fact, the division of the country between East and West has forced different approaches to these units in the initial planning periods. Concentration of modern economic activity on the West Coast of Malaya has drawn further investment to the cities and modern resources exploitation industries (especially in the cities), followed by immigration and the further provision of services to economic activities and for social welfare in these areas. Past and continuing dependence on tin and rubber exports has worried planners, who see diversification of the economy, especially into import-substituting industries as the answer. These have been encouraged to locate in the economically most sound places, i.e. in the already developed parts of the country.

Finally, the racial tensions and national emergency following the riots after May 13, 1969, forced the government to appear active in redressing economic disparities, especially as racially identified. The Second Malaysia Plan embodies at least a resolution to make necessary changes. There are specific areal prescriptions, including the recognition that only in the cities can Malays expect to attain high and rising real incomes of a level which would obviate inclination to despair or envy of the Chinese. That is a major change in conceptual area in policy.

Administrative Area

Malaysia employs a wide variety of administrative units for carrying out her development policy. There is a certain amount of friction, overlap, and blockage in the system; but its very complexity, inherited in large part from the British, is an indication of willingness to innovate and move toward the best workable distribution of powers.

There are really two systems: the hierarchical civil administrative one, in which the states are the key units below the central government, and cities operate under them; and the group of autonomous and semi-autonomous special-function commissions, agencies, and boards. Both of these sets are responsible, ultimately, to the federal government (reserving, in some cases, certain powers), to the respective ministries, and to the Prime Minister's Office which houses the Economic Planning Unit and the Development Administration Unit. They obviously have different areal origins and purposes.

Malaysia's sixteen Ministries plus the Prime Minister's office are all represented in the Development Estimates, and all receive and disburse development policy resources.[1] Their responsibilities are functionally distributed; yet particular departments have through time migrated from one ministry to another (Local Government, for example) with no particular change in functions or even removal of offices. This is to say that individual and powerful departments, such as the Public Works Department (PWD), though integrated into their ministries, operate with a great deal of autonomy, and therefore with particular or even singular impact on the areal pattern of development.

The work of development as planned and financed by the Federal Government flows downward from the Prime Minister in two coordinating systems. In the first, most ministries and departments with heavy development expenditures, particularly Works Posts and Telecoms., Health, Education, Drainage and Irrigation, and Agriculture, have their own federal officers serving as the corresponding State officers--heads of the state departments doing the same job.[2]

---

[1] There were 18 Ministries in 1969. Since then the Ministry of Justice has been reduced to an Attorney-Generalship and many of the responsibilities, such as statistics transferred to the Prime Minister's department; the Ministry of Local Government and Housing has become the Ministry of Technology, Research and Local Government, with housing moved to the Ministry of Home Affairs; the Ministry of Culture, Youth and Sports has become the Ministry of Youth and Sports, with culture moved to the Ministry of Information and the Prime Minister's office; and the Ministry of Lands and Mines has been combined with Agriculture, with cooperatives transferred to National and Rural Development. In 1971 the 16 Ministries apart from the Prime Minister's office are: Ministry of Agriculture and Co-operatives, Ministry of Commerce and Industry, Ministry of Youth and Sports, Ministry of Defence, Ministry of Education, Ministry of Foreign Affairs, Ministry of Finance, Ministry of Health, Ministry of Home Affairs, Ministry of Information and Culture, Ministry of Labour, Ministry of National and Rural Development, Ministry of Technology, Research, and Local Government, Ministry of Transport, Ministry of Welfare Services, and Ministry of Works, Posts and Telecommunications. (See Expenditure Budget 1971, passim, and Malay Mail, Malaysia Year Book 1971 [Kuala Lumpur: Straits Times Press, 1971], pp. 53-130.)

[2] In the formerly Unfederated Malay States (Kelantan, Trengganu, Perlis, Kedah, Johore) there are State (civil) administrative services, as in Penang and Melaka as well which, however, have federal officers in important posts. In the former Federated Malay States (Perak, Selangor, Pahang, and Negeri Sembilan) all state officers are from the federal Home and Foreign and Malay Administrative Services. Until 1958 Education, and Medical and Health duties were State responsibilities, the objects of a large proportion of the high Federal allocations

When yearly budgets, or the five-year plans are in preparation, the State departments send upwards to their federal counterparts their requests, which are put together by the federal functional body into one sectoral request, having individual details of varying refinement, before presentation to the Economic Planning Unit, the secretariat of the National Development Planning Committee.[1] That is vertical coordination.

Then there is horizontal coordination through Malaysia's famous Operations Room-Red Book system. Here, although reporting is inconsistent and attention given to Operations Rooms varies from place to place, there has been, since Malayan planning days, a network of nested development expenditure-project reporting centers culminating in the National Operations Room of the Prime Minister's office. Certain states, such as Sabah have current and extensive data accumulated in maps and charts for ready perusal. Current progress of individual development projects can sometimes readily be seen.[2] Each state has a development officer in charge.

Hence for line-agency activity there is a large degree of (possible) coordination and unity between federal policies and the implementation of them in the States. At the same time, State (or Municipal) development policies, locally financed, can be coordinated with federal ones, as the functional officers, though

---

to States then. This tradition of State power on these matters persists today. (See Lim Heng Boon, "Federal-State Financial Relations in West Malaysia," Graduation Exercise, University of Malaya, Economics and Administration Faculty, 1968/69, fugitive, p. 6.) So far there are few multi-state administrative groupings; although macro-regionalization of medical services, e.g. yielding a Kedah, Perlis and Penang region has been suggested by Tan Sri Sardon, Minister of Health (quoted in the Straits Times, July 4, 1970, p. 7). The Royal Customs and Excise Department organizes West Malaysia into three regions. (See Development Administration Unit, Organization of the Government of Malaysia [Kuala Lumpur: Government Printer, 1967], pp. 86 and 94.) There are West and East Malaysian Departments of Civil Aviation and Posts and Telecoms as well. (Ibid., pp. 194, 205, 218.)

[1] This, of course, has caused problems. Robert Nathan (Malaysian Transport Survey, I, 366) observes: "the spatial pattern of highway investment appears to have been based on proposals by the various states, which were then adjusted downward to fit the amount of funds anticipated to be available. There is no evidence indicating that the adjustments were made systematically on the basis of projected growth in transportation requirements of the various states and substates, on population growth, differential rates of economic development or an analysis of the economic benefit expected to be forthcoming from various projects." This suggests the problem, understandably, that Nathan was hired to correct.

[2] This system is widely copied, for example in Indonesia, but, beyond illuminating blockages, cannot remove them by itself, as is sometimes believed. Malaysia's present lack of interest in the system, after its initial impact, therefore, is not surprising.

from the Federal Service, are responsible, also to the State governments.[1]
Meanwhile, the Constitution of Malaysia lays out Federal and State authority
and responsibilities in Lists. The major powers reserved to States, over
which much complication occurs in development policy implementation nowadays,
are over land (tenure, compulsory acquisition, Malaya reservations, transfer),
agriculture and forestry, water supply, local government (including municipalities), and turtles and riverine fishing. Concurrently, States share responsibilities with the Federal Government for social welfare, animal husbandry, town
and country planning, public health, and drainage and irrigation, among others.[2]

The Malaysian system had adapted to the special problems (and initial
bargaining power as well) of East Malaysia by leaving in the hands of Sabah and
Sarawak much greater autonomy of action and assigned revenue-generating powers. These states regulate incorporation of authorities set up by State law,
ports and harbors other than federal ones, and the Sabah railway. Concurrently,
they control agricultural research, theatres and cinemas, and, in Sabah until
1971, medicine and health. These states are not required to follow the policy
formulated by the National Land Council or of the National Council for Local
Government and are excluded from Parliament's power to pass uniform laws on
these matters.[3] Not surprisingly, under the Prime Minister's Department
there is a Ministry for Sarawak Affairs and an office of the Federal Secretary,
Sabah, whose functions are to look after Federal interests in these States, to
maintain liaison, and to generally supervise the few Federal Departments in
these states.[4] In 1963 the Education Departments in Sabah and Sarawak became
part of the Federal Ministry of Education, receiving Federal Officers, for example. However, these states retain some autonomy even in their educational policies, especially relating to curricula and syllabus as well as the language of
instruction.[5] There are, in fact, far fewer Federal Officers in Bornean State

---

[1]For example, "The Drainage and Irrigation Department operates a Federal Headquarters and 13 state departments . . . all major planning, constitution, design, research, and mechanical engineering services connected with
drainage, irrigation and river conservancy works in the states are provided by
the federal headquarters." Whereas "the respective states are responsible for
financing the construction, operation, and maintenance of water supplies except
those which serve the City of George Town in Penang and those which serve the
Municipality of Melaka." (Malaysia Year Book, 1971, p. 83.)

[2]Malaysia, Federal Constitution (Kuala Lumpur: Government Printer,
1970), pp. 212-17.

[3]Ibid. and p. 97.   [4]Expenditure Budget 1971, p. 36.

[5]English is the official language of East Malaysia until 1973 when that may

governments than in Malaya, and state rather than Federal Service Public
Works Department and District Officers. New State Departments of Drainage
and Irrigation were established in the States of Sabah and Sarawak in January,
1967, with service to them a responsibility, as for other states, of the Federal
DID Headquarters.[1] Lastly, the Bornean states appear to have some say over
immigration to them and greater bargaining power in national development policy-making circles.

The biggest problem for development with regard to states is coordination. Despite the vertical and horizontal systems, or in part because of them,
there has been a proliferation of officers and offices for whom duties and responsibilities are not entirely clear. Every state now has a State Economic
Development Corporation (SEDC), for example, for which a Federal Committee
has been established to coordinate activities.[2] One problem is that of land
administration, which, locally, is the responsibility of the District Officers,
rather than the State Development Officer. This may be changed.[3] Another is
the State Public Works Departments whose job it is to be general contractors
for both the Federal and State Governments. Some Federal departments complain that state projects are given higher priority, leading to even more federal
shortfalls. The solution to this may be more public works constructed, as is
the case of the northern East-West Highway, by federal units. In 1970 the
Minister of Commerce and Industry, Haji Mohammad Khir Johari, warned that
a review of the Federal and State Constitutions might be necessary to overcome
delays by state authorities in dealing with applications to set up new industries.[4]
That same year, the Minister of National and Rural Development, Abdul Ghafar
Baba threatened that Federal Land Development Authority schemes would not be
implemented in Kelantan if that difficult state government refused to consider
lowering its land premium.[5]

---

be reviewed; whereas Malay has been the official language of West Malaysia
since 1967. (Malaysia Year Book 1971, p. 321.)

[1] See Budget Summary, 1969, p. 55.   [2] Second Malaysia Plan, p. 115.

[3] Interview with Dr. Vincent Barnett, Development Administration Unit,
5 October 1971.

[4] Six to nine month delays over land, factory sites or timber or mineral
concessions were experienced after four to six weeks application approval processes by the Federal Government. (Straits Times, March 24, 1970, p. 1.)

[5] Of $50/ac with conditions. (See Straits Times, January 27, 1970, p. 3.,
and November 7, 1969.)

Another problem is state financial ability to develop. This varies considerably from state to state, with the East Malaysian States having far higher development estimates. Actual 1970 development expenditures of state funds by Sarawak were $11.6 million, and for Sabah, $81.1 million, while the total for the 11 West Malaysian states was only $60.7 million.[1] For the 1966-68 period, state development expenditures, including Federal transfers went from $3.2 million by Perlis, $16.7 by Kelantan, and $30 million by Pahang, to $76.8 million by Selangor, and $112.9 million by Sabah.[2] (See Chapter IV.) While Kelantan, Trengganu, and Perlis are hard put to finance any local projects without direct Federal assistance, the East Malaysian states will provide almost all the funds required during the Second Malaysia Plan for water supply projects.[3] The Second Malaysia Plan suggests this principle for the future:

> To ease the Federal Government financial position, States with surplus revenue will be expected to shoulder a larger share of responsibility in financing development projects which are within their purview. States which are in deficit will be urged to examine ways and means of raising more fiscal resources so as to lessen their dependence on the Federal Government.[4]

And much of the burden for State development will have to be borne by the New State Economic Development Corporations. They have a measure of discretion in the disposition of Federal, as well as their own funds.[5]

The problems of the states in finance and coordination and independence of action are multiplied and complicated in the cases of local authorities.[6] Local government is regulated by the states; although a ministry of Local Government coordinates city planning such as it is and distributes certain small funds. The hierarchy of units of local government is remarkable for the inability

---

[1] Economic Planning Unit, 11 October 1971.

[2] See Appendix II.

[3] Second Malaysia Plan, p. 220. A novel suggestion of economic assistance to Pahang from Sabah was mooted by Sabah's Chief Minister, Tun Mustapha, in 1971. He offered help for development of the Port of Kuantan, in connection with Johore's Land Development schemes. This would presumably be loan financing and could be an effective way of equitably redistributing resources, while retaining the financial independence of timber-rich Sabah. (Straits Times, May 31, 1971, p. 12.)

[4] Second Malaysia Plan, p. 78.

[5] The Second Malaysia Plan allocates $45.6 million for all of them. (Ibid., p. 178).

[6] This is common in the world and the United States. (See New York Times editorial "Will Federalism Collapse," November 11, 1970.)

of most of its constituents to remain financially viable during the 1960's. At
higher levels there has been a tendency for take-over by the state governments
for reasons either of malfeasance or insolvency. By tradition the five municipalities have larger budgets, updated rate rolls, and do more for their citizens,
including low-cost housing and even job training and medical services. Of the
37 Town Councils in West Malaysia, 27 are financially autonomous, which
means that they may draw up their own budgets and retain their annual surpluses, if any. "The powers and responsibilities are thus considerably increased when financial autonomy is gained";[1] or they would be if resources
were available to the Town Councils in sufficient amounts. A major problem,
it may be added, has been an inadequate tax rate structure, and non-current
assessments. (Holdings in most local authorities in the 1960's had not been
revalued for a decade or more.) Moreover, towns often do not have the will to
enforce payment that they could rightfully demand. These problems are being
corrected: a central valuation authority is planned; two-thirds of the Town
Councils have had revaluations by mid-1971, and most should be completed by
1973.[2]

In Malaya, local government is not continuous across the area, nor have
government units been standardized or rationalized. Thus great unevenness of
local developmental responsibility and resources prevails--made worse by the
chaotic financial arrangements during the 1960's. Of the four Rural District
Councils of Panang and the three District Councils of Melaka, four are financially autonomous. These bodies cover the area of their states in the manner
of districts in Sarawak[3] and (after 1962) Sabah. In Malaya otherwise, the 289
Local Councils are all financially autonomous and headed by elected Chairmen;
but they by no means provide continuous area coverage. Districts do provide
continuous coverage and are administered by District Officers in an eroded
British manner, but are not local government areas. That is, the duties of
these once all powerful and omniscient officers have been reduced enormously

---

[1] Malaysia Year Book 1971, p. 132. Of the 37 Town Boards, only 6 are
financially autonomous. The others are functionally merely departments of
their state governments, and impecunious ones at that.

[2] Interview with, T. Puvanarajah, Deputy Chief Director, Local Government, 7 October 1971; and Straits Times, June 7, 1970, p. 3.

[3] In Sarawak these Councils have had, through 1971, administration responsibility for primary education. The State Supreme Council has decided,
however, to place them directly under the state government through the Education Department. (Straits Times, October 16, 1971, p. 19.)

as state and federal bodies have assumed responsibility for the needs of their wards. Yet they retain powers to approve budgets and by-laws of Local Councils. In Sabah and somewhat in Sarawak, however, District Officers still are powerful. Whether this is an attribute of comparative underdevelopment or enlightenment, considering the needs for local government reform in West Malaysia, is debatable.

Such problems and needs are not unappreciated in Kuala Lumpur, but a solution, proposed in 1971, could eventually lead to an end of local democracy and traditions of local government in Malaya of great age: the Minister of Technology, Research, and Local Government, Dato Ong Kee Hui, announced that the government is in favor of appointing members to local authorities instead of the present system of electing them (!). The justification is ensurance of "full representation of the people in their areas," and "greater efficiency in the functioning of the local authorities," while attraction of "only public spirited people" to the councils would also follow. He said the Federal Government was also in favor of reducing the number of local authorities.[1] Ipoh, of course, possesses at present one of the few functioning fully elected and not state dominated local governments. It happens to be in the hands of an opposition party (the People's Progressive Party) which is considered to conduct the best-run city government in Malaysia. The President of the Municipality of Ipoh and President of the People's Progressive Party, Dato S. P. Seenivasagam, replied:

> Under the elected system of Local Government the people of Malaysia have been free since Merdeka from the corruption, harassment and sufferings they had before. For no apparent reason, the Government now propose to abolish elected local governments. This decision is due entirely to political reason [sic]. The Alliance knows it cannot gain control of the principal towns in Malaysia by democratic means. It has therefore decided to gain control by destroying democracy. We can never accept this decision as it will mean that the people in their daily life will be at the mercy of officials who may be corrupt and arrogant.[2]

Non-hierarchical administrative units of development cover the range of federal agencies who happen to operate outside the state system (like the Federal Land Development Authority or the Federal Industrial Development Authority), to semi-public, financially autonomous utilities (like the Penang Port Commission, and the National Electricity Board)--all receiving grants and/or capital investment from the Federal Government, but operating basically on their self-

---

[1] Sunday Gazette (Penang), December 9, 1971, p. 1.

[2] Statement following the announcement in Parliament earlier, of 8 July 1971, issued in Ipoh.

generated revenues, to completely private (though invested with private and public funds) non-profit agencies sometimes spawned by the Commonwealth Development Corporation (such as the Borneo Development Corporation and the Malaya Borneo Building Society). The newest form of ad hoc non-line development administrative agency is the water resources-agricultural development management organization. The Muda Agricultural Development Authority (MADA) is the prototype. Kemubu (in Kelantan) should get one like it, as may the areas covered by the Pahang Tenggara and Johore Tenggara projects. The ostensible reason for this innovation (ca. 1970) was the inadequacy of federal ministries (D.I.D., Agriculture, P.W.D.) and state operators to be coordinated enough to bring together the multivarious engineering, human, and agronomic factors in a satisfactory sequence.

The government or statutory corporations at point here have proliferated in the 1960's and into the 1970's. Figures on their operations are somewhat elusive, as their finances are often contained in larger aggregates for government ministries, on the one hand, or are private but occasionally added into totals anyway, on the other.[1] However, we know that in 1966 these bodies used about 25 per cent of the development budget, counting such quasi-independent agencies as the Federal Industrial Development Authority. While for 1966-1968 the four most important independent public authorities (the National Electricity Board, Malayan Railway Administration, Port Swettenham Authority, and Penang Port Commission) spent 20 per cent of total public development funds.[2] In 1965, as this group was picking up steam, government agencies accounted for about 82 per cent of total government sector expenditure, with government enterprises spending another 7 per cent, and public corporations 11 per cent.[3]

The major authorities each operating special areal systems, are important in another way: their surpluses from business are made available to finance their own development undertakings, and planned for accordingly. For example, from 1966 to 1968, the above four public authorities had a combined surplus of

---

[1] For example, Table 10 1966-68 figures from the First Malaysia Plan Mid-Term Review show "public expenditures," including those of public corporations--which is also how the Second Malaysia Plan takes them; whereas Appendix I cites development expenditures taken from the Development Estimates, which only include Federal budget expenditures from Federal revenues; although many transfers are included.

[2] Economic Planning Unit.

[3] See C. T. Edwards, Public Finances in Malaya and Singapore (Canberra: Australian National University Press, 1970), p. 29.

$165.8 million. The Second Malaysia Plan allows:

> The Public Authorities as a whole are expected to increase their current surplus from $340 million during 1966-70 to $550 million during 1971-75. More than half of the surplus will come from the National Electricity Board. The remaining portion is expected mainly from the Sabah Electricity Board, the Sarawak Electricity Supply Corporation, the Port Swettenham Authority and the Penang Port Commission. The current surplus of the Public Authorities, together with loans and other assistance from the Federal Government and from abroad, will be more than adequate to finance their combined development expenditure programme.[1]

The Second Malaysia Plan notes, too, that in recent years the Public Authorities, along with some states have been converting a "suitable quantity" of their accumulated foreign assets to Government Securities.[2]

Listed in Table 7 are the specialized-function public and semi-public bodies which have varying degrees of autonomy in the Malaysian system. These make use of public funds and are important to national development, but operate in areal patterns quite different from those of the Ministry and State line organizations. Their virtue (especially those in Columns B and C) is the ability to mobilize their own resources, often from divergent sources or self-generated, and to zero in on specific functions and targets. They complement and are comparable to the very large agency houses, the two smelting companies, and the private banks whose functions are to keep the export sector rolling along and to channel domestic investment into productive enterprises. The government controls or interferes only minimally with such private or public corporations. The government pushes employment of Malays, taxes, and maintains a British level of business practice in the organizations of columns B and C, while mostly leaving them alone. It puts government investments into all these organizations, and provides government officers and policy instruction to those in columns A and often B and C.

The most important Government Agencies are (1) the Federal Land Development Authority (FLDA), which dates from before Malaysia, and has opened up new land all over West Malaysia, with 60 per cent of its schemes devoted to rubber, and the rest to oil palm; (2) MARA, which assists the Bumiputera (sons of the soil) to "play their part in industrial development" by establishing publicly

---

[1] Second Malaysia Plan, p. 78. By Public Authorities as a whole, the Plan clearly does not mean all statutory bodies, but rather mainly those mentioned. In fact, the Treasury only examined the Estimates of 16 Statutory Bodies in each of the years 1969, 1970, and 1971. (See Expenditure Budget 1971, p. 318.)

[2] Ibid.

TABLE 7

PUBLIC AND SEMI-PUBLIC DEVELOPMENT BODIES, 1971[a]

A. Government Agencies	B. Statutory Bodies (more financially autonomous)	C. Semi-Public Bodies
Federal:	Federal:	Federal:
Family Planning Board	Housing Trust	Cooperative Bank
Malaysian Migration Fund Board	UDA (Urban Development Authority)	Bank Pertanian
South Indian Labourers Fund Board	Worker's Savings Fund	Bank Bumiputera
Port Labour Board	University of Malaya	Bank Negara
Industrial Court	University Kebangsaan	Post Office Savings Bank
Social Welfare Lottery	University of Penang	Employees Provident Fund
Sports Toto	University Hospital	Malayan Banking
National Art Gallery	Agricultural College Serdang	MBBS
Tariff Board	Islamic College	MSA (Malaysia-Singapore Airlines)[b]
MARA	Tunku Abdul Rachman College	
Padi & Rice Marketing Board	Language & Book Center	
FLDA (Federal Land Development Authority)	Industrial Training Institute	
FELCRA	MARA Institute of Technology	
Malaysian Film Unit	Port Swettenham Authority	
Bernama	Penang Port Commission	
MADA	Malayan Railway Administration[c]	
Kemubu Agricultural Development Authority (proposed)	National Electricity Board	
FAMA (Federal Agricultural Marketing Authority)	Rubber Research Institute	
MARDI	MIDF (Malaysian Industrial Development Finance)	
NISIR	MIEL (Malaysian Industrial Estates Limited)	
National Youth Pioneer Corps	National Investment Co.	
National Productivity Council	Cooperative Societies (The National Corporation)	
Capital Investment Committee	PERNAS	
FIDA (Federal Industrial Development Authority)	Malaysian International Shipping Line	
Rubber Marketing Board	Malaysian Rubber Development Corporation	
National Rubber Fund		
Malaysian Wood Industry Board		
Tin Research & Development Board		
Pineapple Industry Board		
National Rubber Stockpile		
Rubber Industry Replanting Board		

TABLE 7--Continued

A. Government Agencies	B. Statutory Bodies (more financially autonomous)	C. Semi-Public Bodies
9 other Rubber Industry funds & boards National Pepper Marketing Board		
State:	State:	State:
13 SEDC's Sabah Padi Board Sabah Land Development Authority	Sarawak Electricity Supply Corporation Sabah Electricity Board Sabah Port Authority Kuching Port Authority Rajang River Port Authority Sarawak Development Finance Corporation Sabah Railway	BDC Borneo Housing Mortgage Finance (Perak River Hydro-Electric Company) (Kinta Electricity Distribution Company) Sabah Foundation

[a]Source: Development Administration Unit, private communication.

[b]In 1972 this split into Malaysian Airlines System (MAS, with Malaysian government share capital) and Singapore Airlines, likewise their flag carrier.

[c]Reorganized as a public enterprise, from a government department under the FMP.

owned enterprises.[1] It was expanded to Sarawak in 1965, beginning with bus routes; (3) Malaysian Industrial Development Finance Corporation (MIDF), and its subsidiary Malaysian Industrial Estates Limited (MIEL), which provide medium and long-term financing to the manufacturing sector and build standard factory units for sale in industrial estates; and (4) the Federal Industrial Development Authority (FIDA), which attempts to "coordinate and strengthen the country's industrial development programs" through the management of incentives and promotion.[2]

Of the statutory bodies the National Electricity Board, Port Commissions, Railway, Universities, and the new shipping line all, as noted, are highly significant to development in general and to particular areas. Whereas the Column A agencies are supposed to operate nationally or in West Malaysia broadly, though with specific areal imperatives (assistance to economically efficient private

[1]First Malaysian Plan, p. 137.   [2]Ibid., p. 136.

industries, for example), these statutory bodies, with the exception of PERNAS, are designed to do specific jobs in specific places or kinds of places, as suggested by their names. The semi-public bodies, by contrast operate broadly in West Malaysia. They, like all of the Federal or national bodies, do not necessarily exist in East Malaysia, which traditionally developed its own institutions, and which has continued that practice to an extraordinary degree. (This is another case of the governments of Borneo possessing superior power of management and over their resources, as states.)

Over the years, and particularly in the Malaysian Plan periods, there has been a trend towards the creation of special institutions for the carrying out of specific kinds of and usually new development policy ventures. Many on the above list are of these. In the First Malaysia Plan period, older institutions, such as the Federal Land Development Authority, Federal Industrial Development Authority, MIDF, and the utilities were relied on most, and two new Bornean Port Authorities created. For the Second Malaysia Plan, however, new bodies have been planned or made up to cope with (or further confuse) the new economic policy needs. PERNAS (actually formed in late 1969), the national corporation, is given the largest responsibility for getting Malays and indigenes into commerce and industry--assuming this rôle despite the existence of MARA.[1] It has been allotted more money than it requested for the next five years,[2] and will be expected to succeed. Likewise, the Urban Development Authority (UDA) has been created. It has little to do with urban development in the broadest sense, but is expected to work with local authorities to improve planning, coordination, and implementation of health, family planning, housing, and other social services which are expanded generally and specially for Malays. It will also "assist in the programme for setting up business premises in the major urban areas to facilitate increased participation in urban activities by Malays and other indigenous peoples." It will work foremost and perhaps exclusively in Kuala Lumpur.[3] The National Padi and Rice Authority for policy and coordination of activities relating to production, processing, and marketing of padi and

---

[1]MARA became most concerned with education of Malays for commercial participation. (See W. D. McTaggart, "The May 1969 Disturbances in Malaysia: Impact of a Conflict on Developmental Patterns," fugitive [1969].) This raises the question of its function under the Second Malaysia Plan, when Malay urban training for participation in the modern economy is crucial.

[2]Dr. Vincent Barnett, Development Administration Unit, interview October 5, 1971.

[3]See Second Malaysia Plan, pp. 74 and 259.

rice will also come into being; and a bonded area will be established in Melaka, to be run jointly by PERNAS, the SEDC, and a local private company.[1]

Scale has a separate meaning and significance as between the civil-administrative and the more autonomous government agencies. In the former, powers are distributed according to old and highly structured forms. There are areas where there is too little authority (e.g. in Pahang), and those where too many governments have responsibilities (Penang before 1966). On the other hand, the public statutory bodies are either areally defined for functional purposes (e.g. the Kuching Water Board, which extends out of town), or they create their own administrative regionalization of the country and expand or contract according to the opportunities. Except nascently in Penang, which is becoming a city-state (see Chapter VII, below), there has been no blending of the two systems areally or, except in the vaguest way, through the central government. Future development imperatives will put great pressure on the systems--to compete or blend. The singularity and independence of Sabah and Sarawak and their institutions will be an added burden, though also perhaps a stimulus to administrative change.

The last development administrative form to be considered is that of foreign and private organizations in Malaysia. As noted, the great agency houses (Sime Darby, Harrisons and Crossfield, Gutheries, Bousted, and the rest), the rubber and tin producing and processing companies (Dunlop, Eastern Smelting, etc.), and the banks and other traders all have enormous importance to the achievement of Malaysia's plan targets. They operate areally primarily according to classical location principles and concentrate their holdings and operations in cities and the export producing areas of West Malaysia.[2] It is believed in Malaysian government circles, too, that major assistance-giving organizations such as the World and Asian Development Banks are uninterested in financing development projects that are not enormous;[3] hence giant electricity generating facilities and water control projects have been born, and located, again, where economically most fitting, from a market viewpoint.

The Commonwealth Development Corporation (CDC) has, since the war,

---

[1] See Straits Times, June 4, 1970, p. 5.

[2] And in 1969 almost 63 per cent of share capital in limited companies was owned by non-Malaysian interests, who can not be so pressured as the government might like to conform their practices to national areal and social imbalance redressing goals.

[3] See First Malaysia Plan, p. 116.

been particularly important to development in Malaysia, especially in Borneo.
It established the Malaya Borneo Building Society (MBBS), which finances housing throughout West Malaysia, and is owned 40 per cent by CDC, 40 per cent by
the Malaysian Government, and 20 per cent by the public. The CDC has been
even more significant in East Malaysia, where it spawned the Borneo Development Corporation (BDC). Until 1963 this corporation was wholly owned by CDC,
after which point the Sabah and Sarawak governments began buying equity, reaching eventually 25 per cent for each. (The same is true with the Borneo Housing
Mortage Finance Company.) BDC provides medium-term loan financing to
industrialists as well as for housing. It is accused of giving preference to Sarawak (where it started) in its activities;[1] although it may be that the Sabah government is not so interested in channelling development through it. It is, in any
case, a great success in Sarawak, for instance in its biggest scheme: the construction of a satellite town for Kuching, Kenalang Park, accommodating 10,000
people in 1,400 houses, 50 shops, and so forth.[2] Elements in the State seem to
prefer it and its manner to the federal organizations who are now grabbing a toe-
hold in East Malaysia.[3]

Malaysia, then, puts administrative power, authority, and responsibility
through a complex areal and capital division of powers. The federal system,
for historical reasons, makes states very important. They have authority over
land and local government, although their powers are blunted by poor finances
and fragmentation of powers within their areas; and they have no particular
developmental responsibility beyond some new coordinative functions, except
for the East Malaysian states, whose independence, ambition, and comparative
strength have been preserved thus far. To counter the decentralizing and devolution of powers tendencies in federal system, the central government, also by
tradition, places its officers in state departments responsible upward through a
line organization, and creates specialized federal bodies with wide authority
and financial power to undertake development activities and to manage location-
specific facilities which can then be run independently and efficiently. It also
allows states, notably the Bornean ones, to do the same.

---

[1] Sarawak Tribune (Kuching), April 24, 1970, editorial.

[2] E. J. Neal, General Manager, BDC, interview, June 18, 1970.

[3] "The BDC has an impressive record of work in the state . . . it goes
about its work quietly with little fanfare . . . while the MIDF has more capital
at its call than the BDC, it cannot be said that the MIDFL has experience in
Sarawak." (Sarawak Tribune, February 21, 1970, editorial.)

It may be said that the Federal government, when confronted with the problem of areal disposition of power and authority displays inclination to centralize authority, while spreading the planning and implementation responsibility downward quite far, perhaps too far. There is, meanwhile, a wealth of coordinating systems alongside individually poorly operating and non-self-sustaining units, because efficiency is rewarded, and this comes easiest with new, flexible and independent (and often semi-autonomous) organizations. These tend to be created; while old bodies abide, resources are dispersed, and confusion proliferates. Nevertheless, one can only marvel at the administrative successes and unquenchable élan of Malaysian development administrators and many of their organizations.

CHAPTER IV

POLICY IN AREA: NATIONAL PATTERNS

The National Area

Development policy expenditure patterns in Malaysia, large and small, are shown in Figures 9 through 19. Expenditures for what may clearly be defined as urban areas and functions (but not counting estate agriculture, roads, etc., as Fryer would, nor necessarily associating them with urbanization[1]) from 1950 to 1968 were almost double those for clearly rural activities (including agriculture and drainage and irrigation). In the three periods, 1950-1960, 1961-1965, 1966-1968, the ratios of urban to rural expenditures declined thus: 5.6:1, 2:1, 1.1:1, for similar quantities of development expenditures.[2] For the First Malaysia Plan period as a whole the ratio was approximately 1:1.1 still, and the planned expenditures in the Second Malaysia Plan were at a ratio of almost exactly 1:1.[3] This reflects both the policy change to emphasis on rural development and, probably more important, the facts that (a) many large urban infrastructural works were completed earlier whereas rural ones like water control were not, and (b) much of the development expenditure for urban functions is borne in Malaysia by statutory bodies not all of whose expenditures are found in the Development Estimates, and by the private sector which itself

---

[1]See D. W. Fryer, "National Development Plans and the Budget: Public Sector Resources for Urbanization, " SEADAG Discussion Paper (New York: The Asia Society, 1969).

[2]The total expenditures in periods have been increasing but the periods shortening. Mappable expenditures (area-specific and available to the researcher) have also been increasing. For the three periods the District maps show respectively 31 per cent, 43 per cent, and 63 per cent of all expenditures, not including those spent abroad. There is a certain indeterminable bias to large projects, urban investments, and POPC expenditures. Rubber replanting, for example, could not be mapped by District. The maps showing expenditures to cities may have a far higher proportion of actual expenditures mapped. Unfortunately, this is also undeterminable. The Economic Planning Unit has nothing like a total list of development expenditures by location. Some ministries do for their particular activities. This is perhaps the best evidence of all that the areal dimension is not significant to Malaysian development planners. (See Appendix II.)

[3]See Appendix I.

117

has been expanding. If one counted all the "urbanizing" development expenditures in 1966-68, including communications, transport, and administration, but not health and education (whose largest expenditures, nevertheless, are in urban areas), the ratio for that period is 1.8:1.

Urban areas are notable for being the locations of higher expectation fulfillment in many development sectors as well. For example, family planning acceptance is from ten to fifteen times proportionally greater in towns, according to the National Family Planning Board. Thrift and credit societies, which presumably are an indication of savings generally have more than three times as many urban as rural members and a growing rather than declining membership. Interestingly, but not surprisingly, even the rural PROB (land development) expenditure--heavily through 1965--favored the more urbanized Southwest Malaya over the poorer North and Northeast.

In the East Malaysian States, during the first three years of the First Malaysia Plan, urban expenditures were almost double those in rural areas and functions; while in West Malaysia they were just about even. This illustrates the basic difference between East and West Malaysian needs and direction of development: the East has required basic social services and transportation; it has no industrialization or small-holder land settlement of note, and is less urbanized.[1] West Malaysia, with 85 per cent of the population had 92 per cent of the total Malaysian cooperative membership. (See Table 5 for relevant comparisons.) At the same time East Malaysia has had much higher revenues and expenditures of state and local authorities (see Tables 8 and 13, and Figure 4): Sabah has been able to afford sharing the financing of her television network now abuilding with the federal government; and has announced plans to take over the timber industry, her biggest dollar earner.[2] These indicate the Borneo States' independent origins and, with less modernization, their traditionally greater need of local government organization. Malaya, of course, has been seen to have gone too far in the direction of shifting power, responsibility, and revenues, upwards through the administrative hierarchy.

---

[1] An Indonesian-styled transmigrasi to internal Sabah might be seriously attempted, but on the basis of experience in both countries so far, it would be expected to work with about as much success. Oil palm and cocoa estate agriculture with highly trained and well-paid workers would seem to be the greater likelihood, considering the already difficult labor shortage in Sabah.

[2] The timber trade accounts for more than 70 per cent of Sabah's total exports, worth $521 million in 1969, and has been in the hands of a few wealthy businessmen and 12 companies the latter of whose leases expire in the next 9 to 13 years. (See Straits Times, August 26, 1970, p. 14; and Newsletter, the Sandakan Chamber of Commerce, No. 28, June 17, 1970, p. 1.)

TABLE 8

MALAYSIA: STATE COMPARISONS

State	1957/60[a] Urban Population	%	1957-67[b] Migration	M$Mil[b] 1965 GRP	1966-68[c] Development Expenditures State/Federal (M$000)	6668POPC[c] State/Federal (M$000)	6668PROB[c] State/Federal (M$000)	6668ECFN[c] State/Federal (M$000)
Perlis	6,362	7	N.D.	55	3,201/1,275	32/803	0/170	3,170/302
Kedah	93,386	13	42,100	437	18,460/141,378	3,603/10,897	3,070/0	11,787/130,527
P. Pinang	356,869	68	16,900	578	32,624/121,011	3,379/5,503	4,998/13,128	24,247/103,579
Perak	276,145	23	-162,000	1,320	58,118/81,321	756/28,787	6,197/1,280	31,165/51,254
Selangor	420,655	42	299,900	2,052	76,800/243,953	35,432/93,435	0/47,838	41,368/102,680
N. Sembilan	77,290	21	91,000	441	12,970/41,114	5,720/19,431	712/0	6,538/21,683
Melaka	69,848	24	1,800	228	14,173/8,837	2,772/5,053	1,425/0	9,976/3,784
Johore	216,808	23	-40,600	954	24,091/39,710	3,662/21,805	3,640/8,558	16,789/9,347
Kelantan	54,662	11	-5,800	221	16,677/21,045	473/7,065	0/80	16,204/13,900
Trengganu	60,948	22	-21,800	198	17,228/9,657	546/4,365	2,169/3,000	14,513/2,292
Pahang	69,105	22	-55,400	394	34,893/13,447	4,254/5,405	3,317/0	27,322/8,042
Sabah	74,350	16	28,900	N.D.	108,021/36,109	4,828/11,387	5,904/638	97,289/24,094
Sarawak	107,330	14	11,900	676	77,850/74,244	3,833/32,415	7,964/4,540	66,053/37,289
Total	1,883,726	(avg)23.5		7,554	495,006/833,101	69,534/246,351	39,393/79,232	366,421/508,171

[a]West Malaysia greater than 5,000; East Malaysia greater than 3,000: <u>towns</u>, not necessarily gazetted areas.

[b]Economic Planning Unit (migration 1960-1970 for Sarawak).

[c]State Estimates 1966-1970 (see Appendix II).

TABLE 8--Continued

State	1961[d] Federal Grants (000)	1969[b] Federal Grants (000)	1966-68[b] Federal Total Development Expenditures (000)	1965 Rev + Expen Local Authorities (000)	1970[e] Population (000's)	To 1969[f] MBBS Loans Released to
Perlis	1,435	1,851	1,275	8,223	121	359,618
Kedah	6,629	9,618	41,378	46,323	955	11,114,865
P. Pinang	5,374	6,445	121,011	28,212	777	Is.:35,923,509 P.W.:11,298,402
Perak	10,515	19,785	81,321	101,436	1,563	49,218,728
Selangor	8,606	13,543	243,953	96,013	1,629	104,695,495
N. Sembilan	4,891	6,340	41,114	37,114	479	3,573,781
Melaka	4,402	4,974	8,837	18,356	404	8,995,234
Johore	8,063	12,898	39,710	91,192	1,274	25,820,392
Kelantan	4,713	7,414	21,045	32,238	681	1,789,543
Trengganu	3,536	9,051	9,657	31,878	406	370,000
Pahang	4,036	9,048	13,447	51,590	503	4,931,994
Sabah	---	19,711	36,109	149,630	655	21,319,189
Sarawak	---	20,906	74,244	112,170	975	21,998,836
Total	62,200	141,574	733,101	804,375	10,422	301,409,386

[d]Federal Estimates 1961, p. 393.

[e]1970 Census, pp. 22-24, 65-66.

[f]In Borneo, to 1969 by Borneo Housing Mortgage Finance.

State	Rubber[g] Replanting (acres)		Manufacturing[h] Industries (M$000)		Pioneer Firms[i] Net Value of Output (M$000,000)		MARA[j] Bus Services 1966		State[k] Expenditures		FLDA[l] Projects to 1970 (acres)	
	1953-67 Total	New Planted	Gross Sales	Salaries & Wages Paid	1966	1968	Route Miles	Buses	% of All West Malaysia Population	State's % of Malaysia Population	Rubber	Oil Palm
Perlis	72,963	2,799	8,328	507	---	---	480	89	1.4	1.3	---	---
Kedah	23,174	335	132,138	8,333	---	---	47	10	10.8	8.7	11,086	---
Penang	148,526	5,709	335,771	27,340	8.7	32.1	24	4	8.9	4.5	---	---
Perak	90,528	1,154	358,339	31,051	6.9	22.3	189	44	19.3	18.7	16,082	7,596
Selangor	105,572	9,692	339,083	125,168	123.4	129.1	37	5	16.4	17.9	7,761	14,094
Negeri Sembilan	93,510	4,199	270,003	13,054	---	---	61	7	5.9	7.2	28,079	---
Melaka	353,070	35,513	82,519	5,511	18.1	26.9	145	24	4.7	3.3	6,571	---
Johore	42,192	4,803	433,802	39,578	---	---	508	135	15.1	16.5	34,300	40,008
Kelantan	29,432	5,337	50,647	4,096	---	---	144	21	7.9	5.9	2,400	---
Trengganu	55,091	9,878	11,209	2,674	---	---	142	29	4.1	6.7	9,791	12,774
Pahang	N.D.	N.D.	56,682	9,645	---	---	174	15	4.9	8.8	34,155	89,531
Sabah	N.D.	N.D.	N.D.	N.D.	---	---	105	12	N.D.	N.D.	---	---
Sarawak (Other)	N.D.	N.D.	N.D.	N.D.	40.4	57.1			N.D.	N.D.	---	---
Total	1,018,058	79,419	3,078,575	266,957	197.5	267.5	1,956	395				

[g] Rubber Industry Replanting Fund "B," Report on Operations for the Year 1967, Appendix a, Table 2.

[h] Census of Manufacturing Industries in West Malaysia 1968, pp. 29-32.

[i] FIDA, private communication.

[j] Robert Nathan et al., Transportation Development in Malaysia, Vol. III, Annex B, p. 23. These statistics, according to the source, are incomplete.

[k] DAU, "State Expenditures: An Analysis" (1969), fugitive, p. 10.

[l] R. Wikkramatileke, "Federal Land Development in West Malaysia," Pacific Viewpoint (May, 1972), p. 67.

Patterns of development policy participation among states illustrate the basic areal realities of Malaysia. There are high correlations between state gross domestic product (GDP) and total (POPTOT) and Chinese (POPCHI) populations. (See Tables 9 and 10.) By 1969 there was less correlation (from .984 in 1961, to .633) between federal grants to states and their population (also to their GDP), indicating a shift in government awareness of the basic inequalities among states. In the Second Malaysia Plan, as noted, we can expect further adjustment to federal assistance to poor states.

TABLE 9

MALAYSIA: STATE ECONOMIC-DEMOGRAPHIC DATA:
PEARSON PRODUCT MOMENT CORRELATION COEFFICIENTS

	61 FED-GRA	69 FED-GRA	67 POP-TOT	67 POP-CHI	67 POP-MAL	5667 MIGN	65 $GDP
61FEDGRA (1961 Federal Grants)	---						
69FEDGRA (1969 Federal Grants)	.915	---					
67POPTOT (1967 Estimated Total Population)	.984	.663	---				
67POPCHI (1967 Estimated Chinese Population)	.902	.501	.910	---			
67POPMAL (1967 Estimated Malay/Indigenous Population)	.730	.198	.691	.442	---		
5667MIGN (1956-1965 Inter-State Migration)	.055	-.070	.105	.158	-.163	---	
65$GDP (1965 Gross Domestic Product)	.833	.627	.862	.862	.375	.493	---
67R+ELA (1967 Revenue + Expenditures of Local Authorities)	.240	.278	.253	.400	-.187	-.116	.151

Source: See Appendix II.

Amount of revenue plus expenditures of local authorities in a state does not correlate significantly with anything, demonstrating that even the poor and agricultural regions of Malaysia are urbanized to a fair degree. It also suggests that states are not regions of urban organization in themselves; nor does their boundary closure follow city systemic patterns.

Otherwise, Selangor dominates most of the other states economically and in expectations fulfillment. (See Figures 6 and 7.) For example, it produced approximately 53 per cent of the net value of manufacturing output in 1967 in West Malaysia and 48 per cent of the pioneer firms' output.[1] With Perak, Johore, and Penang, Selangor has more and functions better: 83 per cent of MBBS loans released through the end of 1969 were in these states.[2] Agricultural household expenditures are twice as high in these states as elsewhere, illustrating the truism that agricultural income is higher in less agricultural regions.[3] But an exception to this development expectation fulfillment pattern is, understandably, MARA bus services. In these services made available specially to Malays, Kelantan, Kedah, and Sabah lead.[4] Another, for obvious reasons is grant rubber replanting, 1953-1967, in which the states ranked thus: Johore (353, 070 million), Perak (148, 526), Negeri Sembilan (105, 572), Melaka (93, 510), Selangor (190, 528), in West Malaysia.[5] And by 1969 the Federal Land Development Authority in approving pioneer companies was turning away from Selangor, perhaps because Petaling Jaya was full. New approvals were 4 in Selangor, but 15 each in Penang and Perak, 21 in Johore, 7 in Sabah (3 in Sarawak), 5 in Pahang, 4 in Negeri Sembilan, and 2 in Melaka.[6]

---

[1] See Department of Statistics, Survey of Manufacturing Industries, 1966-67 (Kuala Lumpur: Department of Statistics, 1968), Appendices I and II.

[2] See Table 7. That is, of course, for West Malaysia. In East Malaysia, Borneo Housing Mortgage Finance Board had by the end of 1969 spent almost identical amounts in Sabah and Sarawak--each about what Johore received.

[3] Development Administration Unit, "State Expenditures: An Analysis," 1969, p. 10, fugitive.

[4] See Table 7.

[5] The rest had: Kedah plus Perlis (72, 963), Pahang (55, 091), Kelantan (46, 192), Trengganu (29, 432), Province Wellesley (16, 976), and Penang Island (6, 198); most planting was in Johore (35, 513), Pahang (9, 878), Negeri Sembilan (9, 692), Kedah plus Perlis (5, 334), Perak (5, 709), Trengganu (5, 337), Kelantan (4, 803), Melaka (4, 199), Selangor (1, 154), Province Wellesley (204), and Penang Island (131). Rubber Industry (Replanting) Board Fund "B, " "Report on Operations for the Year 1967," Kuala Lumpur, 1968, Appendix 10, Table 2.

[6] Federal Land Development Authority, private connection, 6 April 1970.

TABLE 10

FMP DEVELOPMENT EXPENDITURE TO AND BY STATES, 1966-68:
PEARSON PRODUCT MOMENT CORRELATION COEFFICIENTS

	FMP - Federal					
	5667 MIGN	6668 POPC	6668 PROB	6668 ECFN	6668 URBN	6668 TOTL
Federal:						
5667MIGN (Migration)	---	.721	.831	.475	.679	.726
6668POPC (Population Coverage)		---	.912	.435	.825	.802
6668PROB (Problem Area)			---	.498	.918	.815
6668ECFN (Economic-Functional)				---	.634	.882
6668GRBN (Urban)					---	.869
6668TOTL						---
State:						
6668TOTL						
6668AGRI (Agriculture)						
6668LAMI (Lands and Mines)						
6668DRIR (Drainage and Irrigation)						
6668CMIN (Chief Minister)						
6668HOUS (Housing)						
6668RURE (Rural)						
6668PUWK (Public Works)						
6668WATR (Water)						
6668INDS (Industry)						
65M$GDP (Gross Domestic Product)						

Source: See Appendix II.

[1] Lands and Mines. [2] Drainage and Irrigation.

[3] Chief Minister or State Secretary. [4] Rural and Regional.

[5] Public Works. [6] Missing, because Mean 1,000,000.

TABLE 10--Continued

State Expenditures[6]										
6668 TOTL	6668 AGRI	6668 LAMI[1]	6668 DRIR[2]	6668 CMIN[3]	6668 HOUS	6668 RURE[4]	6668 PUWK[5]	6668 WATR	6668 INDS	65M $GDP
.278	.037	-.008	.445	.623	.026	-.527	-.038	.533	.020	.493
.504	.006	-.129	.771	.860	-.281	.117	.066	.914	-.139	.918
.359	-.144	-.187	.717	.844	-.107	-.160	-.131	.811	.153	.815
.197	-.035	-.215	.546	.366	.463	-.116	-.124	.472	.432	.486
.405	-.114	-.199	.784	.793	.091	-.077	-.133	.834	.395	.838
.362	-.052	-.221	.751	.689	.169	-.070	-.088	.778	.249	.788
---	.797	.632	.294	.563	.290	.291	.809	.421	.003	.790
	---	.775	-.222	.030	.468	.180	.951	-.157	-.028	.018
		---	-.315	.065	.325	-.187	.680	-.165	-.195	-.243
			---	.780	-.227	.152	-.199	.878	.062	.804
				---	-.188	.055	.037	.908	-.107	.858
					---	-.189	.336	-.295	.714	-.194
						---	.372	.141	-.118	.263
							---	-.115	-.114	.122
								---	-.111	.938
									---	-.026

National and state development expenditures support the Selangor-centered pattern, with the added exceptional strength of the Bornean States. (See Table 10.) There is high positive correlation between Population Coverage expenditures and GDP, population, Problem Expenditures, and Urban Expenditures over states. State government expenditures for development, however, showed a very different areal pattern. Although expenditures for water and by the Chief Ministers (for government institutions primarily) followed the above pattern, total state development expenditures for 1966-68 had a correlation of only .362 with federal totals for the same period. Sabah, Sarawak, Melaka, Trengganu, Perlis, and Pahang, all had state development expenditures exceeding those of the federal government in their areas. (See Table 8.) Rural and regional expenditures by states are proportionally higher in those states not receiving much assistance from the federal government. These are the unattractive states; as such state expenditures correlate negatively (-.527) with 1957-1967 immigration flows as well.

The Development Map (Figure 8) illustrates large overall 1966-68 policy in area expenditures by the federal government, and the development areas. The largest rural development thrusts are in Pahang and Johore, in out-of-the-way areas, with potential further up the coast in Trengganu. The rice bowls of Kedah and Kelantan, connected by the abuilding East-West highway, have received the rest of the rural problem area attention. A rough urban regionalization (of POPC [Population Coverage] expenditures and urban PROB [Problem Area] expenditures) gives us (1) Penang, (2) Central and Lower Perak, (3) the Kelang Valley, (4) a coastal strip from Seremban to Bandar Penggaram, and the (5) Johore Baharu, (6) Kota Baharu, (7) Kuching, and (8) Kota Kinabalu urban regions. ECFN expenditures, mainly for roads, power facilities, and ports development spread into the Second and Third Divisions of Sarawak, interior Sabah, interior Pahang, as well as to the above localities. A finer look, by

---

This division among rich and poor, dynamic and non-dynamic states does not hold in every sector, however. Relative costs of materials and utilities for construction find higher (above average) levels in the modern states of Johore, Melaka, and Penang, which nevertheless do not have such large-scale activity, and lower levels (below average) in Selangor and Perak, which do. On the other hand, totals of business expenses, as a percentage of gross sales in states finds Selangor highest, and Johore and Perak above average (with Trengganu, perhaps because of its distant but important and costly orientation to Selangor), and Penang and the others below. Penang, with an historically highly developed service sector and a slightly lower cost of living situation emerges comparatively well off here. (J. J. O'Callaghan, "Apparent Cost Differences in Manufacturing Activities in Different States in West Malaysia," Working Paper No. 31, Pahang Tenggara Regional Masterplanning Study [June, 1971], fugitive, p. 2 and Table 13).

districts and cities will be necessary to separate functionally these few very important developments.

Policy in Districts

The 111 Districts are the basic units of areal analysis of Malaysia. They are proportionally much larger in the mountainous and unpopulated interiors of East and West Malaysia, but otherwise tend to a similar size. Thus, area analysis on their basis is useful, particularly since they are the lowest level at which most statistical data are gathered.[1] Later urban analysis is handicapped by the absence of relevant economic and social information collected specifically for and in cities throughout the whole country or even West Malaysia.

The Districts of Kuala Lumpur, Johore Baharu, Port Dickson, and Province Wellesley Utara (Butterworth), dominate Malaysian manufacturing. Kinta, Kuala Lumpur, Ulu Selangor, and Kuantan are by far the largest producers of tin. Iron production is spread and less consequential--among Pekan, Kuantan, Dungun, Muar, Kuala Muda and the tin Districts. And economic agricultural production concentrates in Keluang and the South Coast of Johore, the Districts of Selangor and Negeri Sembilan. Riverine Districts in Kedah, Kelantan, and Perak (also Penang) produce large amounts of rice. (See Figures 2 and 6.)

Population is spread through the two or three tiers of Districts along the West Coast from Johore Baharu to Perlis. Those Districts with larger populations generally have the larger cities. Non-Malay population is also localized in the Western zone of Malaya, though it is not correlated significantly with the size of District population there (at least in 1957--the last year for which racial statistics by districts are now available). (See Figures 3 and 4.) In Sarawak the First Division is predominant, with Sibu following, in all respects save the oil refining and rubber production of Miri. Sabah's two important districts in all respects are Kota Kinabalu, where future growth is predicted to occur, and Sandakan, with rubber production further spread along the Northwest Coast and

---

[1]An alternative, of course, is to impose a smaller and standard hexagonal grid over the whole country, as has Thomas Leinbach. However many of the data important to this study are identified, as to location, only by districts (if at all), such as manufacturing statistics, and school and water works construction expenditures. (See Thomas R. Leinbach, "Transportation and Modernization in Malaya," unpublished Ph.D. Thesis, The Pennsylvania State University, September, 1971.)

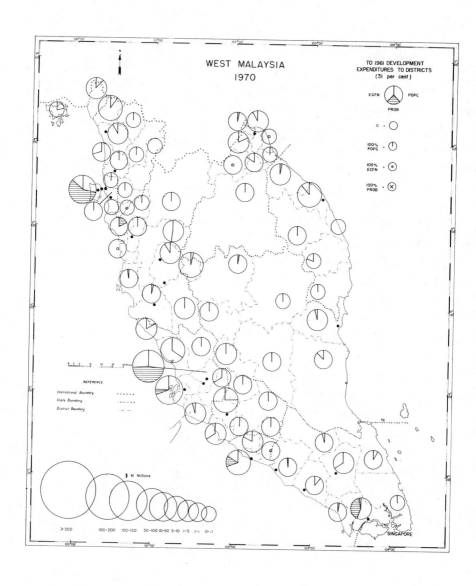

Fig. 9.--Malaysia: To 1961 Development Expenditures to Districts

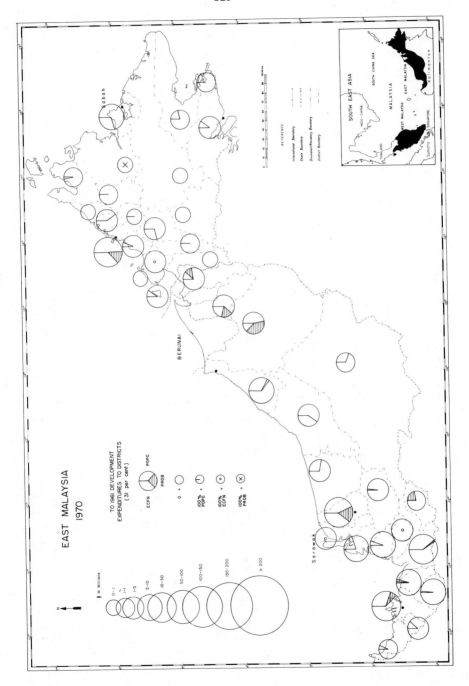

EAST MALAYSIA
1970

TO 1961 DEVELOPMENT
EXPENDITURES TO DISTRICTS
(31 per cent)

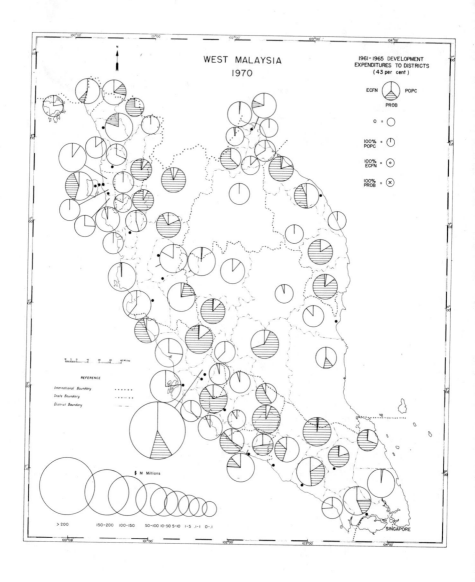

Fig. 10.--Malaysia: 1961-1965 Development Expenditures to Districts

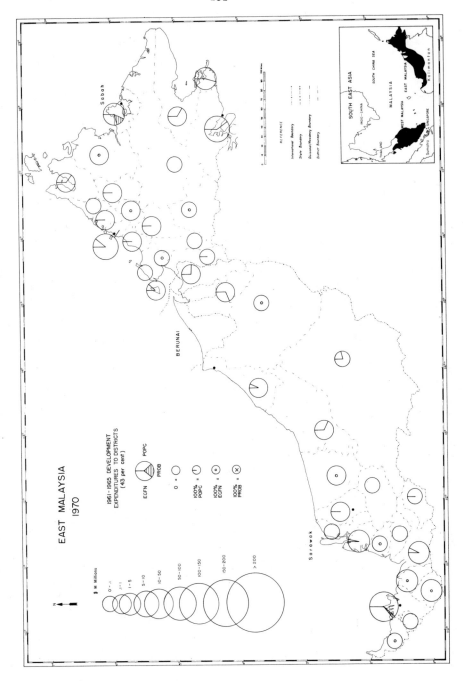

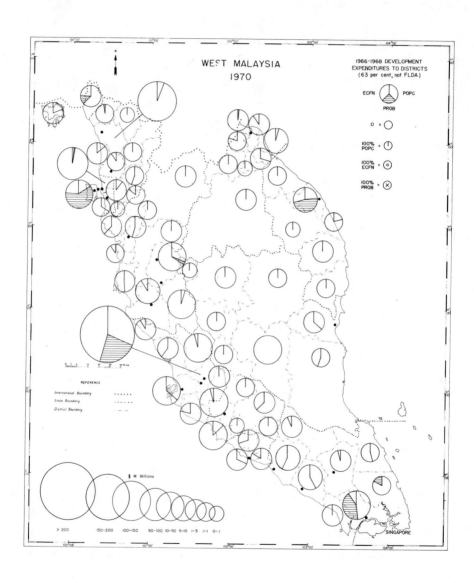

Fig. 11.--Malaysia: 1966-1968 Development Expenditures to Districts

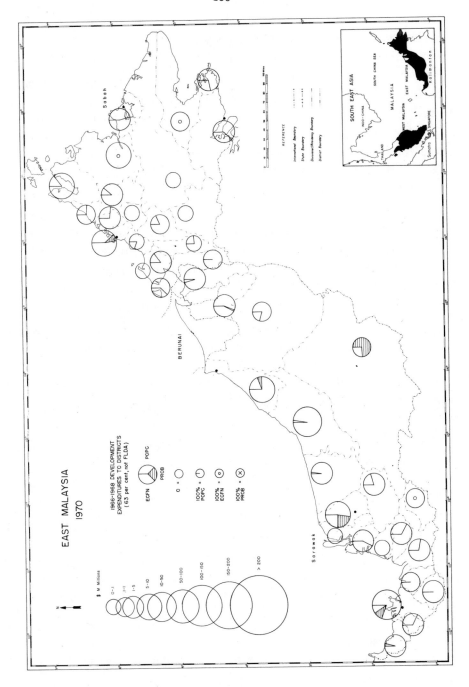

in Tawau.[1]

Tables 1, 4, and 11 show that correlations among the three types of development expenditures to districts during the three periods were only medium high (means of .836, .804, and .758 respectively). There were discernible trends in the composition of development expenditures to area, as well as in their magnitudes. Both POPC (Population Coverage) and PROB (Problem Area) expenditures to large cities (except Kuching) peaked from 1961 to 1965. POPC expenditures generally were proportionally reduced in later years, as economic development policy was pushed outward from the major centers. In the 1961-65 period, Districts' total expenditures correlated highly with POPC expenditures (.954) and with ECFN (Economic-functional) expenditures (.969); while in the 1966-68 First Malaysia Plan period, ECFN was uncorrelated across districts, except with total expenditures, indicating the fruition of planned large water works and transportation projects away from cities. POPC expenditures were correlated in both periods only medium high with 1967 estimated district population (.766 1961-65, .749 1966-68). The traditional magnets for such expenditures, Penang Island, Kuala Lumpur, Kinta, and Kuching, were, in fact, receiving disproportionally more of these social expenditures, particularly in the earlier period. (See Tables 4 and 11, Figures 10 and 11.)

A 6-factor principal components orthogonally rotated factor analysis (communalities no less than .73; and for 6/7 of the 28 variables over .85) of development expenditures and assorted economic-demographic data reveals an unclear distribution of the latter among factors, but a breakdown of development expenditures into three factors accounting for a total of 65.7 per cent of the variance.[2] Factor One contains high factor loadings for expenditures of the to-1961 and the 1961-to-1965 time periods. Factor Two represented 1966 to 1968 (First Malaysia Plan) expenditures save for ECFN, which was isolated in Factor

---

[1]Cadbury's cocoa estate west of Sandakan and the largest State padi scheme in Kinabatangan may shift rural importance away from the West Coast, whereas mortgage assets of the BHMF in districts are still almost four times higher in Kota Kinabalu than Sandakan, and practically nothing in the other districts. Kuching dominates Sarawak to an even greater degree. (See Borneo Housing Mortgage Finance, Annual Report, 1968, passim.)

[2]Factor One percentage of tract = 30.65, Factor Two = 29.691, Factor Three = 5.32. For a discussion of this and the later familiar techniques, see: R. J. Rummel, Applied Factor Analysis (Evanston: Northwestern University Press, 1970); Leslie J. King, Statistical Analysis in Geography (Englewood Cliffs: Prentice-Hall, 1969); R. C. Tyron, "Domain Sampling Formulation of Cluster and Factor Analysis," Psychometrika, XXIV, 113-25; and Jerrold Rubin and Herman P. Friedman, "A Cluster Analysis System and Taxonomy System for Grouping and Classifying Data," Journal of Theoretical Biology, XV (1967), 103-44.

TABLE 11

FMP DEVELOPMENT EXPENDITURES, 1966-1968:
PEARSON PRODUCT MOMENT CORRELATION COEFFICIENTS

	6668 POPC	6668 PROB	6668 ECFN	6668 URBN	6668 TOTL	6760 POPN	65 R+ELA
	DISTRICTS						
6668POPC (Population Coverage)	---	.884	.505	.845	.794	.749	.892
6668PROB (Problem Area)	.899	---	.467	.864	.750	.708	.968
6668ECFN (Economic-Functional)	.793	.822	---	.680	.920	.575	.482
6668URBN (Urban)	.766	.782	.804	---	.865	.750	.867
6668TOTL (Total)	.924	.967	.373	.800	---	.738	.758
6760POPN (1967 Estimated Population - West Malaysia; 1960 Population - East Malaysia)	.813	.906	.335	.777	.770	---	.655
65R+ELA (1965 Revenue + Expenditures of Local Authorities)	.109	.817	.298	.481	.441	.892	---
65R+EPP (1965 Revenue + Expenditures of Local Authorities per Person)	.406	.694	.192	.486	.439	.694	.828
	CITIES						

Source: See Appendix II.

Three.[1] Figure 12 depicts the combinations of these factors, based on scores on districts (high and low being positive or negative z-scores). Districts high on each of the three factors were Kuala Lumpur, Butterworth, and Ipoh--clearly the development points of greatest importance to the government and generally

[1]The unavoidable selectivity of the mapped data favors, as noted already, urban areas; although this bias did not change appreciably over time. The comparatively lesser, proportionally, data available for the first two periods may be a greater fault in the matrices, which would in part account for their separation of Factor One.

136

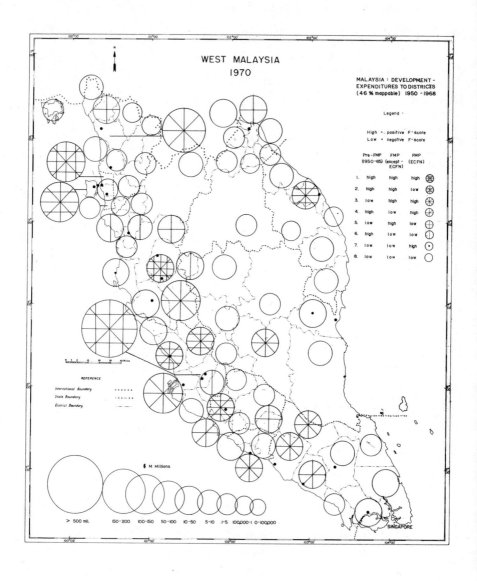

Fig. 12. --Malaysia: To 1968 Development Expenditures to Districts

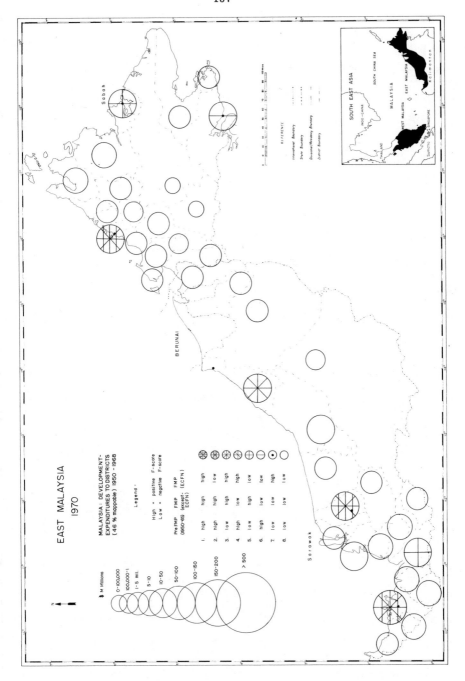

TABLE 12

CLUSTER ANALYSES--DISTRICTS

	All Variables	Population-Economic Data	1950-1969 Development Expenditures	FMP Expenditures	3-periods POPC	3-periods PROB	3-periods ECFN	3-periods URBN
	101	89	105	105	100	108	104	104
Primary Cluster Cluster No. 2	Kuching	Kuching	Kuching	Kuching	Kuching	Johore Baharu	Cameron Highlands	Kuching
Cluster No. 3	Kota Setar, Kinta	Kota Setar	Kelang	Kinta	Kinta, Kota Baharu, Kota Setar, Melaka	Pulau Pinang	Kota Setar	Kinta
Cluster No. 4	P. W. Utara	P. W. Utara	Kinta	P. W. Utara	Hilir Perak, Johore Baharu	Kuala Lumpur	Batang Padang, P.W. Utara	P. W. Utara
Cluster No. 5	Pulau Pinang	Pulau Pinang	Pulau Pinang	Pulau Pinang	Pulau Pinang, Kelang		Kuala Selangor	Pulau Pinang
Cluster No. 6	Kuala Lumpur	Kuala Lumpur	Kuala Lumpur	Kuala Lumpur	Kuala Lumpur		Kuala Lumpur	Kuala Lumpur
Cluster No. 7	Seremban, Johore Baharu	Seremban, Johore Baharu, Kelang	Johore Baharu	Seremban, Johore Baharu	Seremban		Kelang	Kelang, Kota Kinabalu
Cluster No. 8	Kelang	Kinta						
Cluster No. 9		Larut, Kota Baharu						
Cluster No. 10		Melaka Tengah						
Cluster No. 11		Muar, Batu Pahat						
Cluster No. 12		Tumpat						
Cluster No. 13		Kerian, Kuala Kangsar, Hilir Perak, Kuala Muda, P.W. Tengara, Kuala Trengganu						
Cluster No. 14		Sibu						

TABLE 13

MALAYSIA: MIDDLE CITY COMPARISONS

City	POPC				PROB				ECFN				Registered Jan 70 Unemployment	Rank	Admin Status	Rank TO61 TOTL	Rank 6165 TOTL	Rank 6668 TOTL
	TO61	6165	6668	TO68	TO61	6165	6668	TO68	TO61	6165	6668	TO68						
Alor Setar	16	9	6	10	28	8	28	18	13	13	10	15	9,388	6	TC	17	13	10
Sungei Patani	28	22	24	25	28	28	28	28	28	28	28	28	7,288	13	TC	28	23	26
Butterworth	23	23	22	24	23	28	8	13	20	2	1	2	9,799	5	DC	23	2	2
Bukit Mertajam	22	24	27	26	28	28	28	28	28	28	28	28	N.D.	N.D.	DC	22	24	28
George Town	3	3	10	3	2	2	2	2	3	9	6	7	15,890	4	C	2	3	6
Ayer Itam	28	28	28	28	28	28	6	11	28	28	28	28	N.D.	N.D.	--	28	28	24
Taiping	21	16	14	20	28	28	7	12	14	6	12	14	8,368	9	+C	21	14	17
Ipoh	9	12	5	6	28	28	28	28	2	7	4	5	18,064	2	M	12	11	4
Kampor	28	26	25	27	28	28	28	28	28	28	28	28	N.D.	N.D.	TC	28	27	27
Telok Anson	28	25	7	19	28	28	11	16	18	19	28	24	5,551	14	TC	24	25	12
Kuala Lumpur	1	1	1	1	1	1	1	1	2	1	2	1	27,575	1	FC	1	1	1
Petaling Jaya	20	2	26	4	3	4	28	4	7	15	3	3	4,865	15	TB	6	4	3
Kelang	12	11	15	15	5	28	28	9	10	28	28	20	7,406	11	TC	10	16	23
Seremban	14	14	3	5	11	7	28	17	28	28	20	21	7,381	12	TC	16	17	9
Melaka	8	4	21	8	8	3	28	8	9	10	9	12	9,088	7	M	9	6	19
B. Maharani	18	17	9	18	28	28	28	28	19	17	28	23	8,791	8	TC	20	19	18
B. Penggarang	28	21	20	23	28	28	28	28	28	28	15	18	N.D.	N.D.	TC	28	22	20
Keluang	15	19	19	22	28	0	28	28	16	28	28	22	N.D.	N.D.	TC	19	21	25
Johar Baharu	17	6	4	7	10	9	3	3	17	3	14	9	15,929	3	TC	18	5	7
Kota Baharu	10	7	8	9	28	5	12	14	12	18	19	19	7,816	10	TC	13	8	16
Kuala Tenggara	7	8	17	13	28	10	28	19	15	11	17	17	4,030	16	TC	11	12	22
Kuantan	13	13	16	16	6	28	28	28	28	12	5	6	3,997	17	TC	15	15	8
Kota Kinabalu	5	20	18	11	28	6	9	7	11	4	16	8	295	19	TB	4	9	11
Sandakan	4	15	18	12	28	28	28	15	11	16	16	16	127	20	TB	8	18	21
Tawau	19	10	12	17	28	28	28	28	8	8	13	11	33	21	M	14	10	14
Kuching	2	5	2	2	9	4	4	5	1	5	11	4	372	18	TB	3	7	5
Sibu	6	18	11	14	28	28	28	6	6	28	18	13	N.D.	N.D.	TB	5	20	13
Miri	11	27	23	21	28	28	10	10	4	14	8	10	N.D.	N.D.	TB	7	26	15

Source: See Appendix II.

FC = Federal Capital (+Municipality Status); C = City (+ Municipality Status); M = Municipality; DC = District Council; TC = Town Council; TB = Town Board.

TABLE 13--Continued

City	1947 Population	1957/60 Population	1970 Population	% Change 1947-57/60	% Change 1957/60-70	% Change 1947-70
Alor Setar	35,425	52,915	66,179	49	25	87
Sungei Patani	13,175	22,916	35,842	74	56	172
Butterworth[a]	21,255	42,504	61,252	100	54	188
Bukit Mertajam[a]	12,345	24,663	26,679	100	8	116
George Town[a]	189,086	234,903	270,019	24	15	43
Ayer Itam[a]	N.D.	22,369	25,662	N.D.	15	N.D.
Taiping	41,362	48,206	54,603	17	13	32
Ipoh	80,894	125,770	247,689	55	97	206
Kampar	17,499	24,602	26,551	41	8	52
Telok Anson	23,055	37,042	44,668	61	21	94
Kuala Lumpur	175,961	316,230	451,728	80	43	157
Petaling Jaya	N.D.	16,575	92,633	N.D.	459	N.D.
Kelang	33,506	74,649	113,269	126	50	239
Seremban	35,274	52,091	79,915	48	53	127
Melaka[a]	54,507	69,848	86,357	28	24	58
B. Maharani	32,228	39,046	61,203	21	57	90
B. Penggaram	26,506	39,294	53,087	48	35	100
Keluang	15,954	31,181	43,297	95	39	171
Johore Baharu	38,826	74,909	135,936	93	81	250
Kota Baharu	22,765	38,103	55,052	67	44	142
Kuala Trengganu	27,004	29,446	53,353	9	81	98
Kuantan	12,369	23,034	43,391	186	88	250
Kota Kinabalu	11,704	21,719	41,830	86	93	257
Sandakan	14,499	28,806	42,249	99	47	191
Tawau	44,282	10,276	24,184	140	135	465
Kuching	37,800	50,579	63,491	38	26	68
Sibu	9,983	29,630	50,405	197	70	405
Miri	10,949	13,350	35,879	22	169	228
Total	998,213	1,594,655	2,386,403	59	49	139

[a]Town populations.   Source: See Appendix II.

in Malaysia. Secondarily (all but high 6668 ECFN scores), Penang, Kuala Selangor, Ulu Selangor, and Kuala Trengganu in Malaya, and Kuching, Kota Kinabalu, and Sibu in Borneo emerge. It is notable that certain Districts with equal or larger total expenditures for 1950-1968 (such as Alor Setar, Batang Padang, Kota Baharu, Johore Baharu, and Sandakan), do not take on this historical and overall importance. They are either recently emergent recipients

TABLE 13--Continued

1965 Rev+Expen Local Authority (M$000)	(Rank)	1965 Rev+Expen per Capita (M$)	(Rank)	Number of Manufacturing Establishments	Gross Value of Sales of Own Manu Products (M$000) 1967	(Rank)	Fulltime Workers
1,207	(19)	20	(21)	280	63,291	((9)	1,873
858	24	29	19	104	6,885	19	995
N.D.		N.D.		209	151,272	4	5,347
N.D.		N.D.		150	36,852	13	1,365
65,486	1	228	1	807	78,395	7	5,687
N.D.		N.D.		N.D.	N.D.		N.D.
3,373	9	67	7	173	72,883	8	2,564
19,796	3	85	4	518	106,874	5	7,235
1,004	21	38	14	85	9,059	18	764
1,437	18	36	16	240	14,172	17	881
38,073	2	72	6	1,176	541,980	1	20,444
N.D.		N.D.		219	522,262	2	13,631
4,478	7	48	12	171	84,163	6	5,186
2,941	11	51	11	224	42,687	12	2,639
7,640	5	93	3	345	59,392	10	2,569
1,721	15	37	15	173	33,273	14	911
1,686	16	41	13	179	42,325	13	2,122
1,542	17	57	9	106	33,268	15	1,765
5,937	6	64	8	254	174,782	3	10,410
2,106	14	35	17	205	46,713	11	2,698
1,028	20	27	20	172	3,481	20	594
933	22	34	18	97	16,448	16	987
2,249	13	67	7	N.D.	N.D.		N.D.
2,984	10	75	5	N.D.	N.D.		N.D.
932	23	53	10	N.D.	N.D.		N.D.
9,981	4	105	2	N.D.	N.D.		N.D.
3,992	8	N.D.		N.D.	N.D.		N.D.
2,726	12	N.D.		N.D.	N.D.		N.D.
184,110		1,362			2,140,475		90,666

of federal development policy attention, or contain only large special economic-function projects.

The identification of special development districts in Malaysia is borne out by a series of cluster analyses. (See Table 12.) These reveal the very great similarities, almost homogeneity, of most of the Malaysian areas in so far as pattern of government development activity is concerned. For various combinations of variables, the smallest number of Districts in the first cluster extracted was 89 (of 111). [1] Here districts were grouped on the basis of population and economic data only. Seremban, Johore Baharu, and Kelang clustered, as did a group of six rural but important West Coast (plus Kuala Trengganu) Districts. Certain individuals stood out here as in clusters formed on the basis of development expenditure data. The special Districts in respect of individuality of character, if not, so far, strictly magnitude of development expenditures, were, first, Kuching, Kuala Lumpur, Penang, and Johore Baharu, and a second group consisting of Kinta, Province Wellesley Utara, Kota Setar, and Seremban. Other Districts separated out in analyses of POPC, PROB, and ECFN expenditures over the years. Melaka and Kota Baharu received abnormal expenditures. Cameron Highlands, Batang Padang, Kelang, and Kuala Selangor of course took on great ECFN importance, as they were the loci of large electricity and water projects.

As can be seen in Figures 9-11, through time there has been spread of development expenditures culminating in a remarkably wide distribution under the First Malaysia Plan. [2] New policy points of importance in some smaller middle-city regions have arisen. Seemingly, as a development policy matures, it tends to deconcentrate its activity, while pushing a very few city regions (and then perhaps new land development areas) into positions of absolute supremacy.

Policy in Cities

Figures 13-15 depict development expenditures to urban portions (towns of >5,000 population, >3,000 in East Malaysia) of Districts, absolutely, and as a proportion of all expenditures to these Districts. There was, with the maturation of Malaysian development policy, a general decrease in the urban versus

---

[1] Like all the cluster analyses, this reduced the importance of absolute magnitude differences among the districts by converting the variables to rank scores before clustering according to pattern among them.

[2] The 1966-68 District expenditures map is unavoidably misleading, as unlike on the 1961-65 map, land development (Federal Land Development Authority) expenditures have not been shown except in Temerloh (Jengka Triangle), owing to the unwillingness of the government to provide these data. Similar reticence was met in MARA, which shows how politically sensitive Malay politicoes can be. In any case, the policy trend for land development, as noted above, is toward more highly concentrated area development, which began, then, with the Jengka Triangle in Pahang. Under the Second Malaysia Plan we can expect Southeast Pahang and Southeast and Central Southeast Johore to receive large disbursements--for roads and infrastructure, as well as for land-clearing and rubber and oil palm planting and processing, lumbering, and tourism facilities.

rural expenditures ratio but a large absolute growth of urban expenditures in large cities. The exception was Sabah where city development expenditures were stable or declined; whereas urban expenditures as proportions of total district expenditures increased.[1] Certain city districts are seen to be in a decline, nevertheless, relative to others or to their rural areas. They are Kota Baharu, Kuala Trengganu, Kuantan, and Miri--all centers in recognizably poor areas (and below the threshold of dynamism. See below). Leading urban districts in federal attention were Kuala Lumpur, Butterworth, Johore Baharu (the last with increasing expenditures but a varying urban proportion). City Districts with low urban expenditures were Seremban, Kota Setar, and Bandar Penggaram--relatively prosperous agricultural areas.[2]

Figures 16-19 illustrate Malaysian development expenditures to 27 middle cities, plus Kuala Lumpur, the only (proto-) Million City in Malaysia since Singapore was ejected.[3] Certain cities as usual are highly visible as objects of policy over the years--policy which has seen a relative decline in investment in cities, but the increasing dynamism and continued attraction of certain prominent ones. The leaders in development attention are consistently Kuala Lumpur, the Penang Metropolitan Area, and Kuching. In the history of Malaysian development policy these (with emphasis in Penang on Butterworth) also have had the highest expenditures per capita.

Cluster analyses consistently separate these from the other 22-25 similar cities as being special. (See Table 14.) Petaling Jaya and Butterworth come out as singleton clusters over three periods of ECFN expenditures; while George Town and Kuching fall back into Cluster One. Ipoh clusters with Kuching when all variables are considered. But in all variables combinations there is a primary cluster containing more than 3/4 of the cities, showing their basic similarity to one another vis à vis these three to six special cities.

A six factor principle components orthogonally rotated factor analysis

---

[1] This may reflect Sabah's broad underdevelopment, combined with rich timber exploitations--a situation calling for little federal intervention anywhere, so long as the State is so wealthy (even in the absence of massive agriculture development) but with the necessity of making the export outlets operate smoothly.

[2] Keluang acquired a high urban segment of federal money in 1966-68, explicable only in terms of its greater physical needs and the almost complete estate dominance of its hinterland.

[3] Although Kuala Lumpur will not have a million people for some time, its functions as a "Million City" in all policy and increasing centrality respects make it so. Therefore per se it is not within the specific purview of this study.

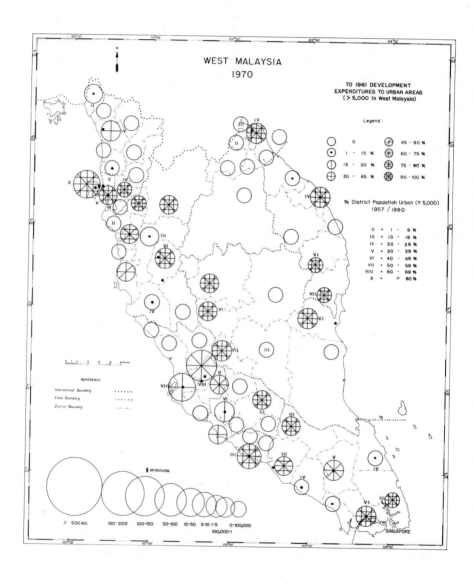

Fig. 13. --Malaysia: To 1961 Development Expenditures to Urban Areas

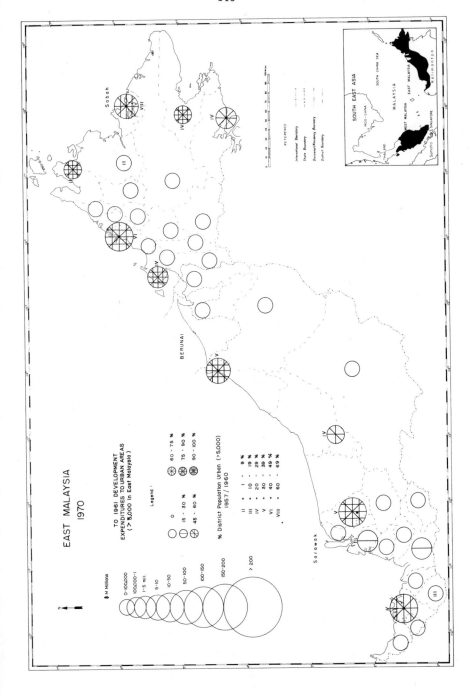

EAST MALAYSIA
1970

TO 1961 DEVELOPMENT
EXPENDITURES TO URBAN AREAS
(> 5,000 in East Malaysia)

Legend :

% District Population Urban (>5,000)
1957 / 1960

146

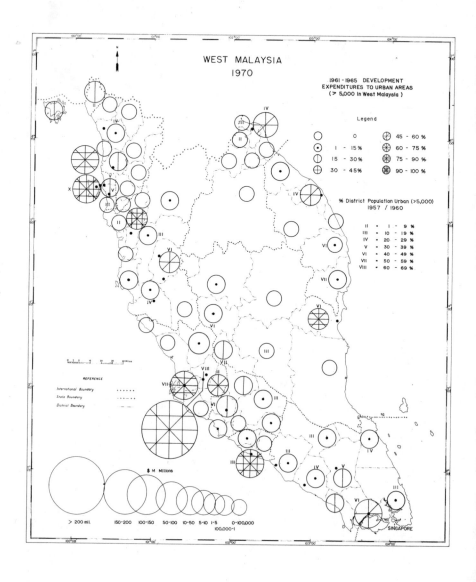

Fig. 14.--Malaysia: 1961-1965 Development Expenditures to Urban Areas

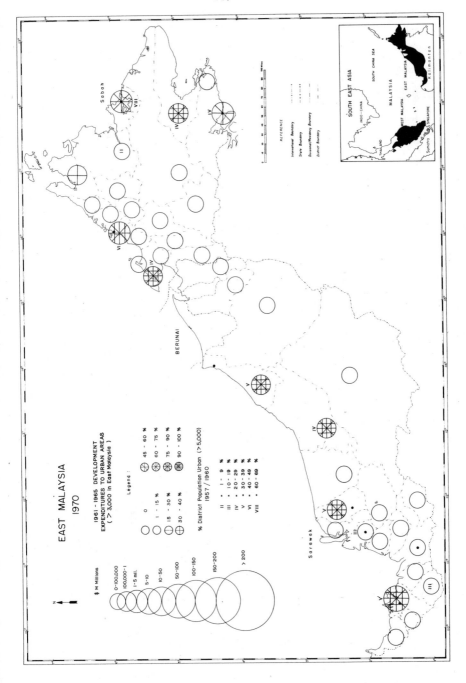

EAST MALAYSIA
1970

1961 - 1965 DEVELOPMENT
EXPENDITURES TO URBAN AREAS
(> 3,000 in East Malaysia)

Legend :

45 - 60 %
60 - 75 %
75 - 90 %
90 - 100 %

0
1 - 15 %
15 - 30 %
30 - 40 %

% District Population Urban (> 5,000)
1957 / 1960

II = 1 - 9 %
III = 10 - 19 %
IV = 20 - 29 %
V = 30 - 39 %
VI = 40 - 49 %
VIII = 60 - 69 %

$ M Millions
0 - 100,000
100,000 - 1
1 - 5 mil.
5 - 10
10 - 50
50 - 100
100 - 150
150 - 200
> 200

REFERENCE

International Boundary
State Boundary
Divisional/Residency Boundary
District Boundary

SOUTH EAST ASIA

148

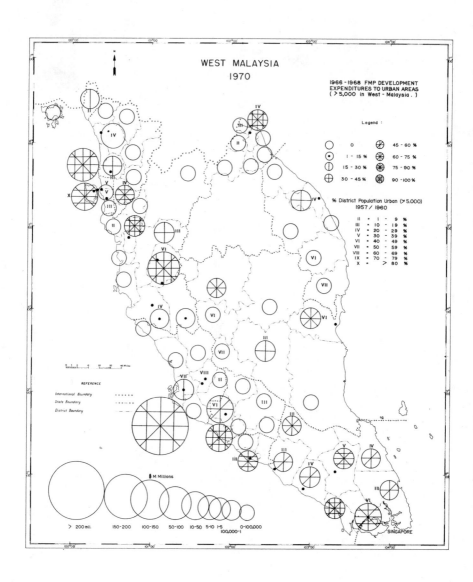

Fig. 15.--Malaysia: 1966-1968 Development Expenditures to Urban Areas

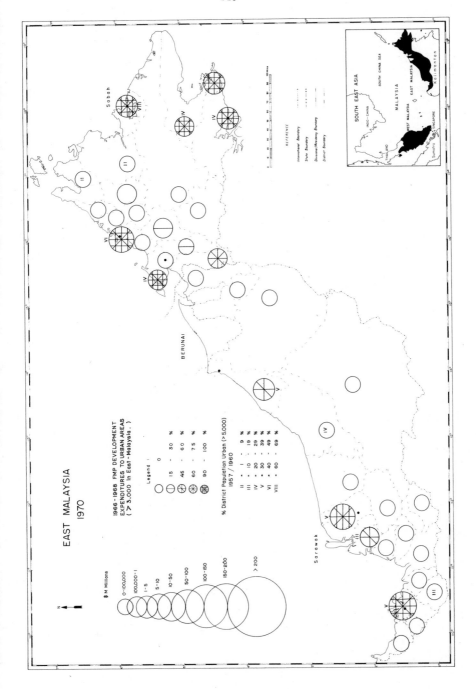

150

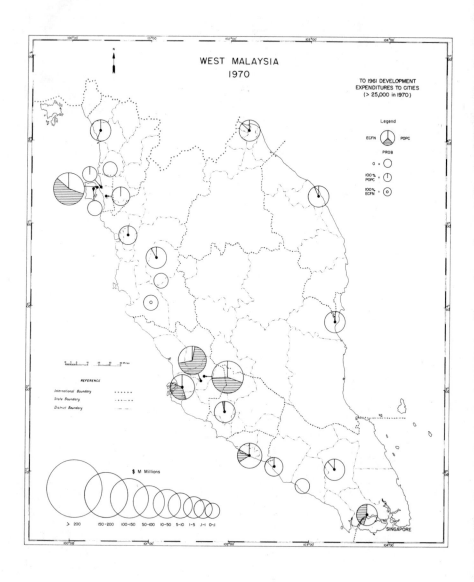

Fig. 16.--Malaysia: To 1961 Development Expenditures to Middle Cities

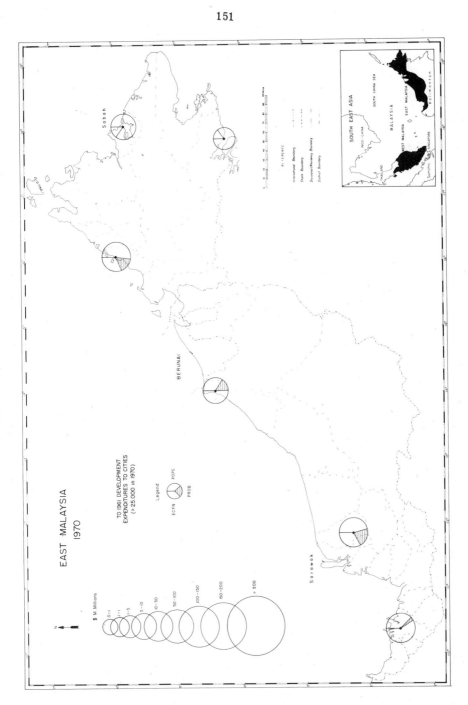

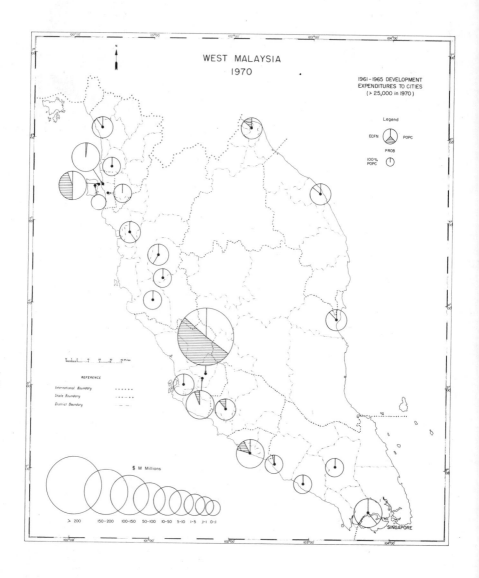

Fig. 17.--Malaysia: 1961-1965 Development Expenditures to Middle Cities

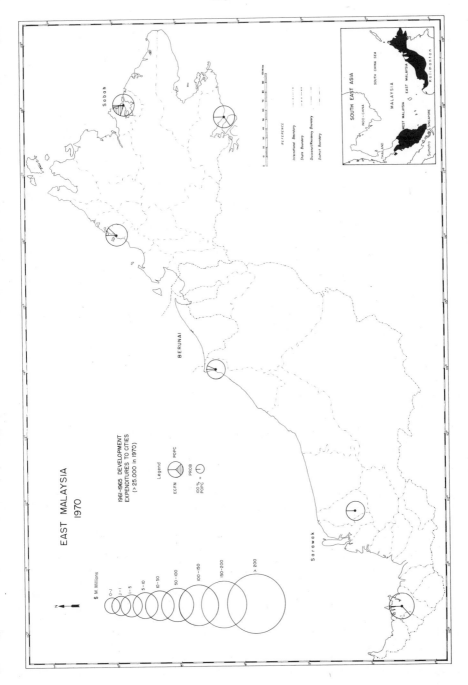

EAST MALAYSIA
1970

1961–1965 DEVELOPMENT
EXPENDITURES TO CITIES
(>25,000 in 1970)

Legend

ECFN   POPC

PROB

100 % =
POPC

$ M. Millions

0–1
1–5
5–10
10–50
50–100
100–150
150–200
> 200

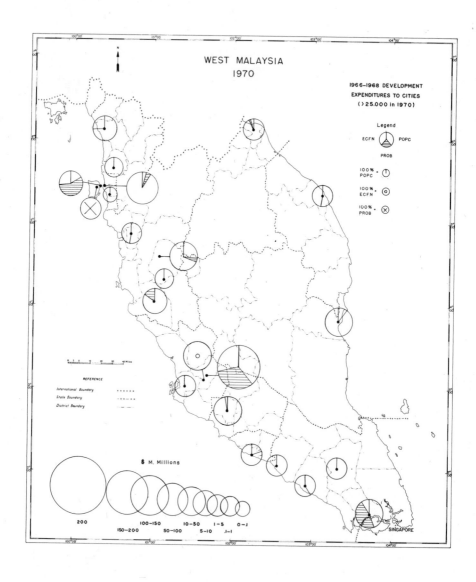

Fig. 18.--Malaysia: 1966-1968 Development Expenditures to Middle Cities

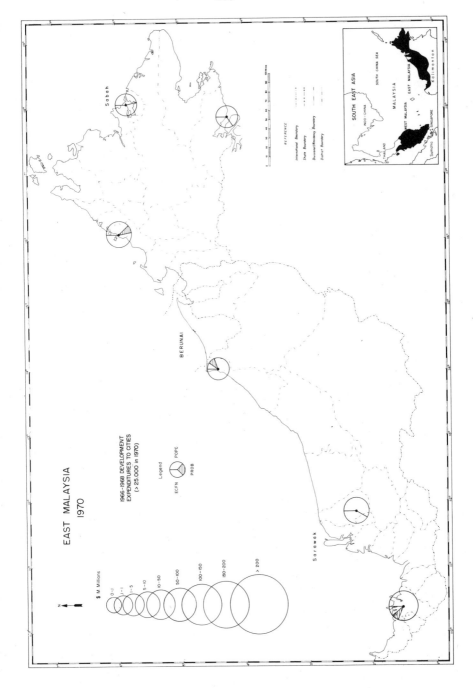

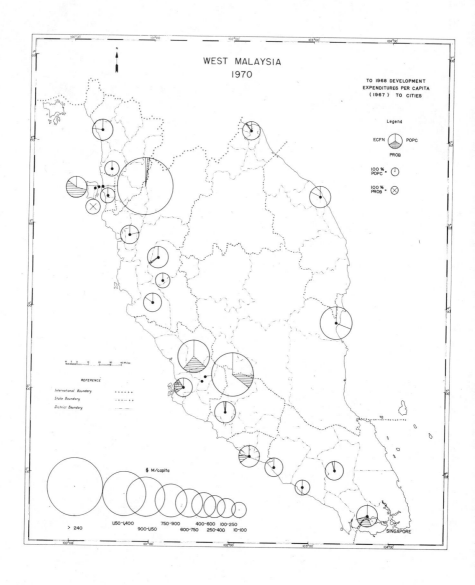

Fig. 19.--Malaysia: To 1968 Development Expenditures per Capita to Middle Cities

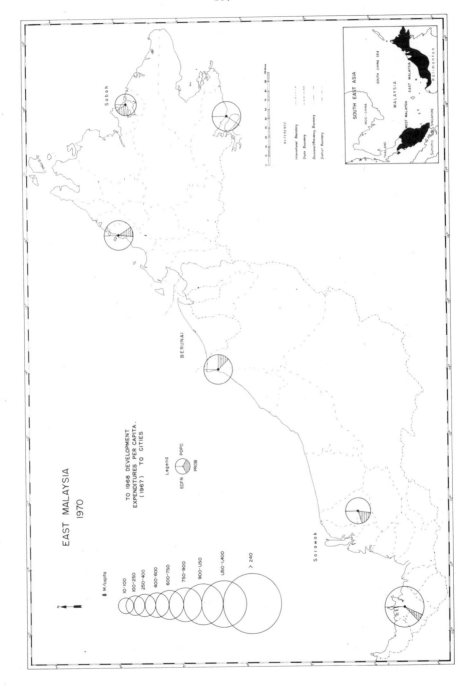

EAST MALAYSIA
1970

TO 1968 DEVELOPMENT
EXPENDITURES PER CAPITA.
(1967) TO CITIES

TABLE 14

CLUSTER ANALYSES--CITIES

	All Variables	Pop-Econ Data	1950-1968 Expenditures	3-periods POPC	3-periods PROB	3-periods ECFN
Primary Cluster	24	22	25	25	26	25
Cluster No. 2	Kuala Lumpur	Kuala Lumpur	Kuala Lumpur	Kuala Lumpur	Kuala Lumpur	Kuala Lumpur
Cluster No. 3	George Town	George Town	George Town	George Town	George Town	Butterworth
Cluster No. 4	Ipoh, Kuching	Ipoh	Kuching	Kuching		Petaling Jaya
Cluster No. 5	Alor Setar					
Cluster No. 6	Melaka, Johore Baharu					

whose fairly evenly distributed tract percentage of variance totalled 88. 87[1] gives inconclusive but interesting support to patterns of similarity and superiority brought out in the maps and cluster analysis. Three cities score positively on all six factors: Kuala Lumpur, George Town, and Johore Baharu. The nature of the factors (see Table 15) is such that population and development policy expenditures are mixed up, thus giving a truer picture of the cities' relative importance--if a somewhat confused one. Butterworth follows, scoring low only on population-related variables, followed by Ipoh, which received similar inattention to 6668 POPC needs, whose larger population weighed in, but which was comparatively ignored in pre-First Malaysia Plan expenditure patterns. Melaka likewise has four positive scores, despite its relative decline in the 1960's as a center of importance. Sandakan, Keluang, and Kota Baharu score surprisingly poorly on these factors; and in Penang State and surrounding areas, the weight of George Town and Butterworth is readily seen.

Inspection of the Pearson Product Moment Correlations of all development expenditures in cities reveals the 1961-1965 Total Expenditure pattern (see Figure 17, Tables 1, 4, and 9) to be the prototype of the distribution of all

---

[1]Also with very high communalities except for 6668 ELFN, which dropped out. See Appendix II.

TABLE 15

CITY FACTOR SCORES

	One Population Density (POPC + 6668 PROB)	Two Second Malaysia Plan (1961- 65)	Three Absolute Population (TO61 Total)	Four 6668 Total	Five 6668 POPC	Six Economic Magnitude
	29.98% of	15.34%	15.37%	10.88%	9.82%	8.46%
Kuala Lumpur	+1.58	+3.69	+1.61	+4.54	+4.20	+2.39
George Town	+1.51	+1.49	+1.08	+0.70	+0.45	+1.38
Johore Baharu	+0.10	+0.07	+0.09	+0.08	+0.18	+0.13
Butterworth	-0.80	+0.86	+0.10	+1.42	-0.01	+0.43
Ipoh	+0.01	-0.29	+0.60	+0.05	-0.19	+0.66
Melaka	+0.09	+0.09	+0.06	-0.55	-0.00	+0.33
Kuching	+1.40	+0.58	-0.78	+0.47	+0.26	-0.01
Kota Kinabalu	-0.12	+0.09	-0.64	+0.28	+0.18	-0.33
Alor Setar	-0.15	-0.45	+0.25	-0.62	+0.12	-0.02
Seremban	-0.07	-0.44	-0.17	+0.52	+0.16	-0.36
Petaling Jaya	-0.57	-0.04	-0.06	+0.72	-0.61	-0.66
Kelang	-0.34	-0.23	+0.05	-0.45	-0.39	-0.72
Kuantan	-0.47	-0.28	+0.07	-0.10	-0.33	-0.68
Bandar Maharani	-0.54	-0.42	-0.56	-0.56	-0.27	-0.58
Kota Baharu	-0.01	-0.24	-0.01	-0.53	-0.01	-0.17
Kuala Trengganu	-0.28	-0.19	-0.22	-0.18	-0.12	-0.45
Taiping	-0.38	-0.25	-0.20	-0.20	-0.25	-0.42
Telok Anson	-0.58	-0.33	-0.15	-0.42	-0.13	-0.50
Tawau	-0.44	-0.16	-0.43	-0.12	-0.20	-0.88
Sandakan	-0.25	-0.19	-0.34	-0.36	-0.27	-0.89
Band. Penggaram	-0.51	-0.39	-0.15	-0.35	-0.19	-0.83
Sungei Patani	-0.57	-0.36	-0.09	-0.35	-0.38	-0.69
Kampar	-0.61	-0.34	-0.25	-0.41	-0.24	-0.78
Sibu	-0.37	-0.16	-0.18	-0.22	-0.21	-1.17
Miri	-0.48	-0.18	-0.30	-0.24	-0.43	-1.19
Keluang	-0.52	-0.38	-0.27	-0.28	-0.35	-1.11
Bukit Mertajam	-0.70	-0.35	-0.26	-0.38	-0.38	-1.16
Ayer Itam	-0.70	-0.38	-0.27	-0.37	-0.37	-1.17

Source: See Appendix II.

Scores rounded from five decimal places, Z-score format, signs made consistent.

expenditures in these periods.[1] Comparing this distribution to that of various functional attributes of the middle cities (see Table 16) suggests that manufacturing towns received relatively more expenditure than they otherwise should (Butterworth, Petaling Jaya, Kelang); those commanding primary and agricultural hinterlands drew less (Kuching, Ipoh, Alor Setar, Bandar Maharani, Seremban, Sibu, Miri). This is not to say that the margins of advantage are devoted directly to manufacturing investment. Rather, Butterworth and Kelang have had port and utilities development, and Petaling Jaya large hospitals; but the direction of large-scale government spending is clear. It includes development of industrial areas, much of the cost of which is compiled in the data. Broadly, cities with multiple functions are best attended to (Kuala Lumpur, George Town, Kuching, Ipoh, Johore Baharu, Melaka, Alor Setar, Kota Kinabalu). They have, generally, the highest unemployment, administrative status, populations, and gross value of sales as well.

Divergences from the 1961-65 Total norms are as follows: Johore Baharu ranks very low in TO61 PROB, and Sibu and Kelang higher; the TO61 ECFN expenditure pattern differs far more, with Kuching, Miri and Sibu way up, Kelang Sandakan, Keluang relatively higher than their norm, and Johore Baharu and Kota Baharu, the old capitals, way down; 6668 ECFN has the most divergent distribution, whereby Ipoh, Kuantan, Miri, and Bandar Penggaram are way up, and Kuching, Johore Baharu, Kuala Trengganu, and Kota Baharu are way down. The differences indicate that: (1) Johore Baharu has been rising in importance as a population but not a development economic center (proximity to Singapore being the presumed reason, although in future planning Johore Baharu is targeted for important industrial development); and (2) East Malaysian, especially Sarawakian, cities have a greater proclivity to being targets of and absorbing extraordinary expenditures.

The figures indicate the following trends over time: (1) increasing dominance of Kuala Lumpur-Petaling Jaya and the Kelang valley corridor within an overall spread effect of development expenditures to cities; (2) an increasing specialization of the super-cities e.g. Kuala Lumpur and Kuching to POPC and the government building component of ECFN; (3) a general decrease (except in Kuala Lumpur and Kuching) in the proportion of POPC expenditure; and (4) a tendency for the larger cities to have the higher proportions of PROB expenditures--understandable considering the urbanization/malaise trends. These are

---

[1]Coefficients of correlation of >.800 for all but TO61 PROB (.755), TO61 ECFN (.676), and 6668 ECFN (as usual the odd ball = .465).

reinforced by patterns, such as they can be discerned, of policy expectation fulfillment among cities. Kuala Lumpur, Ipoh, and the Penang Metropolitan Area had the largest number of MBBS-supported housing units in process in 1968, the largest gross value of sales of their own manufacturing products, and (with Johore Baharu, and Kuching--the scale of the latter of whose industries is far smaller) the most factories constructed in industrial estates.

One may ask, in concluding this chapter: how has the broad location pattern of where things have been done in Malaysia compared with where things were wanted and thought to be? The answer is very well, in the case of expenditures; less well in the case of expectations; and worst, as noted in Chapter III, in the case of administrative efficiency. The major problems with expenditures have been (a) coordination of these from multiple ministries and departments on the ground, and (b) the irresistible attraction of Kuala Lumpur for government-oriented institutional development. The latter is a problem in that other cities and states complain of inattention; and some are declining where added inputs such as these might bolster their growth and morale. The private sector has continued to support the development of three or four cities, to the practical exclusion of all others for activities above the shop, primary products processing, and low governmental levels. It would seem from the persistence of Melaka and George Town and the comparative ignoring of Sibu, Johore Baharu, and Sandakan in expenditure patterns that old ideas of centers of importance, and perhaps in the cases of Melaka and George Town in some respects, the adherence to old stereotypes of dynamism, may by disfunctional. Moreover, Alor Setar, Kota Baharu, Kuala Trengganu, Seremban, Kuantan, Sibu, and Sandakan have not, so far, been asked to do or bear enough responsibility and weight in national development--either for themselves or the nation.

All of this suggests that the Malaysian Middle Cities can be classified broadly into two categories: those above and below a Threshold of Dynamism. Cities only prosper where manufacturing, export, or vast hinterland obtain, and they have multiple functions. Table 16 displays the 28 cities under discussion, rearranged in descending order of importance on the combinations of functions each serves and ten significant variables. The dynamic cities, from the aggregate data, seem to be contributive (generating, even) to national development; the undynamic ones comparatively stagnant. All may have urbanization, urban malaise, and self-development problems. But perhaps the dynamic cities cope with these problems and at the same time make specific and necessary contributions to national development. The undynamic cities would seem to be a drain

TABLE 16

MIDDLE CITIES' THRESHOLD OF DYNAMISM

City	Func-tions[1]					Ranks					
		1968 Manu	Reg. Unem-ploy	Admin Type[2]	1970 Popn	6165 Totl Proto-type	6668 Totl	6668 ECFN	65R+ Expn	65R+ EXPP	47-57 % Pop Growth
Above:											
1. Kuala Lumpur	23456*	1	1	1	1	1	1	2	2	6	14
2. George Town	123456*	7	4	2	2	3	7	6	1	1	26
3. Ipoh	3456	5	2	3	3	11	5	4	3	4	9
4. Johore Baharu	3456	3	3	5	4	5	9	14	6	9	5
5. Kelang	(1) 45	6	11	5	5	16	20	-	7	13	6
6. Petaling Jaya	345	2	15	6	6	4	3	3	n.d.	n.d.	1
7. Kuching	13456*	n.d.	18	3	10	7	4	11	4	2	23
8. Butterworth	1245	4	5	4	11	2	2	1	n.d.	n.d.	11
9. Sandakan	1345	n.d.	20	6	21	18	16	16	10	5	10
10. Kota Kinabalu	2456	n.d.	19	6	22	9	8	7	13	8	4

Below:											
11. Melaka	2456	10	7	3	7	6	12	9	5	3	24
12. Seremban	356	12	12	5	8	17	21	20	11	12	16
13. Alor Setar	2456	9	6	5	9	13	15	10	19	22	22
14. B. Maharani	35	15	8	5	12	8	23		15	16	18
15. Kota Baharu	256	11	10	5	13	14	19	19	14	18	15
16. Taiping	45	8	9	5	14	22	14	12	16	7	27
17. B. Penggaram	5	13	n.d.	5	15	12	18	15	20	14	20
18. K. Trengganu	256	21	16	6	16	20	17	17	8	21 [3]	19
19. Sibu	235	n.d.	n.d.	5	17	25	13	18	18	n.d. [3]	3
20. Telok Anson	35	18	14	5	18	15	24		22	17	7
21. Kuantan	356	17	17	5	19	21	6	5	17	19	12
22. Keluang	35	16	n.d.	6	20	26	22	8	12	10 [3]	8
23. Miri	235	n.d.	n.d.	5	23	23	10		24	20	13
24. Sungei Patani	235	20	13	5	24	24			n.d.	n.d. [3]	17
25. Bukit Mertajam	5	14	n.d.	5	25	27			21	15	25
26. Kampar	35	19	n.d.		26	28			n.d.	n.d.	28
27. Ayer Itam	5	n.d.	n.d.		27				n.d.		
28. Tawau	35	n.d.	21	6	28	10	11	13	23	11	2

1* = multifunctional (≥5); 1 = export port; 2 = rice hinterland; 3 = economic primary products hinterland; 4 = 1968 manufacturing greater than $50 million gross sales of own products; 5 = services center; 6 = state capital.

2 1 = federal capital; 2 = City; 3 = Municipality; 4 = Rural District Council; 5 = Town Council; 6 = Town Board.

3 N. d. here because of discrepancies in urban population–urban revenue+expenditure definitions.

N.B. Blanks mean rank is last, i.e. no absolute score on this variable.

on national and local revenues and patiences--parasites in the national context. [1]

This division of the cities has determined the choice of case-study cities for Chapters V, VI and VII, below. The Small Cities all fall below the Threshold of Dynamism; the Three Singular cities are above this, at this point admittedly somewhat intuitive dividing line. George Town and Butterworth are dynamic, while Ayer Itam is not. These are united in the Penang Metropolitan Area, however, the subject of the last of the three sets of case studies. By looking at these cities' development policy systems, a test of the proposed division can be attempted, and more light shed on the localized conditions contributing to the great difference among Malaysian cities in their rôles in national development.

---

[1]This is not to say they are parasites on their immediate hinterlands. Cf. Bert F. Hoselitz, "Generative and Parasitic Cities," Economic Development and Cultural Change, III (April, 1955), 278-94.

CHAPTER V

AREA IN POLICY: THREE SMALL CITIES

The Three Cities

Alor Setar, Keluang, and Kota Baharu have the following similarities: low gross values of manufacturing sales, lower revenue plus expenditure per capita of the local authority, and lower growth rates and 1970 population than a majority of dynamic cities; and they have lower proportions of non-Malay population.[1] (See Table 13.) Chinese dominate their business and commercial sectors, where, however, unemployment is not so great a problem, owing to lesser immigration, than in larger cities. Industry is scattered and mixed through their areas; there is no technical school or high-order health facility available; and drainage and flood problems are perennial--causing health and housing problems. Being so badly situated in the paths of floods, their comparatively new government and commercial areas have accordingly developed on higher land; while the older settled areas continue to deteriorate. Lastly, they all have plans for but have taken little action on industrial estates, town planning, and regularizing of central city traffic.

As units with high centrality characteristics, the three cities perform service center functions, but have fewer general functions than dynamic cities (an average of three versus four). They are in the shadow of dynamic cities or (in the case of Kota Baharu) just neglected, with almost pure agricultural hinterlands. Their comparative quiescence results from the nature of the rural/city relationship in Malaysia which seems to place greatest importance on the highest service functions of large cities (including supply of technological inputs including education) on the one hand, and of lower order towns for banking and general services especially to the export sector, on the other. This system of large and quite small cities is rather highly developed; the ones in the middle languish, despite some immigration.[2] Partial exceptions to this are state gov-

---

[1] Keluang has the highest, but that exceeds only Johore Baharu among dynamic cities, based on the 1957 census.

[2] Take Pasir Mas, Pasir Puteh, and Machang, for instance, vis à vis Kota Baharu.

ernment activity generally and some agricultural and rural welfare services that emanate from these cities (except Keluang, in the case of state government). The location of state capitals in Alor Setar and Kota Baharu certainly has meant, as well, that these cities are better served with standard health and other welfare activities which naturally have had a tendency to cluster around their state mother bureaucracies. In each city it is the state, in any case, which is the main financier of development in the cities over the years. As objects of development policy, these cities do not attract expectation-fulfilling private enterprise activities such as large-scale housing or industrial projects (except small private processing factories and services) and cannot generate their own public ones. However, the state governments have managed to promote some housing and industrialization themselves.

The cities receive a predominance of POPC (Population Coverage) federal development expenditures, accordingly. Their per capita federal development expenditures through 1968 are comparatively low, but the cities (excepting Alor Setar, because of Muda) receive the overwhelming amounts of development expenditures aimed at their districts. On the positive side, each city is the object now of large external inputs in their agricultural hinterlands--rice double-cropping, water control around Alor Setar (Muda) and Kota Baharu (Kemubu), and integrated land development around Keluang (Johore Tengah), as well as further estate development (especially oil palm) in other sections of Keluang's hinterland.

Nature of the Cities

Alor Setar

Alor Setar is the capital of the State of Kedah, a Town Council which became financially autonomous in 1965 and was Alliance controlled but was taken over by the Mentri Besar (Chief Minister) of Kedah at the beginning of 1970. [1] In the absence of the political problems behind revenue collection of the

[1] The official reason was that the Town Council was "not effective" in administration, mainly in the collecting of rates and looking after urban malaise. Thus the government sub-system of Alor Setar now revolves around the state government, in which resides an Advisory Board to the Mentri Besar, consisting of the Town Council Secretary, who carries on the daily work as usual, Kota Setar (District) Collector of Land Revenue, and the State Engineer, the State Financial Officer, the State Farm Planning Officer, the State Drainage and Irrigation Engineer, the State Land Officer, the Chief Police Officer and the Assistant State Secretary for Local Authorities. (Nor Aman, Assistant State Secretary for Local Authorities, Kedah, interview, August 15, 1970, Alor Setar.)

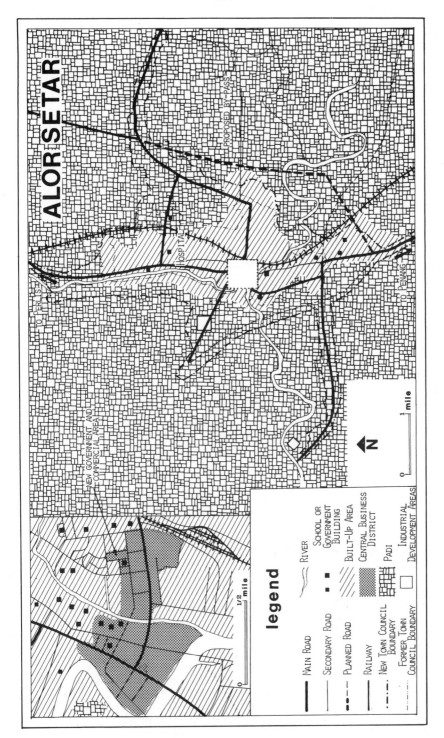

Fig. 20.--City Map: Alor Setar

TABLE 17

ALOR SETAR--REVENUE AND EXPENDITURE 1966-68

	Revenue			
	Regular Income (Rates)	State Deficit Contributions	Project Aid	Total
1966	$ 847, 649	$30, 000	$56, 136	$ 933, 785
1967	905, 704	37, 000		942, 704
1968	1, 019, 512	16, 000		1, 035, 512
Total	2, 772, 865	83, 000	56, 136	2, 912, 001

	Expenditure				
	Salaries	Recurrent Expenditures	Special Expenditure & Projects	Total	Surplus or +Deficit
1966	$134, 876	$ 700, 583	$69, 212	$ 904, 671	+$ 29, 113
1967	140, 109	754, 065	649	894, 822	+ 47, 882
1968	143, 283	740, 333	6, 612	890, 229	+ 145, 283
Total	418, 268	2, 194, 981	76, 473	2, 689, 722	222, 278

Note: Rows may not add, due to rounding.

Source: Majlis Bandaran Alor Setar, private communication.

past, city revenues are now better collected, and the more than one half million dollars in arrears being made up. As can be seen from Table 17 the rates revenue in the 1966-68 period was increasing, and the state deficit contribution declining anyway. The goal has been elimination of the State contribution altogether. Expenditures were almost entirely for routine budgetary matters, with the amount available for special development projects by the city practically nothing by the end of 1968, despite large surpluses.

The population sub-system of Alor Setar (refer to Figure 1, The Development Policy System, and Alor Setar's Profile, Table 18) is heavily Malay in the District, but favoring non-Malays in the city itself; although not by so heavy a proportion as in many cities.[1] City population has been growing at about half

[1] Especially the larger ones. Note that while Alor Setar ranks seventh among cities in population, and, in 1957, sixth in Malay population, its rank for non-Malay population is twelfth.

TABLE 18

MIDDLE CITY PROFILE: ALOR SETAR

	District		City	
	Amount	Rank	Amount	Rank
1. TO61POPC[a]	3,830	12	735	16
2. TO61PROB	0	111	0	28
3. TO61ECFN	357	49	357	14
4. TO61URBN	1,092	22	1,092	19
5. TO61TOTL	4,187	22	1,092	19
6. 6165POPC	12,139	4	2,956	9
7. 6165PROB	1,680	26	48	8
8. 6165ECFN	207	56	207	13
9. 6165URBN	3,211	14	3,211	13
10. 6165TOTL	14,026	11	3,211	13
11. 6668POPC	7,735	7	6,915	6
12. 6668PROB	0	111	0	28
13. 6668ECFN	12,601	1	2,427	10
14. 6668URBN	9,342	9	9,342	10
15. 6668TOTL	134,336	2	9,342	10
16. TO65POPC	15,969	5	3,691	16
17. TO65PROB	1,680	31	48	14
18. TO65ECFN	564	64	564	18
19. TO65URBN	1,705	22	4,303	18
20. TO65TOTL	18,213	13	4,301	18
21. TO68POPC	23,704	5	10,606	10
22. TO68PROB	1,680	31	48	18
23. TO68ECFN	127,165	2	2,991	15
24. TO68URBN	11,047	16	13,645	13
25. TO68TOTL	170,762	2	13,645	13
26. 5760POPN (of 104)	254,147	5	52,915	7
27. 5760MALY (of 104)	207,086	1	20,279	6
28. 5760NONMALY (of 104)	44,061	22	32,636	12
29. 5760POP Density/mi^2	647	7	'65 16,000	4
30. 6760POPN (Estimated, city=6767)	323,742	4	58,134	10
31. 5760Percent URBan	20	29		
32. MANufacturing $SALes ('67)	64,480	8		
33. 65Revenue+ ExpenLocalAuth	1,336	31	1,207	19
34. 65R+EXPer Person			20	21
35. 68HOTelRooMs			N.D.	N.D.
36. JAn70UNEM-ployment			9,388	6
37. 1970 Population	302,539	4	66,179	7

[a]Variables 1-25, 32-34 M$000's.   Source: See Appendix II.

the Middle City average,[1] and represents an extraordinarily small proportion (rank 29th among districts) for a middle-city centered district. The largest parts of this urban population are in commerce, small-scale industry, and services, including government.

The production sub-systems, then, move not around heavy industry, though an industrial estate of sorts is planned, but around local new materials production and markets.[2] Kota Setar District still ranked eighth in West Malaysia sales of own manufactured goods in 1967.[3] Alor Setar, which has been called a regional growth center, is of a city-size group (50,000-89,000) in which J. J. O'Callaghan finds promise for new threshold industrial activities, such as printing and publishing, textile, rubber products, and chemicals. Resource-based industries still predominate (by two-thirds of employment of the 280 total establishment).[4]

The areal pattern sub-system causes the biggest problems of Alor Setar. City development and urban malaise as real factors in Alor Setar are associated with problems of land uses and ownership, the port, water and flooding problems, sewerage, and the further need for migration of the business center to open new high land. Circulation moves through a north-south axis along a highway and the railway, with a cross axis; and the conjunction of two rivers, the Sungei Kedah and the Sungei Anak Bukit, makes the old city center. Naturally the site there is low and subject to floods, but nevertheless there also are the old government buildings and banks. A new center, to the west of the old is being developed (centering on the corner of Jalan Tunku Ibrahim and Jalan Badlishah), with new state government buildings and a new shopping complex. A

---

[1] There are 1,070 more males than females, in 11,281 households, growing, in aggregate 110 per cent from 1947 to 1970 (60.1 per cent from 1921 to 1931). (See Federation of Malaya, A Report on the 1947 Census of Population [Kuala Lumpur: Government Printer, 1947], p. 44.)

[2] Including straw board and paper, bricks, starch from banana stems, mill stores, fabrication of agricultural machinery and farm equipment (near Alor Setar), cattle and poultry feed, and rice-milling, motor workshops, ice cream, printing, and tire retreading. (Ibid., pp. 4-10.)

[3] And ninth as a town in 1968. See Tables 8 and 16.

[4] There are 210 employees in rubber and coconut oil basic processing plants, 20 in sago and tapioca and 816 in large rice mills, and 197 in saw milling. See "Town Sizes and Thresholds for Manufacturing Activities in West Malaysia," Pahang Tenggara Regional Master Planning Study, Working Paper No. 39. Data are from the Census of Manufacturing 1968 (Kuala Lumpur: Department of Statistics, 1971), p. 33, et passim.

North-South by-pass--east of town--is proposed. Ribbon development is also apparent along the access highways to the padi area surrounding the city. The very small wharf sends some rice 8 miles to the sea and beyond, but it is in no condition to absorb heavier or larger scale traffic at present. Land and its use is a special problem, lately overcome to a degree: 90 per cent of the city land is Malay Reserved; Malays have not been about to spring into business, so a policy of leasing land for commercial development by non-Malays has been instituted. It was also possible for the state government to alienate some of its own land for commercial development in this new business center particularly. Traffic is another heavy problem, especially as there is increasing demand for shopping and entertainment by visitors from the hinterland. Therefore more traffic lights and hawker and trishaw controls have been instituted. [1]

The centrality function of Alor Setar is that of a city servicing a vast intensively farmed rice lowland, in which water control is becoming increasingly important as a means of raising output. Its containing environment (or the region of which it is not necessarily the center) basically is the State of Kedah or Kedah/Perlis. Its generated environment (or the region it uses) is the Muda rice area on the one hand, and the rice-consuming cities to the south on the other. Thus it is surrounded by rural settlements which are mainly rice-milling and low level commercial centers, and the loci of farm population residences. [2] The commercial hinterland of Alor Setar must extend northward at least to the Perlis border and for certain functions (such as publications distribution) through Perlis. Its extension southward is met by the strong distributional force of the Penang Metropolitan Area. [3] The area's big export, of course, is rice, of which the Alor Setar and north region sends 51.4 per cent to Kuala Lumpur/Port Swettenham, 18 per cent to Port Dickson/Melaka, 15 per cent further South, and 13.3 per cent to Kuala Krui/Tumpat mostly by rail. [4]

The major centralizing function of Alor Setar, then, is associated with

---

[1] Interview with Syed Mansor bin Syed Salim, Town Council Secretary, Setar, July 29, 1970.

[2] Seven are particularly important and have a combined population of 19,569--giving the greater Alor Setar area a total population of 85,748 in 1971. (See Malaysia, Statistics Department, Urban Connurbations--Population and Households in Ten Gazetted Towns and Their Adjoining Built-up Areas [Kuala Lumpur: Department of Statistics, 1971], p. 26.)

[3] Sungei Patani can be assumed to orient toward Butterworth for all but Kedah State government inputs (such as housing development).

[4] Source: Economic Planning Unit, "Rail Origin and Destination Study," 1967.

its most significant function as an object of national development policy: the development of the Muda agricultural--double-cropping rice--scheme. Whereas the numerous smaller centers (including Kangar) in the region lessen Alor Setar's hold on regional commercial and services center powers, the Muda project surrounds the city. Alor Setar has become the administrative and supply center for this vast project and will be the direct recipient of the multiplier effects of the expected rise in incomes of the rural population. This project is Malaysia's largest agricultural development project. It is designed to enable the double-cropping of more than a quarter of a million acres of existing padi land spanning the states of Kedah and Perlis.[1]

Initially Muda was managed in parts by the Drainage and Irrigation Department, the Ministry of Agriculture, and several authorities. Coordination was a serious problem when water for double-cropping became available in the first phase areas and the farmers were not prepared to take advantage of it. A bureaucratic innovation was then proclaimed: the Muda Agricultural Development Authority, gazetted in May 1970. This corporation administers the $228 million agricultural scheme, with overall powers to make on-the-spot decisions from offices just outside of Alor Setar.[2] It supposedly is "clothed with the power of government, but possessed of the flexibility and initiative offered by private enterprise."[3]

However, agricultural hinterland development will not be enough for Alor Setar. The State government recognizes this, even if the Federal government does not. Thus, the liberal non-Malay land policy has been initiated, and certain low-cost housing units have been completed in the city (two sets, one of 144 units, one of 59). Lighting, drainage, and employment opportunities proj-

---

[1] As the Muda Agricultural Development Authority puts it: "The project area has a long tradition of single crop padi cultivation which forms the main source of income and economic activity for about 50,000 farmer families. Indirectly, padi cultivation in the project area provides income and employment opportunities for thousands more persons in input supply industries, rural shopkeeping, rice-milling, etc." Muda Agricultural Development Authority undated information release, 1970.

[2] See Straits Times, June 23, 1970, p. 4; and August 8, 1970, p. 2; and Malay Mail, April 7, 1970, p. 2.

[3] It will undertake coordinated socio-economic planning "in connection with the adaptation of Muda's rural economy to modern agriculture," including regional planning in water control and related agricultural fields, especially the organization of farmers into "dynamic communities" on the basis of Farmers' Associations, and the design of publicly owned facilities. Muda Agricultural Development Authority, "Proposal: Organization and Management Policy" (Alor Setar, May, 1970), pp. 2, 8.

ects also have been undertaken by the state since taking over of the Town Council,[1] and industrial areas at Seberang Terus west of the Sungei Anak Bukit planned. Although there have been problems with land speculation, electricity supply, and in coordinating the Public Works Department and MARA inputs, these seem promising, at least for rice and timber-based industries. The problem with such developments and the expansion of the town along the arteries outward is competition for land with the Muda Agricultural Development Authority.[2] New town boundary changes in the 1960's have spread its control in all directions along roads, heightening the non-agricultural occupance of rich, water-provided padi land.[3]

The Federal government has also been allocating expenditures to Alor Setar. Its district is of far greater national importance, but in the to-1961 period over $1 million were spent in the city, mostly for police and government buildings and welfare. In 1961-65, there was a similar pattern, with the largest item ($2.6 million) going to a regional hospital. Under the First Malaysia Plan the city received in 1966-68 enlarged amounts of Federal funds. Approximately $4.1 million in Federal funds were spent on POPC (Population Coverage, mainly Social) items, of which the largest part ($2.9) went for water supply on the basis of a loan to the State Government. Six hundred thousand dollars were allocated for the industrial estates, and about $559 more for other ECFN (Economic-functional) projects, along with $709 from the State for roads and $435 for offices. Table 15 shows Alor Setar as the only one of our three small cities to have had a positive factor score in the city factor analysis. This is reflected in the positive score, as well, on the 6668 POPC expenditure factor which, because it has separated itself out, takes on a certain added importance. Although POPC and city population variables are not extremely highly correlated for cities (in the low .800's), here is a city which has managed to attract significant POPC expenditures, apparently because of special needs perceived by the central government, probably related to its regional service rôle.

---

[1]The Straits Echo (Penang), July 20, 1970, p. 5, opines that the take-over has apparently been justified, taking quick improvement to the town as a criterion. Now there is less indecision, and more money spent.

[2]Interview with Enche Tamin, General Manager, Muda Agricultural Development Authority, Alor Setar, July 30, 1970.

[3]Interview with Lin Tee Seong, Kedah State Town Planner, July 29, 1970.

Keluang

Keluang is a Town Council in central Johore. It has not been taken over by its state government.[1] Mis-management or inability to collect funds have never been problems. Even though there is a deficit budget each year (with the small balance made up by the state government--"Misc.," in Table 19) this is not for lack of rates collected.[2] Keluang has always been a prosperous Town Council area, as indicated by the larger per capita expenditures and revenue of the Council.[3] The Town Council spends considerable monies on education, markets, roads and grounds, and abattoirs--all traditional duties of a Town Council. They are just higher in this more prosperous town. Like all local authorities, most of the town's revenue comes from assessments and goes to administration, though in a decreasing proportion in the 1966-68 period (when the balance carried forward, especially, has risen).

The 1970 population of Keluang was 43, 297, and its district 133, 317. In 1957 the population was about one quarter Malay and three quarters non-Malay in both city and District, with a large Indian population associated with the railways and service functions to the Tamil rubber-tapping population of the hinterland. The town's population growth rate from 1947 to 1970 was 171, very close to the over-all middle-city average for the period, but considerably less than the 1921-31 increase of 349 per cent.[4]

Keluang ranked eleventh in District manufacturing sales of self-produced manufactures in 1967, and fifteenth as a town in 1948, the majority of manufac-

---

[1] With the resignation of four of the six near-majority Socialist Party members in 1969, the Johore government has appointed three Alliance members to replace them, yielding a new 9-man Alliance majority out of 12.

[2] The Town Council employs its own solicitors to collect rates every year. (Interview with Ibrahim A. Ghani, Town Council Secretary, Keluang, August 4, 1970.)

[3] Despite the name of the town meaning bat (flying fox), and its having during the Emergency "one of the most unsavoury reputations in the country," and being, perhaps, "sullen," and "gripped like a vice by the Communist machine." (See Noel Barber, The War of the Running Dogs: The Malayan Emergency 1948-1960 [London: William Collins, 1971], pp. 239-40.)

[4] Growth rates of Bandar Penggaram and Bandar Maharani were 100.per cent and 89 per cent in the 1947-1970 period respectively, and Johore Baharu's, 250 per cent; while for 1921-31 the rates were 108, 52.2 and 40.2 respectively. Keluang was taking off and Johore Baharu leveling off in the 20's and 30's, with the west coast areas holding their own. Since the war Johore Baharu has become dominant in population, and the proximity of all these secondary cities and the narrowness of hinterlands have undoubtedly contributed to Keluang's lower growth rate in this period.

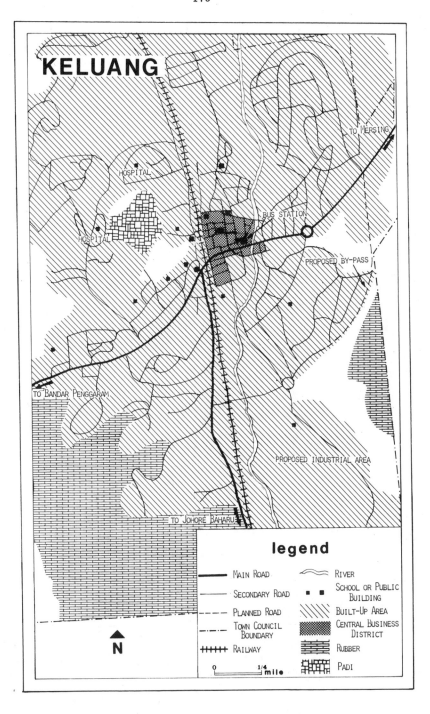

Fig. 21.--City Map: Keluang

TABLE 19

REVENUE AND EXPENDITURE OF KELUANG 1966-1968

Revenue

	Assessment	Conservancy	Abattoirs	Fees, Rents, Licenses	Misc.	Balance Brought Forward	Total
1966	422,000	70,000	21,000	142,000	934,000	121,000	1,710,000
1967	438,000	62,000	19,000	131,000	991,000	110,000	1,881,000
1968	555,000	46,000	19,000	145,000	1,014,000	53,000	1,832,000
Total	1,515,000	178,000	59,000	418,000	2,939,000	284,000	5,393,000

Expenditure

	Adminis-tration	Conser-vancy	Abattoirs	Scavenging	Education Rates	Markets	Roads, Grounds	Other	Balance Carried Forward	Total
1966	316,000	61,000	5,000	268,000	---	28,000	110,000	812,000	110,000	1,710,000
1967	195,000	46,000	4,000	267,000	37,000	21,000	165,000	1,063,000	53,000	1,851,000
1968	180,000	42,000	4,000	298,000	5,000	19,000	81,000	1,047,000	156,000	1,832,000
Total	691,000	149,000	13,000	833,000	42,000	68,000	356,000	2,922,000	319,000	5,393,000

Note: Figures rounded.

Source: Majlis Bandaran Keluang, private communication.

tures being rubber and timber processing, and bricks, tiles, textiles, furniture, and crafts manufacturing, with new palm oil mills coming up.[1] There is a greater specialization in household manufacturing than Alor Setar or Kota Baharu have, despite the rich resources-producing hinterland of Keluang. But in 1956 it appeared that there was comparatively little existing, or prospect for, secondary industry in Keluang; and that appears to still be the case.[2]

A past significant feature of the production sub-system of Keluang's Development Policy System was the British armed forces garrison, once the second largest in Malaya. The garrison occupies 839 acres partly in and partly outside the Town Council area. More than 5,000 British personnel and dependents resided there; and although much of their consumption was of externally supplied materials, they still kept a large service community at work in Keluang. And they built a considerable amount of public facilities, including playgrounds, as part of local good-will activity. Their gradual replacement by the Malaysian military has already caused a depression in housing and a halt in new construction. The Malaysian counterparts are expected to spend far less for luxuries, though perhaps more for basic needs, in the local economy. Unemployment is a problem, but despite the British pull-out, not an overwhelming one as seen by the Town Council.

The areal pattern sub-system of Keluang resembles those of Alor Setar and Kota Baharu, in having cross-axial roads and a rail line, complicated by a river. There is a gazetted town plan, however. The low land along the river is subject to flooding, and squatters there are frequently rendered homeless. This problem is being tackled through canalizing of the river and the establishment of a new settlement area on higher land, which however may not be adequate. Because of the development of the town center, its moving toward higher land northward, and the consequently increasing congestion, a ring road by-pass, east-west (like that of Alor Setar) is proposed.[3] The natural expansion of

---

[1] Keluang is below J. J. O'Callaghan's population threshold for regional manufacturing activity, but within the group (30,000-50,000) that can be expected to have general industrial activity, primarily in primary products processing. Thus, 106 manufacturing establishments employ 1,765 full-time workers, of whom, however, only 304 are found in resource-based industries (105 in rubber primary processing, and 199 in sawmills). Loc. cit.

[2] The scope is for further development of primary products processing and for the production of consumer items, e.g., a pineapple cannery, and rubber goods. See J. Nicholls, State Planning Officer, "Keluang Town Plan: Report on Survey Description of Plan" (Johore Baharu: Town and Country Planning Department [1958], pp. 8-11.)

[3] B. Fernando, Town Council Building Inspector, interview, August 4, 1970.

the town is toward the east along the railroad and north up the west bank of the river, the Sungei Mengkibol.

The railroad, as in Alor Setar, is important for the movement of the products of Keluang and its hinterland. The surrounding area, a containing environment, and a hinterland apparently coinciding closely with the boundaries of Keluang District, [1] possibly extending beyond them eastward and southeast-ward, produces latex and palm oil from estates. Keluang District, in fact, had the largest acreage of oil palm (50, 590) in the country in 1968, and ranked third (behind Johore Baharu and Segamat) in rubber-estate acreage (with 76, 703 acres). [2] (See Figure 6.) An intensification of estate activity, especially rub-ber replanting now being completed, speaks well for Keluang's continued cen-tral importance in rural Johore.

For Keluang, like the other small cities in this chapter, the biggest development policy event will be found not in the city itself, but in its hinter-land--an agricultural project of vast proportions. The Johore Tengah project, part of the larger proposed Johore Tenggara integrated land development scheme, will take off immediately southeast of Keluang. Keluang is the largest city in the development region. [3] In all, between 1972 and 1987 281, 500 acres of roll-ing forest land will be cleared for the development of 249, 800 acres of oil palms, rubber, and various new agricultural activities. There may also be timber complexes, tourist resorts, 30-40 new villages, 6 larger central villages and two new towns, as well as expansion schemes in Keluang and Kota Tinggi. In Keluang planned expansion will concentrate on Public Works Department water works. It may be noted that the preponderance of oil-palm planting over rubber (58 per cent to 23 per cent) is in line with the Federal government's intention to concentrate oil-palm production in Johore and rubber further north. This should mean a specialization of Keluang in the handling and possibly the secon-dary processing of palm oil, as well as its transshipment for Singapore. The

---

[1] Keluang Town Plan, p. 2.

[2] Since 1956 the area in rubber estates has declined (from 123, 133) and the amount in small holdings (1956=29, 549) seemingly held steady; while oil palm acreage has jumped (from 36, 864), portraying the trend in hinterland development--though not particularly a changing role for Keluang. Palm oil can be and usually is processed in mills on estates, and transported much as latex is.

[3] This is an area within a ten to fifteen mile radius of Keluang between the eastward and southward highways, and southeast on either side of Kota Tinggi and further southeastward in underdeveloped southeast Johore.

TABLE 20

MIDDLE CITY PROFILE: KELUANG

	District		City	
	Amount	Rank	Amount	Rank
1. TO61POPC[a]	1,006	24	1,006	15
2. TO61PROB	0	111	0	28
3. TO61ECFN	519	42	121	16
4. TO61URBN	1,127	20	1,127	18
5. TO61TOTL	5,525	35	1,127	18
6. 6165POPC	782	50	577	19
7. 6165PROB	3,166	23	0	28
8. 6165ECFN	31	77	0	28
9. 6165URBN	577	28	577	21
10. 6165TOTL	3,979	41	577	21
11. 6668POPC	1,236	38	1,100	19
12. 6668PROB	0	111	0	28
13. 6668ECFN	54	76	0	28
14. 6668URBN	1,100	27	1,100	25
15. 6668TOTL	1,290	62	1,100	25
16. TO65POPC	1,788	41	1,583	19
17. TO65PROB	3,166	23	0	28
18. TO65ECFN	550	66	121	20
19. TO65URBN	1,704	23	1,704	21
20. TO65TOTL	5,504	49	1,704	21
21. TO68POPC	3,024	39	2,683	22
22. TO68PROB	3,166	25	0	28
23. TO68ECFN	604	78	121	22
24. TO68URBN	2,804	24	2,804	24
25. TO68TOTL	6,794	53	2,804	24
26. 5760POPN (of 104)	91,929	24	31,181	16
27. 5760MALY (of 104)	23,483	57	7,437	17
28. 5760NONMaly (of 104)	68,446	13	23,744	17
29. 5760POPDensity (of 104)	84	46	N.D.	N.D.
30. 6760POPN (Estimated, city = 6767)	97,068	32	26,976	23
31. 5760Percent URBan	34	16		
32. MANufacturing SALes ('67)	43,482	11		
33. 65Revenue+ ExpenLocalAuth	1,542	24	1,542	16
34. 65R+EXPer Person			57	9
35. 68HOteLRooMs			N.D.	N.D.
36. JAn70UNEMployment			N.D.	N.D.
37. 1970 Population	133,317	21	43,297	20

[a]Variables 1-25, 32-34 M$000's.   Sources: See Appendix II.

Master Plan predicts a 1990 population for Keluang of 150, 000-200, 000, the higher figure for which should certainly be attained. [1]

As an object of past and present development policy the town of Keluang itself has so far attracted most of the national development expenditures in its district, except in the period 1961-65, in which land development and rubber replanting accounted for the large rural expenditure. This is not to say Keluang looms large. In fact it has the third lowest sum of city factor scores on variables in the middle-city factor analysis. [2] In town, water projects and health and telecoms development have predominated. Keluang ranks low among all middle cities for every category of expenditure over the years (see Tables 13 and 16), which must be explained by her position in the shadow of Johore Baharu. On the other hand, Johore is one of the two states (with Kedah), which take particular care to give assistance to their Town Councils. [3] The state of Johore, moreover, has selected Keluang as one of the three industrial development towns of the state (with Bandar Penggaram and Johore Baharu). However, no state-sponsored industrial estate has been mentioned for Keluang. Possibly it is too near Johore Baharu, and not Malay enough. To remedy this the Town Council has designated an area near the by-pass as an industrial area; but developments there are and will be slow.

Kota Baharu

Kota Baharu is the state capital of Kelantan. It has an elected Town Council, formed in 1953 from the town Board, with an Alliance Party majority in this otherwise PMIP (Pan Malaysia Islamic Party)-dominated state. This Town Council is in the worst financial position of the three discussed here; although her rank in revenue plus expenditure per capita is not so bad--13th of 28. Nevertheless, the money available to the Council to perform its statutory

---

[1] Hunting Technical Services Ltd, Binnie and Partners, Johore Tenggara Regional Master Plan (Kuala Lumpur [?], 1971), pp. 5, 6, 9, 38, 86.

[2] See Table 15.

[3] State grants in aid have been for local roads, and the state has built four blocks of multi-storey low-cost housing of a larger project in the by-pass vicinity. The $600,000 needed for completing bridges along the by-pass route and paving will come in time, from the state; although state grants have been diminishing, and impatience has been rising in recent years over radicalism in the Town Council. State land has been alienated in and outside of the town for shophouse and other commercial development--not yet begun, but committed. As pointed out by Enche Puvanarajah, interview, idem.

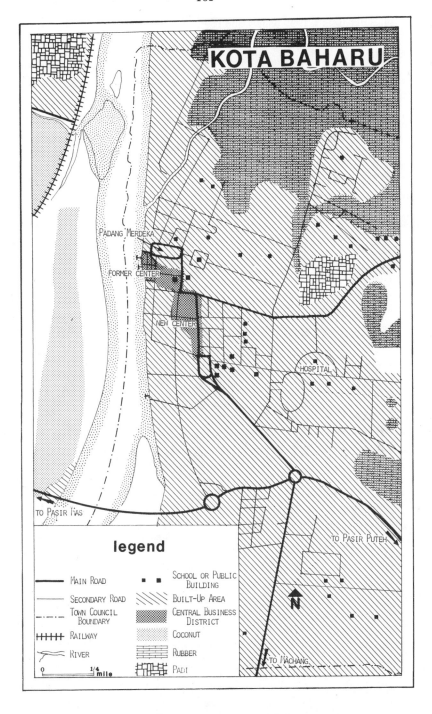

Fig. 22.--City Map: Kota Baharu

TABLE 21

REVENUE AND EXPENDITURE OF KOTA BAHARU 1966-1968

	Revenue						
	Tax Receipts	Revenue Producing Services	Grants & Grants in Lieu of Rates	Misc.	Special	Brought Forward	Total
1966	432,610	172,346	173,757	313,681[a]	30,400	5,703	1,128,489
1967	523,687	121,532	55,858	39,098	- - -	14,691	754,867
1968	560,077	135,816	82,690	66,771	350	4,312	849,516
Total	1,516,365	429,691	312,305	419,050	30,750	24,706	2,732,872

	Expenditures[b]									
	Admin	Interest in Loans	Cleansing	Grounds	Special	Health Services	Markets	Misc.	Carried Forward	Total
1966	204,803	- -	339,748	144,673	290,591[c]	25,842	60,002	51,855	14,691	1,128,489
1967	199,410	12,659	299,363	81,273	1,860	24,461	61,367	45,163	4,312	754,867
1968	210,366	26,321	299,719	124,584		26,304	66,813	63,933	31,477	849,516
Total	613,859	38,980	938,830	347,530	292,451	76,607	188,182	160,951	50,480	2,732,872

Note: Rows may not add, due to rounding.

[a] Includes $300,000 State Government loan for new central market.

[b] Include capital and recurrent expenditures.

[c] $289,001 for Kota Baharu Central Market.

duties is pitifully short, a situation made worse by the poverty of the state government itself. The source of the financial plight of the city (whereby the street lights had to be run in 1970 at half full because National Electricity Board bills could not be paid otherwise) has been unsuccessful collection of rates and antiquated assessment rolls. The Town Council estimates that, with the lowest property tax rate in the country, Kota Baharu has $500,000 uncollected in assessed rates. Poverty of the populace is blamed.[1]

The population of Kota Baharu in 1970 was 55,052, with 124 more males than females. Population growth 1947-1970 was 141 per cent, somewhat below the national average for middle cities of 175, but considerably better than the 1931-47 growth of 53.4 per cent.[2] In 1957 there were twice as many Malays as non-Malays in the town, and nine times as many in the district--the fourth largest in Malaysia in Malay population, while tenth in total population. (See Table 22.)

The economy of Kota Baharu is depressed, despite her regional containing environment. It ranks twentieth as a district in local manufactures sales, but eleventh as a town in 1968. Kota Baharu has a considerably smaller range of industrial activities and manufacturing employment than other centers in her size range. Ice, matches, biscuits, building materials, and batik and other handi-crafts predominate. About five-ninths of the fulltime employment is in resource-based industries, divided evenly between rubber and coconut-oil processing and saw-milling. Rice-milling clearly goes on out of town.[3] Rice trade is very important to the city, nevertheless, as are local services such as coffee shops and beauty parlors. Tourism is practically unborn, despite the charm of the people, beaches, and arts and curios.

Areal sub-systems of Kota Baharu's 4.4 square miles resemble those of the other Malayan undynamic cities. East-west and north-south roads connect in the city center. The town parallels the river (Sungei Kelantan), on the other side of which, oddly, is the railroad, and, further, the depressed harbor of Tumpat. There is, as is common, an old administrative and business area near the river on low ground, northwest of the presently growing center to which business and the state government have moved in the last ten years. Those old areas are subject to the worst flooding and squatting. (There are over 2,000 illegal

---

[1] Interview, in the Town Council, Kota Baharu, July 22, 1970.

[2] See Table 7, and Report on 1947 Census, loc. cit.

[3] See O'Callaghan, ibid., and p. 29.

TABLE 22

MIDDLE CITY PROFILE: KOTA BAHARU

	District		City	
	Amount	Rank	Amount	Rank
1. TO61POPC[a]	3,494	13	3,344	10
2. TO61PROB	0	111	0	28
3. TO61ECFN	569	39	464	13
4. TO61URBN	3,808	12	3,808	13
5. TO61TOTL	4,063	23	3,808	13
6. 6165POPC	4,868	13	4,005	7
7. 6165PROB	640	33	640	5
8. 6165ECFN	1,275	30	3	18
9. 6165URBN	4,648	8	4,648	8
10. 6165TOTL	6,783	31	4,648	8
11. 6668POPC	3,909	13	3,864	8
12. 6668PROB	80	15	80	12
13. 6668ECFN	200	66	200	19
14. 6668URBN	4,144	15	4,144	16
15. 6668TOTL	4,189	31	4,144	16
16. TO65POPC	8,362	10	7,349	8
17. TO65PROB	640	38	640	10
18. TO65ECFN	1,844	40	467	19
19. TO65URBN	8,456	14	8,456	14
20. TO65TOTL	10,846	30	8,456	14
21. TO68POPC	12,271	13	11,213	9
22. TO68PROB	720	41	720	14
23. TO68ECFN	2,044	58	667	20
24. TO68URBN	12,600	14	12,600	15
25. TO68TOTL	15,035	29	12,600	15
26. 5760POPN (of 104)	150,903	11	38,106	14
27. 5760MALY (of 104)	135,133	3	25,306	4
28. 5760NONMaly (of 104)	15,770	50	12,800	25
29. 5760POPDensity (of 104)	961	4 '65	63	8 (of 13)
30. 6760POPN (Estimated, city = 6767)	208,182	9	59,586	9
31. 5760Percent URBan	25	23		
32. MANufacturing SALes ('67)	18,545	20		
33. 65Revenue+ ExpenLocalAuth	2,106	15	2,106	13
34. 65R+EXPer Person			35	14
35. HOTelRooMs			63	8
36. JAn70UNEMployment			7,816	10 (of 21)
37. 1970 Population	208,076	12	55,052	10

[a]Variables 1-25, 32-34 M$000's.   Sources: See Appendix II.

houses according to the Town Council.) The movement of business, modern housing, and manufacturing such as they are, is to the south and southeast along the highways.[1] A lack of developed main thoroughfares, except to the new bridge, causes traffic congestion, not helped by the total absence of zoning.

There are three hinterland activities of importance to Kota Baharu: (1) the Kemubu rice double-cropping scheme, which is similar to that of the Muda, though later and smaller; (2) the northern East-West Highway; and (3) the Malayan Tobacco Corporation's operations. The Kemubu scheme is priced at about $78 million, with an initial $10 million loan from the World Bank. In the project area to the south of Kota Baharu, 55,000 acres are being converted from single- to double-cropping. It, and likewise the Muda, are expected to raise the average net incomes of farmers in their areas from about $140 per annum (in 1965) per acre to $430.[2] There is nowhere other than Kota Baharu to spend such money. Thus, Kota Baharu may in due course experience a small boom.

Similarly, the East-West Highway, which was begun in 1971 and will be opened during the Second Malaysia Plan, is expected to "accelerate development of the northeast region of West Malaysia, the northern interior hinterland and the Penang/Butterworth industrial area."[3] It should energize exporting and importing interests in Kota Baharu and provide easier markets for West Coast and interior primary products, especially wood, and locally manufactured handicrafts like batik. The Malayan Tobacco Corporation began in 1959, not as an estate, but as an organizer and buyer of high grade tobacco, which is grown on higher, non-padi land south of Kota Baharu. The acreage is expected to increase from 3,250 to 5,000 acres in ten more years. Sixteen curing factories and the company as a whole directly employ 10,000. Everything needed for tobacco production in Kelantan is purchased in Kota Baharu.[4]

The two enormous federal projects signal a change in attitude toward Kelantan by the federal government. The Kelantanese regard themselves as

---

[1] See Map: "Location of Existing Industries" (Kota Baharu: Jabatan Peranchang Negeri, 1969).

[2] First Malaysia Plan, p. 116. Here the price is put at $40 million-- clearly an underestimate, unless what is meant is the World Bank's expected contribution.

[3] Second Malaysia Plan, p. 190.

[4] Interview with M. Strevens, General Manager, Malayan Tobacco Corporation, Kota Baharu, July 23, 1970.

having been neglected during the 1950's and 1960's. This view is supported by the pattern of development expenditures in Kota Baharu and its vicinity. In mappable expenditure totals to 1968, the Kota Baharu District ranks 29th, and the town 15th (of 111 and 28 respectively). Kota Baharu's centrality and state capital status have saved it from utter ignominy in development policy. But it is notable that almost all expenditures (11/12ths over time) have been for POPC needs, specifically the hospital, teachers' college, schools, water and government buildings, mostly the first. While Kota Baharu has a negative score on every factor in Table 15, its highest scores (-0.01) are in the population and POPC factors, like those of Alor Setar--showing again that a certain population weight combined with state capital and broad regional significance can attract social expenditures (as was not the case in Keluang).

The State of Kelantan traditionally has done what it could for development in Kota Baharu. In 1966 the State Economic Development Corporation was established, then reorganized in 1970. Since 1969 it has built a plywood factory with pioneer (tax advantage) status at Kuala Krai and has started work on a $1 million hotel and shopping complex in Kota Baharu. It plans an electrical appliances factory there to be set up with PERNAS (The National Corporation). The state also has received a $1 million loan from the Federal government for general developments in Kota Baharu and Tumpat in 1970. Indeed, this increased activity, in the face of not much reduced intransigence of the PMIP state government, must be attributed to the New Economic Policy views of the federal government. Although there are fewer Malays in Kelantan than in Perak, it is certainly a "Malay State" in the true sense of the the expression, [1] and therefore now may expect special attention from the federal government. Malaysia Industrial Estates Limited already considers establishment of an electronics factory and bonded area in the Kota Baharu area. [2]

The Development Policy Systems Compared

These three undynamic small cities are unimportant in national development. They are not major immigration targets. [3] They do not produce essential

---

[1] Kelantan, like Trengganu, for example, follows a Malay week: Thursday and Friday as Saturday and Sunday.

[2] Straits Times, August 20, 1970, p. 4; and Town Council interview, idem.

[3] Although their population growth while below the average for middle cities is still (excepting Alor Setar) considerably above the annual natural growth rate since 1947.

manufactured goods; although they process essential foods and other exports.
And they have not received significant national development policy expenditures.

Generally the same flows and blockages occur in the Development Policy
Systems of all three cities. Without making too strong a general small city
case for Malaysia or the world, it would seem safe to generalize for Malaya
thus: (1) POPC expenditures from the Federal and State governments to small
middle cities work, i.e., are spent, and the projects, such as hospitals, are
built and meet major needs reasonably efficiently; (2) ECFN expenditures, for
roads and the like, likewise are carried out, generally by the Public Works
Department with dispatch. Larger ones, such as for industrial areas or power
stations, are rarely attempted, but even the railroad and port facilities of these
cities are run down and of limited usefulness; (3) the generated (market) environments of these cities, being the objects of large public and private investments,
take on huge importance to them--which means use of the cities as organizing
entities for the rural schemes. But this does not mean that the cities will succeed in topping off the cream of the hopefully large incremental boosts in rural
family incomes; for although (4) large scale integrated management organizations, centered in the towns, have to be instituted to manage the rural projects,
(5) Alor Setar and Keluang lie in the large trade and service shadows of powerful, dynamic, and nationally important metropolises, i.e., the Penang Metropolitan Area, and Johore Baharu/Singapore. Kota Baharu, although near a
smaller rural development project anyway, finds itself in the enviable position
of being the only place for trade to go or go through. Yet, even there, the East-
West Highway may benefit other cities, like Pasir Mas, just as much.

These cities do not operate at a scale to provide expectation fulfillment
at the level desired by the Central government. In fact such problems as local
revenues, land management, state government relations, and health and water
needs prevent these cities from expending what they might on the kinds of training, industrial employment, or even infrastructural improvements which would
help make economic-social disparities disappear. In short, the natural growth
potential of these cities is not great; their environments, generated and containing, are too limited. Indeed they may be simply too small.

What of the federal government's areal logic? It wants cities, by themselves or possibly with state assistance, to grow economically, and thereby to
create opportunities for improvements in living for both present and future residents. These three cities, and their class cannot do so now. There is little
room for the kinds of urban commercial expansion which would allow inept Malay

entrepreneurs to survive unaided (as, perhaps they may in Kuala Lumpur). Education, of the technical or higher varieties, is unavailable; and the modern business set-up is dominated by a hard core (as in Keluang) of tough business-men who have taken a long time to succeed and who would tolerate state-sup-ported competition with ill grace, if unaccompanied by enhanced economic dynamism of the cities.

Another assumption of the central government has been that large-scale rural development projects can be made to work without concern for the capa-bilities of local cities to provide services for them and help organize their activities, especially marketing and processing. This has caused problems to Muda development. At least more realization of local needs and of rôles for local urban areas in the planning and implementation of these projects is neces-sary. Whether or not that forthcomes with the more complex (though perhaps less urbanizing) Pahang and Johore Tenggara projects will be interesting to see.

CHAPTER VI

POLICY IN AREA: THREE SINGULAR CITIES

The Three Cities

It is more difficult to generalize about Ipoh, Sandakan, and Kuching. But these cities do most of the things the smaller cities are apparently not doing, and more information is available about their activities. They were selected to portray a wider variety and more important side of Middle City experience in Malaysian development than the smaller ones could. Their city budgets accordingly distribute far more of the revenues to engineering and health departments. As Ipoh and Kuching are Municipalities, there is much more to spend, as well.

The two Borneo cities have had significant PROB expenditures. All have benefitted from proportionally greater ECFN expenditure and higher than average central government expenditures in general. [1] All three are notable for the importance in their hinterlands of public authorities and private firms directly involved in development (the Kuching Port Authority, and Water Board, the Borneo Development Corporation, and the Borneo Company; the large tin companies, the Malaya Borneo Building Society, and the Perak River Hydro-Electric Power Company in Ipoh; the timber and prawn exporters, the Harrison's and Crossfield Company in Sandakan).

These cities support a wide variety of public amenities and city-development enterprises, such as public libraries, parks, health clinics (and free ambulance service in Ipoh), some slum clearance and relocation of families (Sandakan--also State-supported), and public housing (Kuching and Ipoh). They have industrial estates or areas, zoning, and, yet, strip development outward, with unemployment not so severe a problem as in Kuala Lumpur and Penang (but bad enough in Ipoh). The cities have their own city planners and also make use of state planners, a major concern of whom is the construction of ring roads

---

[1] PROB are expenditures to areas viewed as having special problems; ECFN expenditures are those to places whose economic-functional characteristics make them right for particular expenditures or projects; POPC expenditures, by contrast, are those aimed to serve needs presumably distributed according to population size.

around each city between major production and transportation points. This is a common need which smaller cities with development pretensions consider, but might be more active in meeting. A major problem is the shortage of skilled labor in the cities, despite the presence of technical schools.

Nature of the Cities

Ipoh

This Municipality sits in the middle of the richest tin-producing area in the world. It has been prospering since the late Nineteenth Century.[1] The Municipal government has never been in any danger of being taken over by the State of Perak. Indeed, Ipoh is regarded as the best-run city in the country. Nonetheless, the city feels that both the state and federal governments ignore its needs--possibly for political reasons.[2]

In 1965 the revenues and expenditures of Ipoh were the third highest in the country (behind Kuala Lumpur and George Town) and the fourth highest per capita. From 1966 to 1968 there was a steady increase, with revenues increasing from the General Rate source, but declining from other governments' contributions in lieu of rates, and fees and taxes; Ipoh has become even more self-reliant. Expenditures increased significantly in health, education, and low-cost housing. These indicate the functions that Ipoh's government can and does perform: refuse disposal and sanitation, housing, protective services, health inspection, communal services (e.g. lighting), social and trading services (e.g. markets), road building and maintenance, and general town planning and developmental promotion.[3] In addition to building low-cost housing and strictly enforcing building by-laws, the Municipality maintains child and health clinics and the famous free 24-hour ambulance service, and has designed two industrial estates, one of which (Tasek) is operating successfully under Ipoh ownership and management.

---

[1] In 1893 Ipoh's first government, the Ipoh Sanitary Board, was established by Sir Frank Swettenham following the tin rush of the 1880's. The town government became financially autonomous in 1956. It became a Municipality with a fully elected council of 18 Councillors, a majority of whom are members of the People's Progressive Party, in 1963. (See Ipoh Municipal Council, Ipoh: The Town That Tin Built [Ipoh: Pheonix Publications, 1962], passim.)

[2] Meanwhile, the Municipality stations two Councillors on duty in the Majlis Bandaran building every work day to take complaints and carry on Municipality business.

[3] In 1921 Ipoh was the only town in Malaya to have completed a town plan.

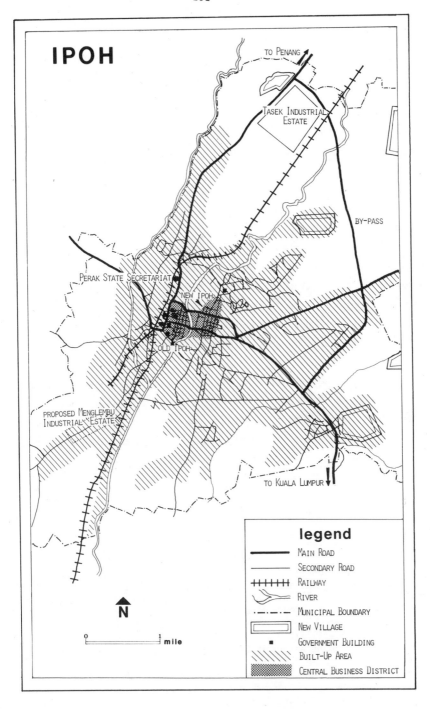

Fig. 23.--City Map: Ipoh

Ipoh is also the capital of the state of Perak, a distinction that is owed to the Japanese who transferred state administration there from Taiping in 1942. The State government, which is controlled, of course, by the Alliance Party, has the responsibility under law to approve the budget and by-laws of the Municipality. All loans from the federal government, too, as for Town Councils, must be approved by the state government. And this has, in the views of the Councillors, caused undue delay and annoyance in the past, although it seems that there is a basic laissez-faire relationship between the two governments and a good deal of cooperation.[1]

The population of Ipoh in 1970 was 247, 689 in 43, 840 households.[2] In 1957 and since, Ipoh was the third largest city in Malaysia, and the population was divided more than five to one non-Malay to Malay. The employment situation is difficult. Insufficient skilled labor is available for Tasek and other industrail operations: yet Ipoh had the second highest registered unemployment (i. e. job-seekers) in January 1970.[3] (See Table 24.) Indeed, although Ipoh only increased in population by 44. 3 per cent from 1921 to 1931, and by 52. 1 per cent from 1931 to 1947, it has since been growing rapidly (by 206 per cent from 1947 to 1970), catching up on George Town, at a rate three times the natural increase.

The labor force produced manufactured products in 1968 with a gross value of sales of $106. 9 million, fifth in the nation after Kuala Lumpur and Petaling Jaya, Johore Baharu, and Butterworth/Prai. But Ipoh does not involve itself in heavy industries, to its regret. In the Tasek Industrial Estate, which is three-quarters full, there are 60 different factories, producing concrete,

---

[1] Interview with Dato S. P. Seenivasagam, President of the Municipal Council, July 18, 1970, Ipoh.

[2] When the adjacent Mukim Ulu Kinta is added, the built-up area's population totals 257, 309.

[3] Bachelor land schemes have had to be opened up to try to draw off city-ward migrants. (Straits Times, August 4, 1970, p. 15.) Employment in 1962 in the Municipality found 41, 932 males and 12, 005 females, 32. 83 per cent of male and 48. 43 per cent of female full-time workers, employed in services; 14. 95 and 13. 91 per cent respectively in manufacturing; 13. 26 and 8. 28 per cent in mining and quarrying; and 4. 6 and 10 per cent in agriculture. Not only are there a lot of working women in Ipoh, and as large a service sector as one would expect, there is, thus, a significant population in mining, which in part lends to Ipoh its special character, one of vigor and seeming opportunity, despite the unemployment problem. Full-time here means greater than 24 hours per week. (See Department of Statistics, Report on Employment, Unemployment and Underemployment [Kuala Lumpur: Department of Statistics, 1962], Table 5. 1. 1.)

TABLE 23

REVENUE AND EXPENDITURE OF IPOH 1966-1968

General Revenue

	Municipality	General Rate	Contributions in Aid of Rates	Fees and Taxes[a]	Interest	Licenses	Misc.	Total
1966	---	$3,768,002	$ 919,096	$ 471,623	$136,155	$ 136,119	$ 186,855	$ 5,617,832
1967	$ 104,850	4,146,839	928,266	355,581	171,648	139,384	118,570	6,088,146
1968	104,750	4,540,975	909,169	362,969	223,058	139,073	110,586	6,398,697
Total	209,600	9,463,836	2,756,531	1,190,173	530,861	414,576	416,011	18,104,675

Expenditure

	Government	Engineering	Health[b]	Superintendent	Low Cost/ Housing	(Fed'l) Education	Misc.	Total
1966	740,286	1,043,064	1,052,658	1,910,722	71,352	379,000	477,543	5,665,625
1967	767,624	2,193,128	1,113,783	1,953,374	149,836	390,000	422,524	6,990,270
1968	755,544	2,122,357	1,160,341	2,022,653	132,850	515,000	497,518	7,206,276
Total	2,263,454	5,358,549	3,326,782	5,886,749	354,038	1,275,000	1,397,585	19,862,171

[a]Does not include remunerations from certain health services.

[b]Includes remunerative services.

Note: Rows may not add, due to rounding.

Source: Municipality of Ipoh, Accounts, 1966, 1968.

TABLE 24

MIDDLE CITY PROFILE: IPOH

	District		City	
	Amount	Rank	Amount	Rank
1. TO61POPC[a]	4,188	11	4,042	9
2. TO61PROB	0	111	0	28
3. TO61ECFN	431	45	401	13
4. TO61URBN	4,443	11	4,443	11
5. TO61TOTL	4,619	20	4,443	12
6. 6165POPC	8,391	7	2,594	12
7. 6165PROB	0	111	0	28
8. 6165ECFN	1,730	22	1,730	7
9. 6165URBN	4,596	9	4,324	11
10. 6165TOTL	10,121	21	4,324	11
11. 6668POPC	9,193	6	7,674	5
12. 6668PROB	905	7	905	7
13. 6668ECFN	20,272	6	20,272	4
14. 6668URBN	28,851	3	28,851	4
15. 6668TOTL	30,370	4	28,851	4
16. TO65POPC	12,579	8	6,636	10
17. TO65PROB	0	111	0	28
18. TO65PROB	2,161	34	2,131	11
19. TO65URBN	9,039	11	8,767	11
20. TO65TOTL	14,740	18	8,767	11
21. TO68POPC	21,772	6	14,310	6
22. TO68PROB	905	36	905	12
23. TO68ECFN	22,433	8	22,403	5
24. TO68URBN	37,890	6	37,618	6
25. TO68TOTL	45,110	9	37,618	6
26. 5760POPN (of 104)	367,096	2	125,761	3
27. 5760MALY (of 104)	65,860	14	19,333	7
28. 5760NONMaly (of 104)	301,236	2	106,428	3
29. 5760POPDensity (of 104)	499	11	'65 8,871	10
30. 6760POPN (Estimated, city = 6767)	539,064	2	232,260	3
31. 5760Percent URBan	45	8		
32. MANufacturing SALes ('67)	130,264	5		
33. 65Revenu+ ExpenLocalAuth	18,848	2	19,796	2 (K.L. = N.D.)
34. 65R+EXPer Person			85	4
35. 68HOTelRooMs			175	4
36. JAn70UNEMployment			18,064	2
37. 1970 Population	482,567	2	247,659	3

[a]Variables 1-25, 32-34 M$000's.   Sources: See Appendix II.

metal work, consumer items, and cement pipes, rubber goods, and plastics, among other products. At Menglembu, another planned industrial estate, lighter industries (like iron foundries) are intended. This seems to be the way for Ipoh to create employment and reduce its economic dependence on tin and rubber produced by its hinterland and shipped through it.[1]

The Municipality of Ipoh occupies 31 square miles (cf. 33 square miles for Kuala Lumpur) of densely packed shophouses surrounded by a green belt of residential area, and further surrounded by the literally fantastic Kinta Valley landscape, notable for tin mines, caves and mountains. In 1964 the boundaries of Ipoh were expanded, to encompass surprisingly large amounts of tin-mining and even rubber-tapping within the city limits. This expansion incorporated seven new villages into the city as well, which had been Local Councils since inception during the Emergency, but much in need of facilities. They were absorbed, on the periphery of the town proper on all sides, and required heavy investment by the Municipality in lighting, roads, and drains.[2]

Ipoh's areal pattern is one having an old town, located between the river (Sungei Kinta) and railroad, the site of which was too small, resulting in a "new town" across the river to the east. In the old town are the government buildings,

---

[1] An additional manufacture of Ipoh, it may be added, is electricity, through the Perak River Hydro Electricity Company, which is locally distributed by its subsidiary, the Kedah Electricity Distribution Company. Here is a colonial remnant, 70 per cent owned in Britain, which produces and sells electricity at higher rates for consumers than the National Electricity Board charges, yet has a monopoly in the Ipoh area. It was established originally to supply tin mines in 1926. Since then it has come to supply Ipoh and the Tasek Industrial Estate, though not the Kinta Valley as a whole. It is blamed, because of its rates, for scaring away of one carbide factory from Ipoh and for excess costs to Tasek Cement of $40,000 to $50,000 per month. The Federal Government plans to nationalize it when its present concession ends in 1975. Undeniably, this company has been important in the development of modern tin-mining in the Ipoh area and the channelling of investment there in the past. It is a case, however, of an organizational variant which may have outlived its usefulness to the local economy. (Interview with D. Hunter, Chief Engineer, Perak River Hydro, October 3, 1970, Ipoh; and with Ipoh Municipal Councillor Khong Kok-yat, August 1, 1970.) The Company supplies 575 consumers, including KED which in turn supplies 52,909 consumers, and it sells bulk electricity to the National Electricity Board--power which that utility shortly will not need from that source. Net profits have been increasing, and in 1967 were £970,000 Sterling. (See The Perak River Hydro Electric Power Company Ltd., Reports and Accounts, 1969 [London, 1970], pp. 5, 14-15.)

[2] Such development may not be over: Acting Prime Minister Tun Ismail announced in October 1971 that owing to subversionary threats severe measures would be taken. The Perak State government almost simultaneously began granting land leases to Chinese squatters in the Ipoh/Sungei Siput area. (See James Morgan, "Malaysia Bracing for a Long Haul," Far Eastern Economic Review, October 9, 1971, p. 18.)

including the State Government Secretariat, new in 1970 and the banks and older institutions. In the new town are more modern shophouses, and proceeding outward, ribbon commercial development, and good quality detached residences. Ipoh is regarded as an extremely well-laid-out town (thanks to early planning) and a beautiful and functional one, in which parks and wide streets organize it efficiently for commerce and recreation. As usual, traffic is congested downtown, and through traffic is encouraged to use a new by-pass from Tasek to the Kuala Lumpur road south. A major problem, therefore, is traffic and parking. Another is the absence of a water-borne sewerage system.[1]

Ipoh dominates the Kinta Valley's 700 square miles of tin production and rubber-tapping. The city is bounded on the east and west by land over 250 feet, including mountains, but the elongated valley is filled with tin-mining and good roads--or it has been. Tin deposits are being exhausted rapidly, and the hope of new technology to revive them seems somewhat distant. Yet, newer iron-mining industries have been developing on former tin land; and an ambitious 20-mile diversion of the Kinta river immediately downstream from Ipoh is being financed by tin miners with the intention of gaining access to new tin deposits. Ipoh is contained, hence, in an environment of past and present vigorous resources exploitation, to which it supplies capital and management services and for which it provides serene urban amenities.

The most important elements in Ipoh's development beyond tin mining and certainly the most problematical are those created by the State and Federal governments' development policies. Ipoh is the epitome of those urban areas which have been regarded as able to look after themselves. In fact, Ipoh does very well at this, but it is not enough. Besides providing exemplary city services including a free library, the Municipality builds low-cost housing (Star Park, in conjunction with MBBS) with more than $1,040,000 invested in 1966-68. The Municipality has built the Tasek Industrial estate, planned the Menglembu Light Industrial Estate, compiled funds for sewerage system development, and built roads in profusion in the city (including the Menglembu by-pass).[2]

---

[1]One has been planned and proposed by the Municipality with State agreement since 1962, but as yet is without federal sponsorship, even though the Municipality has a two-million-dollar fund awaiting the go signal. (Interview with F. L. Cowie, Ipoh Municipal Engineer, July 17, 1970, and Lim Thiem-poh, Municipal Secretary, Ipoh, July 18, 1970.

[2]Capital projects cost the city $632,819 in 1968, and $2,007,412 for the 1966-68 period. (See Majlis Bandaran Ipoh, Laporan Tahunan [Ipoh: Municipality of Ipoh, 1966, 1967, 1968], passim.) During the Second Malaysia Plan main city roads are to become dual-carriageways (!).

Fig. 24.--Ipoh and Kinta Valley: Chinese Shophouse Architecture

Yet, the State government (while spending approximately $1,577,600 between 1966 and 1968 in Ipoh for identifiable projects, such as the new mosque and channelling another $2,780,544 in federal funds for the Ipoh Central Post Office), gets in the way of Ipoh's own development.[1] The Menglembu Industrial area is a case in point. The State Economic Development Corporation has decided to take over development of it, after the Municipality planned it, removed and relocated squatting occupants, realigned roads, and so forth, having mooted the idea as early as 1959 and having been given original development authority over it. In switching to state direction, the project has been set back at least two years.[2] Likewise, the State has decided to take over the Kinta Heights low-cost housing projects, which the Municipality would be perfectly capable, with

---

[1] Perak, Anggaran Kumpulan Wang Pembangunan Negeri, 1969 (Kuala Lumpur: Government Printer, 1969), p. 34. In November, 1972, the Asian Development Bank approved a loan to Malaysia of US$6.1 million for "Greater Ipoh water supply" development, almost certainly to be managed by the State. (ADB, Quarterly Newsletter [January, 1973], p. 10.)

[2] Interview, Councillor Khong Kok Yat, Ipoh, October 13, 1971.

Menglembu, of financing itself, with federal loan support.[1] The old policy of leaving town development to Ipoh has seemingly been abandoned by the state in the cases of glamorous projects whose success is assured.

Meanwhile, over the years, central government development expenditures have been moving to ECFN from POPC. Roads, industrial estate loans, and buildings have replaced hospitals and schools in importance. Expenditures per capita to 1968 have been of similar magnitude to those for Johore Baharu and George Town. The Kinta District has high readings on all three District Factor Analysis factors, but Ipoh city has only low positive scores on four of six factors in the city Factor Analysis. Thus, it appears that despite Ipoh's important population, it is indeed neglected nationally on a relative basis, although absolute rank in expenditures 6668 is fair.[2]

Sandakan

Sandakan, next to George Town, is the most singular of the cities treated in this study. It was for a long time the capital of North Borneo under the Chartered Company. It is dynamic because of the timber industry, which in turn is responsible for its otherwise impractical location and its charm.

The Sandakan Town Board operates under the Sabah Local Government Ordinance of 1961, there being no Town Councils.[3] Revenues come primarily from rates, with small income from government contributions and fees. (See Table 25.) Expenditures by the Board have been increasing in 1967 and 1968, with special capital expenditures in decline, however. Health, markets, miscellaneous services (like cleansing and lighting) receive most developmental

---

[1]In fairness it should be pointed out that projects require federal loans, for which the state must take approving responsibility--not that Ipoh's credit is not of the best.

[2]One reason for the unexciting national development policy expenditure activity in Ipoh may be the vigor of the private and semi-public enterprise system there. MBBS finances numerous housing estates besides the Municipality's Star Park, among which are Shatin Park, Merdeka Park, and Ipoh Gardens; four industrial firms from Malaysia, Japan, the Philippines, and Hong Kong have joined to establish a $2-million garment factory in Ipoh (see Straits Times [February 28, 1970], p. 4); and, with no urban renewal plan, all housing development is in private/MBBS hands. 7,246 housing units were completed in 1967. (Municipality of Ipoh, private communication, July 18, 1970.)

[3]It is given authority for licensing of houses and hotels, restaurants, and laundries, regulation of advertising, and promotion of arts and recreation. Of thirteen members of the Board, seven are elected and five are appointed by the Ministry of Local Government; there also is a District Officer.

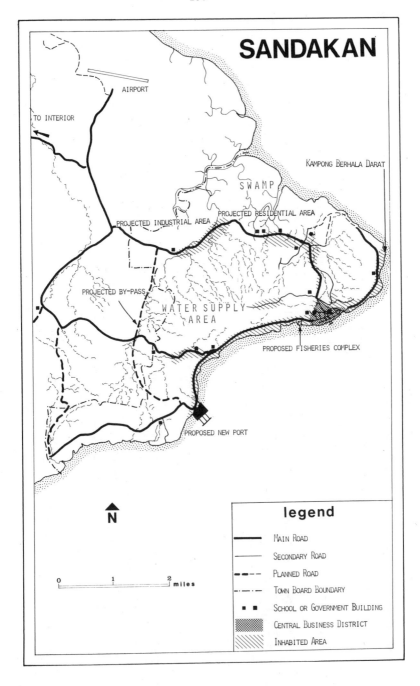

Fig. 25.--City Map: Sandakan

TABLE 25

REVENUE AND EXPENDITURE OF SANDAKAN 1967-1968[a]

Revenue

	Rates	Government Contribs.	Sundry Fees and Fines	License Fees	Rentals	Misc.	Total	Net Total
1966	N.D.	N.D.	N.D.	N.D.	N.D.	N.D.	N.D.	N.D.
1967	1,006,220	152,434	161,100	86,256	98,200	10,405	1,514,615	1,113,785
1968	1,110,260	164,405	189,850	86,756	101,700	9,795	1,760,716	1,225,926
Total	2,116,480	316,839	350,950	173,012	199,900	20,200	2,275,381	2,339,711

Expenditure

	Admin	Health	Markets	Misc. Services	Street Lighting	Payment to Gov't	Cap Special	Misc.	Total	Net Total
1966	N.D.	N.D.	N.D.	N.D.	N.D.	N.D.	N.D.	N.D.	N.D.	N.D.
1967	201,253	163,683	157,500	134,300	121,000	400,820	519,500	104,600	1,802,656	1,401,836
1968	241,563	192,120	121,800	157,010	128,500	438,840	161,030	117,800	1,508,663	1,511,014
Total	442,816	355,803	279,300	291,310	249,500	839,660	680,530	222,400	3,361,319	2,912,850

Note: Rows do not necessarily add because of estimations discrepancies.

[a]Estimated 1967, revised; estimated 1968.

Sources: Sandakan Town Board "Estimates" and, for net total, 1969 Sabah Annual Bulletin Statistics (Kota Kinabalu: Government Printer, 1970), pp. 150-51.

attention.[1] Revenues plus expenditures per capita in 1965 were the fifth highest in the country, indicating the extraordinary activity of this Town Board.

The population of Sandakan in 1970 was 42,249, that of a small city with a just above average growth rate 1947-1970, but with a projected population of 100,000 in 1990 for the urban region, assuming continued prosperity.[2] Of the estimated 1967 population of 39,331, the work force comprised 10,616, or 27 per cent.[3] Yet, labor availability problems are among the greatest worries of the city. Nearby estates are searching for labor; the timber industry has had to import workers from Indonesia and the Philippines; and city service and manufacturing jobs go wanting.[4] Immigration from West Malaysia has not been notably successful. The population, in 1960, was overwhelmingly Chinese.[5]

The production sub-system of Sandakan includes the handling and processing of the major exports--wood and prawns (also bird nests),[6] and the production of consumables and services for itself and its hinterland. When the city region grows to 60,000 or so, it is expected to become "self-generating" as regards service and light industries.[7] This is dependent, as everything else in Sandakan on growth in the productive environment. Currently there are three plywood/veneer factories, but production costs are so high that two of them lose money. Light industry for export is not really an attractive proposition in Sandakan at this time.

---

[1]In Sabah local authorities undertake to collect certain State revenues, hence the payments to government expenditure.

[2]Valentine, Laurie and Davies, Sandakan Traffic Study (Kota Kinabalu, 1969), p. 8.

[3]Ibid.

[4]Interview, R. Turner, Manager, The Chartered Bank, Sandakan, June 25, 1970. Sandakan ranks twentieth in registered job seekers, out of 21 cities. (See Table 13.)

[5]Sandakan ranked 20th in 1970 city population, but 16th in non-Malay population, versus 23rd in Malay and indigenous, in a district 64 per cent urban (third ranked on this variable). (See Table 26.)

[6]Sandakan is the largest exporter of all these in Malaysia. Exports of frozen prawns from Sabah in 1970 were expected to exceed 1,600 tons worth $9 million in 1970 (Malay Mail, September 9, 1970, p. 1); and Sabah's round timber production, 40 per cent of Malaysia's, rose to 5 million tons in 1970, almost all from the east coast, primarily Sandakan. (Second Malaysia Plan, p. 122.)

[7]Sandakan Traffic Study, loc. cit.

TABLE 26

MIDDLE CITY PROFILE: SANDAKAN

	District		City	
	Amount	Rank	Amount	Rank
1. TO61POPC[a]	6,338	5	6,388	4
2. TO61PROB	0	111	0	28
3. TO61ECFN	2,635	21	1,081	11
4. TO61URBN	7,419	8	7,419	8
5. TO61TOTL	8,973	8	7,419	8
6. 6165POPC	1,963	25	1,963	15
7. 6165PROB	448	36	448	6
8. 6165ECFN	1,013	35	40	16
9. 6165URBN	2,451	17	2,451	18
10. 6165TOTL	3,424	49	2,451	18
11. 6668POPC	1,117	43	1,117	18
12. 6668PROB	0	111	0	28
13. 6668ECFN	1,324	40	1,324	16
14. 6668URBN	2,441	19	2,441	21
15. 6668TOTL	2,441	42	2,441	21
16. TO65POPC	8,301	12	8,301	6
17. TO65PROB	448	41	448	12
18. TO65ECFN	3,648	30	1,121	14
19. TO65URBN	9,870	10	9,870	10
20. TO65TOTL	12,397	24	9,870	10
21. TO68POPC	9,418	18	9,418	12
22. TO68PROB	448	43	448	15
23. TO68ECFN	4,972	34	2,445	16
24. TO68URBN	12,311	15	12,311	16
25. TO68TOTL	14,838	30	12,311	16
26. 5760 POPN (of 104)	45,296	48	28,806	19
27. 5760MALY (of 104)	11,294	85	4,413	23
28. 5760NONMaly (of 104)	34,002	31	24,393	16
29. 5760POPDensity (of 104)	51	55	'65 2,871	19
30. 6760POPN (Estimated, City=6767)	N.D.	N.D.	39,331	17
31. 5760Percent URBan	64	3		
32. MANufacturing SALes ('67)	N.D.	N.D.		
33. 65Revenu+ ExpenLocalAuth	3,140	9	2,984	9
34. 65R+EXPer Person			76	5
35. 68HOTelRooMs			42	11
36. JAn70UNEMployment			127	20
37. 1970 Population	72,430	45	42,249	21

[a]Variables 1-25, 32-34 M$000's.   Sources: See Appendix II.

Trading and production for local consumption, however, do pay. Harrisons and Crossfield Company has its main Borneo office in Sandakan, servicing its plantations and competing with the Chinese small businesses. The largest European company in the area, it trades diversely in automobiles, detergents, Greyhound Bus tickets, as well as palm oil and timber. Housing construction in Sandakan tends to be for middle-income home owners, and is concentrated in estates, for instance the Po Hing Estate south of town. While construction of shophouses and multi-story flats declined in the late 1960's (55 in 1967 to 7 in 1969; and 561 in 1967 to 180 in 1969, respectively), detached residential buildings grew from 27 built in the Town Board area in 1966, to 146 in 1968. [1]

As a service center, Sandakan's hinterland stretches over land approximately to the boundaries of the Residence, [2] and beyond by sea to the smaller cities further down the east coast and into the Philippine archipelago via smuggling as well as legal trade. At present the frozen prawns, logs, and veneer and plywood go to Japan (66 per cent), South Korea, Taiwan, and Hong Kong, plus a little wood to Sarawak. A neat arrangement for logs and prawns by-passes the antique harbor facilities. Logs are floated out to ships which lift them on board. Prawns are carried to the ships in motorboats and stowed in freezing lockers. Future growth will depend on the diversification of agricultural production in the Sandakan Residency. A beginning is the Cadbury's cocoa plantation, and some oil-palm planting. [3]

However, two problems loom: (1) the timber boom, which, after all, is crucial for maintaining the dynamism and level of services of the town, may have peaked; and (2) transportation through Sandakan is very difficult. In the summer of 1971 it became apparent that the bottom, at least temporarily, had dropped out of the plywood market. While timber exports from Sabah sold for more than $300 million in 1970 (4/5 of the state's export revenues), in six months the price at Tokyo mills was halved. The hardwood log market tumbled

---

[1] Indicating the growing prosperity of the town in general, but its saturation in service and small productive businesses. (Sandakan Town Board, private communication, June 25, 1970.)

[2] Valentine, Laurie and Davies, p. 9.

[3] Sir Bruce White and Partners/Sabah Public Works Department, remark, "Studies [a report by Gutheries] relating specifically to future projected growth in agricultural products derived from Sandakan Peninsula indicate that there will be spectacular developments in the production of oil palm in particular, also rubber, coconut and other products," in Report on the Development of Sandakan Harbour (Kota Kinabalu: Sabah Public Works Department, 1963), p. 2.

as well. One problem has been Indonesian-Bornean competition, in an industry
where Malaysian relatively superior efficiency is not very important.[1] Journal-
ists predict the end of Sandakan's boom,[2] not counting, presumably, on significant developments from French oil explorations off Sandakan.[3]

The circulation problem through Sandakan relates to its site constraints
and lay-out. The city was leveled during World War II and rebuilt (giving it a
modernity and high-rise aspect that is salutory) in situ. Its site, unfortunately,
is at the foot of an escarpment whose wooded slopes (40 per cent of the Town
Board area) must be preserved almost entirely as a catchment because drinking
water is scarce in the area. Some housing is allowed there. The sewerage
system meanwhile, is confined to the central business area. The coastal strip,
including the business area, is a quarter of a mile at its widest, and has had
some area added by reclamation (and by building houses over water). But this
"constitutes the biggest immediate problem facing Sandakan, namely down-town
congestion, serious parking problems, and the need to examine critically the
intensity of land use, existing and proposed."[4] In the escarpment zone no new
development will be permitted. Thus development outward is lineal and dispersed, and follows the main lines of communication. Industrialists find suitable sites almost non-existent. Further reclamation is a possibility along the
coast north of the central business area.[5] But at present, industrial landscape
is found only along the coastal strip south of the city center and along North
Road between large residential areas.

The New Port of Sandakan, at Pavitt Point south of town, will be built

---

[1] Ironically some of the Indonesian timber enterprise has been assisted,
even undertaken, by Sabahan private interests. And the Japanese logging boat
methodology, developed in part because of Sandakan's poor port (see below)
facilities, should work well in Kalimantan's even worse ports.

[2] All this may presage the end of Sandakan as an improbable but sparkling
nightlife and commercial sex arena, "The New York of Sabah." See Jack Foisie,
reporting from Sandakan in the Singapore New Nation (Singapore), September 28,
1971, p. 6.

[3] $5 million were spent on preliminary investigations before 1970, and
$20 million in drilling operations were planned in six months, 1970/71. See
Straits Times, July 18, 1970, p. 15.

[4] Valentine, Laurie and Davies, p. 4. Kampong Berhala Darat was built
up since 1965 to accommodate fishing communities from the very central and
bothersome kampong Gelam Mata village. The new facility is occupied, and the
old one is reoccupied--crowding log pools and preventing land reclamation put
south of the CBD. Housing in the cover photograph is in the escarpment area.

[5] Arthur Kinkade, Chief Surveyor, Sandakan District, memorandum, 1969.

Fig. 26.--Sandakan: Fishing Village and Log Pools in City

during the SMP at a cost of at least $27.6 million. This will relieve the severe congestion and difficulties around the present wharf in the middle of the city, where ships have often to wait as much as a week to be unloaded.[1] It will further solidify the development of this area as the overseas processing and transshipment point of Sabah.[2] The goal is to construct an access road from the North Road direct to this center, by-passing the CBD and connecting the port, then, with the airport and the Labuk Road.

In common with the three small cities of Chapter V, Sandakan as an object of development policy is mainly to be considered in terms of its hinterland and developments there or associated with them. The object, with timber in a decline, will be opening up land around Sandakan to agricultural use. For this,

---

[1] Despite the fact that the SMP claims the wharf capacity is sufficient for present demand (op. cit., p. 202). According to FIDA, the "island" wharf will be 600 feet long by 400, with two wharves, and a 490-foot bridge to land. All berths will be able to handle both general and containerized cargo.

[2] In this section already there is a petroleum jetty, a palm oil storage facility, and a veneer and plywood factory.

the Cross-Sabah interior road is key. It will be a long time before it crosses
the Crocker Range and connects the east and west coast, [1] but meanwhile the
Australian government has financed the Telupid-Ranau sector, scheduled for
completion in 1973 at a cost of at least $21.7 million, while the Sandakan-
Telupid sector has been upgraded at a cost of $13 million. [2] Hence the interior,
as approached from Sandakan, is opening up fast. Cadbury's new cocoa and
Unilever's oil-palm plantations have sprung up, with both products moving to
Sandakan for storage and transshipment.

Attention to the city itself has come from the federal and state governments in moderate and variable amounts over the years. At the end of 1970 a
new electricity generating facility was completed by the Sabah Electricity Board.
The state Estimates for 1970 reported sewerage project expenditures of $628,000
from 1966-68. And according to FIDA, the state government is reclaiming 100
to 500 acres of swamp land in an attempt to alleviate the shortage of industrial
land: although financing has been difficult.

Federal development expenditures, set out in Table 26, have been higher
in the pre-Malaysia period than since. POPC (water supply, hospital, and education) projects took more than half of the total expenditures to 1968. The real
and especially the proportional amounts of Economic-functional (ECFN) expenditures rose steadily over the years, with attention especially to roads, air, and
sea communications, indicating the more dynamic quality of Sandakan as perceived by the Federal government. Since 1950, the town received more than
four-fifths of the district's expenditures. This proportion should remain about
the same in the future, as hinterland expenditures will be mainly private, and
new port, industrial reclamation, and further housing projects will be placed in
the city.

Kuching

Sited on the banks of the Sarawak River where small hills rise above the
surrounding swamps and some eighteen miles from the sea, the State capital . . . the largest town in Malaysian Borneo . . . [with] the longest history . . . already by the late 1880's a well built and planned town [had]
sprung up, with good roads, handsome public buildings and efficient policy. [3]

---

[1] The Mid-Term Review of the FMP mentions a feasibility study to identify
an adequate road crossing of the Range. (Op. cit., p. 94.)

[2] Ibid. Meanwhile the SMP prominently mentions developing and upgrading
of feeder roads in the Sandakan area, and the figure of $22.3 million for the
feeder program there and around Lahad Datu and Tawau. (Op. cit., p. 201.)

[3] Jackson, Sarawak, p. 67. See his discussion and that of Lee Yong-leng,

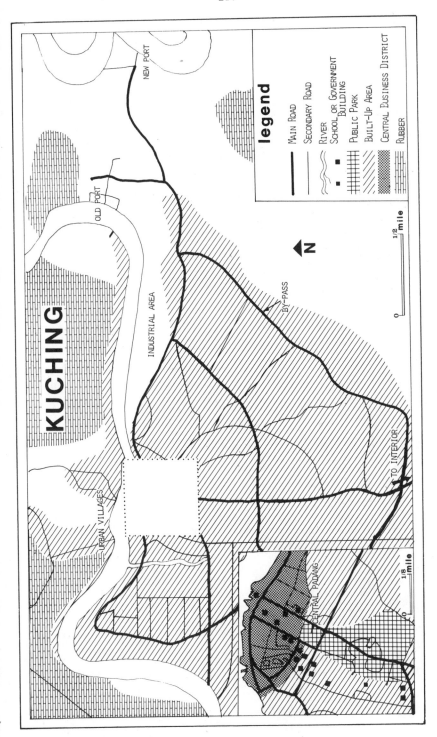

Fig. 27.--City Map: Kuching

Kuching has a history of imperial capital importance unknown to any other city in Malaysia. It is the star area in the individualistic State of Sarawak, a Municipality, and a city of infinite charm.

The Kuching Municipal Council is the only local authority in Sarawak with autonomous status.[1] Its 27 Councillors have powers, defined by the Kuching Municipal Ordinance, over reconstruction and maintenance of roads, provision of street lighting, provision and maintenance of public playgrounds and open spaces, public health controls and cleansing, maintenance of markets and licensing.[2] Table 27 shows that revenues come from rates, and in a larger than usual measure from the state government. Expenditures follow the responsibilities listed above, with the notable addition of primary education (11 schools), which was still a local responsibility in Sarawak in the FMP period and which accounts for a portion of the state grant aid.

The government sub-system of Kuching is complicated and enriched, as portrayed in Chapter III, by the presence there of several authorities, notably the Kuching Port Authority, the Sarawak Electricity Supply Corporation (SESCO), the Borneo Development Corporation (BDC), and the Kuching Water Board. More than in any other city in Malaysia this division of responsibilities among local semi-independent units contributes to stability and dynamism of growth. The Kuching Port Authority was established in 1961 to operate the new facilities at Tanah Puteh.[3] In 1966 the Port's revenue was \$4,632,063, an increase of 6.25 per cent over the previous year, and an income almost equal to that of the Municipality; while expenditures were up 10 per cent, to \$2,656,571.[4] The

---

Population and Settlement in Sarawak, pp. 229-36, for physical descriptions.

[1] Prior to 1921 the functions of the Municipality were in the hands of the Public Works Department of Sarawak. In that year the Kuching Sanitary and Municipal Advisory Board was constituted, becoming a Municipal Authority in 1934, though still a department of the government. This Board was made an autonomous Municipal Council in 1953, a body corporate with perpetual succession and a common seal.

[2] Details from a talk by the President of the Council, Cr. Song Thian Cheok to the students of Batu Lintang Training College, July 9, 1969.

[3] The initial cost of these was approximately \$7 million, which was vested in the Port Authority by the Sarawak government free of charge. Since 1964 plans for a new port have been underway (see below). See Sarawak Development Office, Sarawak Development Progress 1964-1967 (Kuching: Government Printer, 1968), p. 34.

[4] Kuching Port Authority, Report and Accounts for the Year 1966 (Kuching, 1967), p. 2.

TABLE 27

REVENUE AND EXPENDITURE OF KUCHING, 1966-1968

			Revenue			
	General Revenue	Licenses	Grants etc. from Gov't	Transfer from Reserves	Misc.	Total
1966	2,289,669	194,525	2,248,050	82,238	120,625	4,935,107
1967	2,348,301	196,383	2,215,368	325,971	276,673	5,312,696
1968	2,381,928	209,430	2,449,584	154,956	262,447	5,458,344
Total	6,019,898	600,338	6,913,002	563,165	659,745	15,756,147

			Expenditure			
	Admin	Primary Education	Health	Public Works	Swimming Pool	Misc.	Total
1966	737,674	2,188,792	739,888	775,093	38,520	122,036	5,046,131
1967	588,377	2,293,933	961,217	1,217,095	26,993	277,389	5,377,013
1968	609,430	1,908,766	772,332	1,525,877	39,173	225,393	5,152,286
Total	1,935,481	6,391,491	2,473,437	3,518,056	104,686	674,818	16,575,430

Note: Rows do not add because of rounding.

Source: Kuching Municipal Council, Annual Reports, 1967, 1968 (pp. 10-11).

Port has benefitted from a loan of US$5 million in 1969 for expansion from the ADB.[1]

The Kuching Water Board was established in January, 1959, to provide treated water to an area which since 1959 has expanded from 17.3 to 35 square miles (Kuching Municipality occupying 7.5 square miles).[2] Major investments have been made possible by a CDC (Commonwealth Development Corporation) loan of $2,693,875 in 1966.[3] Unlike the water (and electricity) supplies of George Town and vicinity which are provided by that city and which yield, therefore, a far larger city budget than it would ordinarily have, the Kuching Water

---

[1] Newsletter, loc. cit.

[2] The total services have risen from 1,472 to 9,554 and revenue from $782,641 to $2,481,086. To the end of 1967 the Board will have spent $7,475,245 on capital works and $1,744,297 on renewals. (See Sarawak, Kuching Water Board Annual Report, 1967 [Kuching, 1968], pp. 1, 7.)

[3] Sarawak Development Progress, p. 22.

Board is independent, and will remain so. The Municipality has considered taking it over and rejected the notion as too expensive and complicated--an uncharacteristic failure of nerve by Kuching.[1]

Likewise, the SESCO is an independent authority, whose job it is to supply electricity throughout Sarawak, and with large investment in the Kuching area.[2] The BDC operates throughout Sarawak and Sabah, and especially in Kuching and Kota Kinabalu. The Sarawak Development Finance Company, which is state owned, does agricultural financing. It performs the function in Sarawak of Bank Pertanian in Malaya. It also promotes land development, beginning in 1968 when it took over land schemes started by the state and began functioning like the FLDA--with the assistance in 1969 of a $2-million federal loan.[3]

Finally, as noted in Chapter III, many of the line departments of the Sarawak government have independence of action and financing denied to those in West Malaysia. Thus the Public Works Department is independent of the Federal PWD,[4] and the Lands and Surveys, Agriculture, and Forestry Departments are similarly autonomous. All of this independence of action, centered in Kuching among development agencies, makes the First Division and Kuching city far more open to development attention and understanding than any of the rest of the city areas in this study. Interviews give the impression that working relations are good, and there is general agreement among the Sarawakian institutions on the needs and ways to attainment of development.

The population of Kuching in 1970 was 63,491 and that of the district 214,797, with respective ranks of tenth and ninth in Malaysia. This population has been growing at an exceptionally slow rate (by 67 per cent from 1947, or

---

[1]This has meant that Water Board revenue excesses have been unavailable to the Municipality. On the other hand greater service to the hinterland has probably resulted from this division of powers. Interview with the Kuching Municipal Secretary, Tan Nyet-chin, Kuching, 16 June 1970.

[2]It also has been expanding and modernizing in smaller town and rural networks, with new networks at Siburan, Kundu, Beratok, Julau, Tapah, and Lawas, and improvements during the 1960's in Simmangang, Sibu, Bintulu, and Marudi. But, again, its financial resources are not in the hands of the Municipality. (Sarawak Development Progress, p. 32.) That, too, has been with ADB loan assistance--of US$98 million in installments approved in 1969 and 1972. (ADB, Newsletter, loc. cit.)

[3]Interview with Amin bin Haji Satem, Director, Sarawak Development Finance Corporation, Kuching, June 19, 1970.

[4]Indeed it claims to feel no pressure from Kuala Lumpur even to standardize construction forms in line with those of West Malaysia. It is doing so, however, to a degree, anyway. (Interview with Chai Boon-poh, Deputy Director, Public Works, Sarawak, Kuching, June 17, 1970.)

2 per cent per year, indicating slight net out-migration). This holds for the district population between 1960 and 1970 as well. Although Kuching has been primarily a Chinese city in the Twentieth Century, the proportion of Malay and indigenous population is comparatively high, almost one-fourth in 1960 in the Municipality and as much as one-third in the "agglomeration."[1]

The Municipality of Kuching fronts on the Sarawak River. Circulation to the interior goes up river and by road east, west, and south, and down the river to the sea. Across the river and to the west are Malay kampongs, the latter connected by oar-powered ferries. There is no bridge on the river here, and none is contemplated. (A pedestrian bridge crosses the river at a narrower point west of town.) So Kuching has the odd and pleasant phenomenon of a rural village within three minutes of its city center.[2] The main constraints on the development of the urban area are the river, the swamps on all sides, a hill and overcentralization in the dense city center, and the extremely low population densities beyond which make provision of public transportation (to relieve the traffic problem) difficult. Other problems are drainage and sewerage (there is no water-borne sewerage system; although an $18-million one is proposed), and squatting on state land southwest of town and in Pending,[3] the site of the new port.

---

[1] Jackson opines that "rural-urban migration has been a significant process in post-war Sarawak," within which "all available evidence suggests that there was, in fact, a very substantial increase in the number of Malays residing in the Kuching urbanized area." (See Sarawak, p. 69; see also Lee Yong-leng, Population and Settlement in Sarawak, pp. 228-29.)

[2] That center, of course, begins at the water's edge, with river traffic wharves and markets, just inward from which are the old colonial government buildings. (The White Rajah's istana or palace is across the river.) Further inward are dense blocks of shop-houses. Beyond on a radial street pattern are open areas with the newer government buildings, the cathedral, and further yet the library and museum and residential and school areas. The larger urban area pattern includes the present Kuching Port down river and the new one, at Pending point across the neck of a peninsula from it, further down. The airport is south of town. A striking similarity to Sandakan arises in the juxtaposition of these with the dense and traffic-aggravated city center. A by-pass will presumably be perfected by 1973 to connect the port and the new industrial estate, Padungan, with the airport and the roads to the interior. Between the old port and town are oil jetties. Although Kuching does not have anything like Sandakan's escarpment and watershed problem, the central town is bisected by Bukit Mata (partly owned by the state and partly by the Borneo Company)--a hill which can only accommodate residential use at present. East of town on both sides of the river are mangrove swamps which provide a considerable barrier to site expansion.

[3] Interview with Henry T. P. Kon, Director, Planning Section, Land and Survey Department--First District, Kuching, June 19, 1970.

In Kuching's very small industrial area[1] in 1967 there were 227 manufacturing and commercial establishments, employing 8,777 people (comparing to Sibu's 63 and 2,939),[2] which processed timber and other natural products, and did small-scale (less than 10 workers per establishment) manufacturing of soap, shirts, footwear, and so forth. Three industrial areas are developed or developing: Padungan, directed by the Borneo Development Corporation with 6.8 acres, Bintawa of which 47 acres have been taken over for development by Wee Hock Teck Development Corporation, and Pending, adjacent to the new port, which will occupy about 50 acres. Whether these can be filled is a big question.

The exports of Kuching, mostly going to Singapore for transshipment, include rubber, sago flour, pepper, canes, foodstuffs, and semi-processed wood products of which rubber, pepper, and vegetable oil yield by far the largest tonnage.[3] The centrality of Kuching may be enhanced in the export environment sense, however, if, for example, bulk coal handling facilities are deemed desirable, as has been suggested, at the Port. Coal production is being developed by the Japanese in Selantek; and the world's largest antimony smelter is being set up at Buso, 22 miles southwest of Kuching at an investment cost of $3 million.[4] The port of Kuching, which can currently receive vessels up to 2,500 tons, traditionally serves the double function, then, of entrepôt for much of Sarawak and its raw materials, and as trade center for its hinterland.[5] The most important imports, in order of tonnage in 1968, are consumer goods, cement, fertilizer, rice, and sugar.[6] Unfortunately, it is not possible to clearly delineate this

---

[1]The Greater Kuching Master Plan (which exists in the absence of a Town and Country planning law) makes land use estimates from 1969 aerial photographs thus: 48.67 per cent residential, 15 per cent mangrove and nipah, 5 per cent government, 3.4 per cent schools and training grounds, 2.6 per cent open space, 3 per cent industrial, 1.67 per cent commercial, and 1 per cent warehouses and power. (Land and Survey Department, Sarawak, 1970, passim.)

[2]Sarawak, Annual Bulletin of Statistics (Kuching: Department of Statistics, 1968), p. 47.

[3]12,165, 11,647, and 5,969 tons respectively in 1968 (Kuching Port Authority, private communication, June 20, 1970).

[4]Borneo Bulletin (Kuching), June 20, 1970, p. 1.

[5]See Jan O. M. Broek, "Trade and Trade Centers of Sarawak," Department of Geography, University of Minnesota, fugitive, n.d., p. 2.

[6]112,466; 23,985; 18,964; 18,580; and 15,112 tons respectively. (Kuching Port Authority, ibid.)

hinterland. Certainly it contains the First Division. There, 33 per cent of the gross regional product of the state is concentrated; while 45 per cent of the tertiary sector of Sarawak is concentrated in the Kuching urban area itself, [1] and must serve needs as far as Sibu. It is believed that the hinterland stretches at least to Lubok Antu to the east. [2] It extends by way of barter trade across the border into Indonesia to the south and west. Sibu is the natural competitor of Kuching for interior markets and port development assistance. [3]

As an object of development policy expenditures and expectations, Kuching has a unique function as the premier center for almost all modernizing and dynamic elements in its large and backward state. International organizations, both public and private, are at work to open up the hinterland of Kuching, while furthering its port and distributive function. [4] Housing is well developed for upper- and middle-class dwelling, thanks to the BDC and private developers. Low-cost housing, partly because of the inordinately high land and construction prices in Kuching, has not come along as quickly as the Municipality would like. Kuching has been unable to organize projects of its own which really meet the problem, particularly when relocation is desired.

The problems with developing Kuching as a modern city are associated with thresholds for growth industries. The Wageningen Team identifies these limiting factors on development: (1) limited size of the domestic market; (2) absence of an industrial tradition; (3) prevalence of family-oriented business organization; (4) competition of imported goods; (5) high land and utilities prices; and (6) absence of a consistent industrialization program. [5] Since the State is incapable of mounting an industrial program by itself, national development policy comes to the fore. But a major problem from the federal viewpoint is insufficient data on the economy of Sarawak. To Sarawak's regret the federal government has rejected some projects the state has suggested, such as a sago-process-

---

[1] Study Team of the Agricultural University Wageningen, Netherlands, "Regional Planning Study of the First Division of Sarawak--Interim Report, Notes for Discussion" (Kuching, March 3, 1970), p. 2.

[2] Interview with Andrew Chan, Director, Kuching Port Authority, June 19, 1970.

[3] As the Rajang Ports Authority begins to operate, we shall see how the boundaries between the two ports' areas will be fixed.

[4] Including the Asian Development Bank, which in addition to the loan for the new Kuching Port, approved in 1970 a US$3.5 million loan for Sibu port expansion. (ADB Newsletter, loc. cit.)

[5] "Regional Planning Study," p. 15.

TABLE 28

MIDDLE CITY PROFILE: KUCHING

	District		City	
	Amount	Rank	Amount	Rank
1. TO61POPC[a]	12, 701	4	12, 701	2
2. TO61PROB	1, 543	6	1, 076	9
3. TO61ECFN	24, 071	2	20, 015	1
4. TO61URBN	33, 792	3	33, 792	3
5. TO61TOTL	38, 315	3	33, 792	3
6. 6165POPC	5, 648	12	5, 648	5
7. 6165PROB	239	37	0	28
8. 6165ECFN	3, 298	17	3, 278	5
9. 6165URBN	8, 926	7	8, 926	7
10. 6165TOTL	9, 185	22	8, 926	7
11. 6668POPC	20, 706	2	20, 706	2
12. 6668PROB	2, 417	5	2, 417	4
13. 6668ECFN	2, 517	21	2, 417	11
14. 6668URBN	25, 539	4	25, 539	5
15. 6668TOTL	25, 640	7	25, 539	5
16. TO65POPC	18, 349	4	18, 349	3
17. TO65PROB	1, 782	29	1, 076	9
18. TO65ECFN	27, 369	5	23, 293	3
19. TO65URBN	42, 718	4	42, 718	3
20. TO65TOTL	47, 500	4	42, 718	3
21. TO68POPC	19, 055	3	39, 055	2
22. TO68PROB	4, 199	20	3, 493	5
23. TO68ECFN	29, 886	7	25, 709	4
24. TO68URBN	68, 257	4	68, 257	5
25. TO68TOTL	73, 140	6	68, 257	5
26. 5760POPN (of 104)	149, 456	12	50, 579	9
27. 5760MALY (of 104)	22, 831	58	12, 000	9
28. 5760NONMaly (of 104)	126, 625	6	38, 579	12
29. 5760POPDensity (of 104)	158	38	'65 7, 550	11
30. 6760POPN (Estimated, City=6767)	N. D.		60, 399	7
31. 5760Percent URBan	33	16		
32. MANufacturing SALes ('67)	N. D.	N. D.		
33. 65Revenu+ ExpenLocalAuth	14, 659	3	9, 981	3
34. 65R+EXPer Person			166	2
35. 68HOTelRooMs			N. D.	N. D.
36. JAn70UNEmployment			372	18
37. 1970 Population	214, 797	10	63, 491	9

[a]Variables 1-25, 32-34 M$000's.   Sources: See Appendix II.

ing mill.[1] The Sarawak Cement Company, however, may begin a large import substitution production facility at or near the new port (mostly with local financing).[2] A major Kuching problem is underscored:

> At present the bulk of the raw material of this region, particularly timber, is leaving the region in an unprocessed condition representing a great loss in revenue for the states. This also reflects the large amount of employment opportunities which can be made available with the proper financing, planning and exploitation of raw materials.[3]

How has national development expenditure treated Kuching's problems? Table 28 shows that whereas Economic-functional (ECFN) expenditures were important prior to the creation of Malaysia, they have taken a declining proportion and were less than one-eighth of Population Coverage (POPC) mappable expenditures from 1966-68. This partly reflects Kuching's extraordinary ability to attract social expenditures (ranking second in this 1966-68), but also the unattractiveness, in the Federal view, of Sarawak and Kuching as generators of modern economic development. Water, health, education, broadcasting, and some housing have taken the POPC expenditures through the years. Government buildings, the airport, and port have taken ECFN, in declining amounts, although planned port and road expenditures after 1968 should redress this to a degree. Kuching district (expenditures to which are almost all urban) not surprisingly has high factor scores on the two factors not 6668 ECFN expenditures in the district factor analysis, and has positive city factor scores on all factors except those associated with absolute population and modern economic magnitude.

The Development Policy Systems Compared

Ipoh, Sandakan, and Kuching are used in various ways in the national development policy system, and are reasonably successful at performing their urban functions. They all have as their most important function the funneling of raw materials, mostly unprocessed, to export markets in the rest of the world. Secondarily, they provide efficient and smooth, local and regional governmental services. As centers of the newer urban economic growth activities, they are for the most part left on their own. National industrialization policy, whether it be for industrial estates or bumiputera business, hardly touches them. Never-

---

[1]Interview with Richard Lye, Secretary, Sarawak Industrial Development Committee, June 17, 1970.

[2]Interview, Andrew Chan, idem.

[3]Editorial, Sarawak Tribune, April 24, 1970.

theless, each city is undertaking industrial, if only light industrial, development of its own, including industrial estate development and infrastructural development, with some federal assistance. In their private sectors the housing, commercial, and transportation segments are limited in what can be done locally by too much competition with other centers and, in the case of the Bornean cities, hinterlands far too limited in buying power and the provision of skilled labor.

Flows in the Development Policy Systems of these cities are excellent in local government and, as one would expect, among the constituents of the export trades. Information about the needs and self-perceptions of the urban communities seemingly does not easily flow upward to the state (except from Kuching) and federal governments. One would wish, on behalf of these cities, for more decentralization of thinking (and then centralization of implementation) in the cases of specifically urban projects. In the cities themselves, high land costs, high labor costs (in Borneo), and inadequate technical training institutions provide major systemic blockages. In none of these cities, however, is "excessive" urbanization--gross numbers of migrants arriving and finding nothing to do, and having attendant psychological problems--or urban decrepitude, a major problem. Indeed, labor shortages are a bit of a problem in each, but confined more or less to skilled occupations.

These middle cities, though differing from one another greatly in character, have so far succeeded in avoiding the major urban problems of Malaysia and the world today. They perhaps are very lucky, but certainly have traditions and organizational excellence going for them. And most important of all, they are perhaps of the right size and location in Malaysia's system of cities to continue to avoid hard problems, while paying the eventual and acceptable price of being overshadowed in glamour (and industrialization) by Kuala Lumpur, Penang, and possibly Johore Baharu. Thus whereas dynamic cities such as these do receive proportionally more ECFN expenditures than those in the lower category, and they are growing, thriving service centers, they do not find themselves receiving those expenditures that excite industrial development; and as systems they do not have the mass, or backing to do any more than they already are to inspire rapid economic growth.

CHAPTER VII

POLICY IN AREA:

THE PENANG METROPOLITAN AREA

Nature of the Area

Penang is the Pearl of the Orient.[1] Penang, including in its urban ag-

glomeration--Butterworth, Prai, Ayer Itam Village and parts of three adjacent

Mukims, as well as George Town--is the most significant of all Malaysian Mid-

dle City areas. With a combined population of 375,752 in 1970 it has 53 per

cent of the population of the Kuala Lumpur Municipality and adjoining built-up

areas, including Petaling Jaya.[2] So with the overwhelming dominance of the

Kuala Lumpur area (and its development corridor to Port Swettenham), Penang

is appropriately definable as middle in function and importance. It is particu-

larly important because (a) it is functionally the only rival of Kuala Lumpur,

and (b) it is in the process of constituting itself a city-state, a condition revolu-

tionary in Malaysian city and Southeast Asian development.[3]

The Penang Metropolitan area, and George Town in particular, are

multi-functional (six of six functions, see Table 13). The Metropolitan area has

---

[1] The name refers both to the island of Penang and to the State: both in
Malay are Pulau Pinang. The State, besides the island contains Province Wellesley on the mainland. In all it is 402.7 square miles, or 3 per cent of the national
areal total. The island is 15 miles long by 9 miles wide, or 110 square miles.
Province Wellesley is 45 miles long by between 6 and 8 miles wide; and there is
a strait of between 2 and 8 miles between them, at the narrower part of which is
the harbor of Penang. Province Wellesley is a low flat coastal plain. The island
is commanded by Penang hill near its center, with coastal plains and uplands
around, 30 per cent in tropical forest. Beautiful beaches, highland spice plantations, the cool reaches of the hill, tropical gardens, the Chinese and British
buildings and Malay kampongs have made the island a favorite stopping place for
travelers for almost two centuries.

[2] See Urban Conurbations, pp. 24-25.

[3] Singapore, of course, already is a city-nation. But the absence of a
national environment containing varieties of development phenomena, including
a separate national government concerned with rural and backward region development, removes it from consideration.

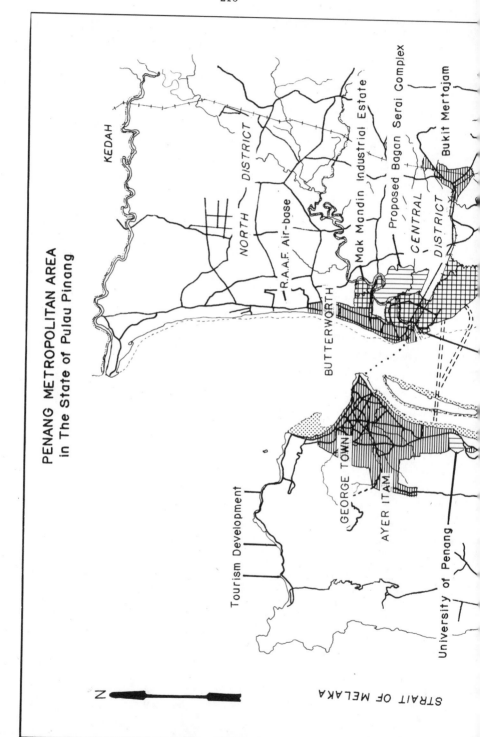

PENANG METROPOLITAN AREA
in The State of Pulau Pinang

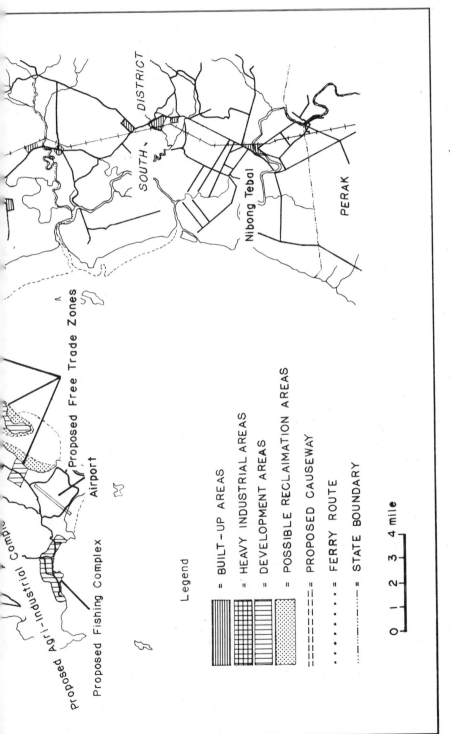

Fig. 28.--Regional Map: The Penang Metropolitan Area

Legend

= BUILT-UP AREAS	
= HEAVY INDUSTRIAL AREAS	
= DEVELOPMENT AREAS	
= POSSIBLE RECLAIMATION AREAS	
= PROPOSED CAUSEWAY	
= FERRY ROUTE	
= STATE BOUNDARY	

0 1 2 3 4 mile

73 per cent as many manufacturing establishments as Kuala Lumpur/Petaling Jaya (but only 22 per cent of Kuala Lumpur's gross value of manufactured products in 1967, and 51 per cent of the number of banking offices of Kuala Lumpur). It is approached in importance only by Kuching as a Middle City regional center and point of dynamism. But these calculations are made difficult by the disaggregation of the Penang Metropolitan Area into town and District Council units, which is exactly what the Penang government has seen, symbolically and really, as the major organizational problem of Penang state: a non-functional distribution of activities, and an absence of a comprehensive approach to state development. Comprehensive state development is possible as a goal because of the smallness of Penang, and the largeness within it of George Town on the island, and Butterworth/Prai joined to it on the mainland by heavily travelled ferries. Thus the theme of this chapter is the treatment of Penang as a city-state, and its reorganization and potential along that line.

The government of the state of Penang has the customary powers of a state in Malaysia, including powers over local government and land; but it also has been impecunious, especially in contrast to the Municipality of George Town. George Town is the oldest local government unit in the country, the first to have a fully elected council and to be given city status.[1] And its expenditures in 1965 and through the 1966-68 period were almost 2 1/2 times those of the State. In 1966 the State vested all the functions of the City Council in Penang's Chief Minister--to enable a Commission of Enquiry to investigate allegations of maladministration, malpractices and breaches of law committed by the City Council since the end of 1958.[2] Thus during the FMP the City was managed by the State and local/state government consolidation began, but George Town functioned as a separate entity through 1969 anyway, with its own civil service, sources of revenue, and development plans.

Counting George Town, there were five local governmental units in Penang, the other four being Rural District Councils, one on the island and three in Province Wellesley. Like the other Malaysian Straits Settlement, Malaka, Penang has both districts (5), in the usual sense, and these comprehen-

---

[1] It is the only officially City in Malaysia at the moment; although Ipoh and Kuala Lumpur are working on gaining this cachet.

[2] See Commission of Enquiry to Enquire into the Affairs of the City Council of George Town, Penang 31st December 1958 up to 30th June 1966, Part I of Report by the Commission (Alor Setar: Government Printer, 1967), p. 65 et passim.

TABLE 29

REVENUE AND EXPENDITURE OF GEORGE TOWN 1966-1968

Revenue

	Rates	Contribution from Elec Dept	Town Cleansing	Road Grant	Taxes and Licenses	Other Revenue	Transportation Department	Water Department	Electricity Department	Total
1966	6,724,072	1,600,000	1,011,862	933,233	410,082	2,567,661	2,434,172	4,002,364	14,240,187	33,923,623
1967	7,134,966	---	1,034,721	977,540	413,972	2,540,704	2,279,510	4,036,588	13,363,358	31,781,361
1968	6,672,680	1,500,000	1,091,450	998,908	409,350	2,885,340	2,281,186	4,087,454	13,631,055	33,557,373
Total	20,531,718	3,100,000	3,138,033	2,909,681	1,233,406	7,993,705	6,994,868	12,126,406	41,234,600	99,262,357

Expenditure

	Contribution to Capital	Market, etc.	Fire Services	Town Planning and Building	Administration and General	Treasury and Valuation	Health and Veterinary	Engineer's Department	Town Cleansing
1966	633,549	528,970	560,047	638,773	987,796	571,495	1,831,807	2,900,998	3,013,617
1967	706,330	585,125	604,914	923,679	843,113	1,683,314	1,902,897	2,844,139	3,102,956
1968	1,204,375	573,323	612,413	907,031	760,786	1,727,064	2,002,433	2,726,558	3,245,967
Total	2,544,254	1,687,418	1,777,374	2,269,483	2,591,875	4,981,873	5,755,137	8,471,695	9,362,590

	Transportation Dept			Water Dept			Electricity Dept			Total
	Contribution to Reserves	Loan Charge	General	Contribution to Capital	Loan Charge	General	Contribution to Capital	Loan Charge	General	
1966	---	(132,449)	2,475,688	378,532	1,528,547	1,846,225	1,357,000	2,325,247	10,072,117	32,783,031
1967	(146,952)	(109,863)	2,347,876	830,100	1,421,023	1,812,504	2,684,300	2,138,942	7,428,178	32,543,206
1968	(166,452)	(118,079)	2,333,676	590,371	1,421,023	1,877,037	2,511,737	2,165,374	6,893,699	33,389,398
Total	(313,240)	(360,391)	7,157,240	1,799,003	4,370,593	5,535,766	6,553,037	6,629,563	24,393,994	98,715,635

TABLE 30

MIDDLE CITY PROFILE: GEORGE TOWN

	District		City	
	Amount	Rank	Amount	Rank
1. TO61POPC[a]	13, 598	3	11, 216	3
2. TO61PROB	28, 240	2	28, 240	2
3. TO61ECFN	6, 651	7	6, 463	3
4. TO61URBN	45, 919	2	45, 919	2
5. TO61TOTL	48, 490	2	45, 919	2
6. 6165POPC	13, 171	3	11, 014	3
7. 6165PROB	9, 392	8	9, 392	2
8. 6165ECFN	1, 613	24	1, 479	9
9. 6165URBN	21, 885	4	21, 885	3
10. 6165TOTL	24, 176	7	21, 885	3
11. 6668POPC	3, 259	14	3, 164	10
12. 6668PROB	12, 228	2	12, 228	2
13. 6668ECFN	4, 998	12	4, 998	6
14. 6668URBN	20, 485	6	20, 390	6
15. 6668TOTL	20, 485	10	20, 390	6
16. TO65POPC	26, 769	3	22, 230	2
17. TO65PROB	37, 632	2	37, 632	2
18. TO65ECFN	8, 265	12	7, 942	5
19. TO65URBN	67, 804	2	67, 804	1
20. TO65TOTL	72, 666	3	67, 804	2
21. TO68POPC	30, 028	4	25, 394	3
22. TO68PROB	49, 860	2	49, 860	2
23. TO68ECFN	13, 263	12	12, 940	7
24. TO68URBN	88, 289	3	88, 194	3
25. TO68TOTL	93, 151	5	88, 194	3
26. 5760POPN (of 104)	296, 566	4	234, 903	2
27. 5760MALY (of 104)	60, 691	15	26, 757	3
28. 5760NONMaly (of 104)	235, 875	3	208, 146	2
29. 5760POPDensity (of 104)	2, 624	1	30, 575	1
30. 6760POPN (Estimated, City=6767)	410, 034	3	286, 104	2
31. 5760Percent URBan	96	1		
32. MANufacturing SALes ('67)	59, 124	9		
33. 65Revenu+ ExpenLocalAuth	68, 159	1	65, 486	1 (K. L. = N. D.)
34. 65R+Exper Person			228	1 (K. L. = N. D.)
35. 68HOTelRooMs			412	2
36. JAn70UNEMployment			15, 890	4
37. 1970 Population	433, 760	2	270, 019	2

[a]Variables 1-25, 32-34 M$000's.   Sources: See Appendix II.

sive administrative Rural District Councils.[1] On the first of January, 1971, the State Government transferred the functions of all four of Penang's Rural District Councils to the Chief Minister of the State, completing the consolidation of local authority with that of the State, and the second step toward the legal and administrative creation of the city-state.[2]

The advantages of greater administrative unity are many. First, the Rural District Councils have not been particularly well financed. Their budgets (see Table 31) have been adequate for rural support, but not for industrializing and infrastructural developments needed in their large areas, especially that of Province Wellesley North (Butterworth/Prai).[3] The State sees George Town in

---

[1]On Penang Island there are the North-east District (containing but not administering George Town) and the South-west District, both of which are administered for purposes of non-urban local government by the financially autonomous and formerly fully elected Rural District Council, Penang Island, headquartered in George Town. On the mainland there are three Districts which are practically identical to the corresponding three District Council local government areas: Province Wellesley North, whose administrative center is Butterworth and which is financially autonomous and formerly elected; Province Wellesley Central, with headquarters at Bukit Mertajam; and Province Wellesley South, with its administrative center at Nibong Tebal. For mapping purposes Penang Island has been treated as one district.

[2]This was a measure to enhance efficiency, with no apparent implication of former District Council malpractice.

[3]The finances and duties of the District Councils are organized to provide minimal urban amenities and rural capital investment on a very small scale. The revenues come from rates and taxes primarily. The expenditures go for administration of service and works. Of these, the Province Wellesley North District Council, which has been Alliance controlled, is the most important; but it has been unable to do the kinds of urban planning and control that would give best support to development there. For example, building plans cannot be processed by the council for lack of staff, and cleansing is not up to George Town's level. The District Council is mainly used as a complaints department by the local manufacturers. (View from interview with Khoo Keat Then, Secretary, Province Wellesley North District Council, Butterworth, September 9, 1970.) See Robert Nathan et al., Penang Master Plan, Vol. I (draft) (George Town: State of Penang, 1970), which states that none of the five independent planning authorities in the state "has the capability to perform its delegated statutory functions," let alone "extra-statutory" coordinating functions (p. 133). On 10 December 1969, the Straits Echo reported that "the Integration Committee of the State of Penang to Look into the Coordination of the State Services has strongly recommended that the Local Councils be suspended forthwith. It is felt that in view of the small geographical area of Penang, these Councils would function better if controlled by the center--the Penang State Government; and that there would be increased efficiency and accelerated development if all the resources of the local councils were exploited to the full in furtherance of the economic plans of the State Government" (p. 2).

TABLE 31

REVENUE AND EXPENDITURE OF PENANG DISTRICT COUNCILS 1968

	Revenue				
	Taxations	Commercial Undertakings	Misc. Sales	Allocations and Grants	Total
P. W. Utara	988, 000	12, 000	325, 000	142, 000	1, 467, 000
P. W. Tengah	440, 000	181, 000	101, 000	82, 000	804, 000
P. W. Selatan	217, 000	78, 000	55, 000	---	350, 000
Penang Island Rural	1, 002, 000	---	571, 000	---	1, 573, 000
Total	2, 647, 000	271, 000	1, 052, 000	224, 000	4, 194, 000

	Expenditure			
	Ag & Forestry	Public Works	Admin Depts	Total
P. W. Utara	8, 000	445, 000	1, 582, 000	1, 835, 000
P. W. Tengah	6, 000	273, 000	523, 000	802, 000
P. W. Selatan	---	141, 000	208, 000	348, 000
Penang Island Rural	12, 000	983, 000	1, 054, 000	2, 050, 000
Total	26, 000	1, 842, 000	3, 167, 000	5, 035, 000

Note: Rows do not add, due to rounding.

Source: Robert Nathan, Penang Master Plan, Table 26.

the reverse light: as an enormous and administratively highly efficient unit (if formerly truculent and crooked politically). In 1969, with 40 per cent of the population, the revenues of the City were 61.2 per cent of the combined revenue of the State, the City, and the District Councils.[1] The State has noted its own lack of technical staff and financial resources for development.[2] Taking over George Town has made the city's revenues and more importantly her flexibility available to the state planners.[3]

---

[1] Nathan, Penang Master Plan, Vol. II, Part 1, p. 75.

[2] Mohd. Ishak bin Haji Mohammad Ariff, State Planning Officer, Penang, "Urbanization in Penang State (with Special Reference to Problems of Physical Planning)," paper prepared for SEADAG Conference, George Town, 1970, p. 16.

[3] For example, the state, through the City, has been able to introduce vocational training for youths, connected with employment as human parking meters (see Figure 30), while preparing them for specific jobs in state-organized business.

George Town has a long history of self government, the prominent feature of which has been the development of city services of a high order, particularly electricity and water which charge lower rates than the federal agencies.[1] The finances of George Town are set out in Table 29. This indicates the very high level of financial operation of the Electricity and Water Departments, and the importance of the rate fund. The Transportation Department (which operates extensive bus services through the city and environs) and the Cleansing Department are not financially self-sufficient; health services and a large portion of the roads are also paid from general rather than just their own revenues; and contributions to capital and transfers from the profit making departments loom large ($11,214,742 total in 1966-68).

The Penang Port Commission is the most important semi-public authority in Penang, and was established by ordinance in 1955. It was the second most financially important government in the state in the 1966-68 period, operating at about 45 per cent of the level of the City, with slightly higher revenue plus expenditures than the State (but with State budgets closing in).[2]

The population of Penang state in 1970 was 776,770, making it the sixth most populous state in Malaysia and three times denser than the next most densely populous state (Melaka, and 4.3 times Selangor).[3] A steep population density gradient moves downward away from George Town. The City of George Town, with 270,019 people in 1970 had a 15 per cent growth change from 1957, indicating net out-migration. The District (in this case meaning the Island as a whole) however, grew in population by 46 per cent, or 3.5 per cent per year, clearly absorbing much of the George Town emigrants and more. In 1957 21 per cent of the population were Malay on the Island, 11 per cent in George Town,

---

[1] Five to ten per cent cheaper on electricity rates. Water and electricity are provided by George Town to much of the Island, but none to the mainland. The State Public Works Department provides some water, too, to rural areas on the island, and to Penang Hill. (See Penang Master Plan, Vol. II, Pt. 1, pp. 108-11.) Interview, Anwar Fazal, Assistant to the Chief Minister for City of George Town, October 11, 1971. The City also maintains 113.5 miles of streets and lanes, 9 Child Welfare Clinics, an isolation hospital, and public dispensaries.

[2] In 1968 the PPC's gross operating income was $17,013,363 (including $3,836,648 from General Charge and Port Dues); while operating expenditure amounted to $12,914,226 (including $2,280,884 for General Charge and Port Dues). See Penang Port Commission, Thirteenth Annual Administration Report and Accounts (Penang: PPC, 1968), p. 14.

[3] That population was distributed among the district areas as follows: 373,086 in the North-east of the island, and 60,674 in the Southwest; P.W. North, 161,605; P.W. Central, 117,759; and P.W. South, 63,646.

49 per cent in Province Wellesley North, and 24 per cent in Butterworth. (See Tables 30 and 32.) Penang is thus a rural, mixed racial state, housing an enormous non-Malay city.[1]

The most important population matter in Penang at present, rather than race per se, however, is employment. Unemployment in the State is almost twice as great urban as rural, with discrimination in favor of white-collar workers. Employment, reflecting the mercantile and self-sufficient past of Penang, finds 20 per cent in commerce and trade, 20 per cent in services in the urban areas.[2] Industry has the highest unemployment rate and seems to be the failing sector, whereas services are holding their own in employment. And this fits into the general production sub-system picture of Penang. Low rates of both generation of employment and production growth are associated by the Nathan Associates with five factors: (1) shortage of agricultural land, (2) heavy dependence on regional and international trade, (3) remoteness from the major consumer market, (4) high urbanization, and (5), in the past, lack of effective programs.[3] Of these (3) and (5) have been the worst problems--both arising initially from (2).

Penang's gross regional product, as computed by Robert Nathan, was composed in 1969 of 57.5 per cent in trade and services, 16 per cent in agriculture, etc., and 12 per cent in manufacturing. This parallels the employment pattern, but with higher employment, proportionally, of course in agriculture.[4]

---

[1] Perhaps surprisingly, the rural Penang population is almost exactly evenly divided between Malays and non-Malays, on both sides of the harbor. (Source: State of Penang.) In the urban conurbation, a survey shows that racial interaction is less prevalent than in Kuala Lumpur, especially among Indians-- a significant commercial minority in George Town. This is one reflection of the traditional style of the city--outward-looking insouciance--which must change. See Alvin Rabushka, "Racial Stereotypes in Malaya," Asian Survey, XI, No. 7 (July, 1971), 709-16.

[2] In the State, 48 per cent of labor is employed in trade, service and government, 31 per cent in agriculture, forestry and fishery, 20 per cent in manufacturing, and 6 per cent in transportation and communication. City unemployment in industry is 39 per cent (versus 29 and 22 per cent respectively in Kuala Lumpur and Ipoh), services, 26.4 per cent in George Town (versus 34 Kuala Lumpur and 33 Ipoh), manufacturing, 17 per cent (versus 16, and 15), and transportation, 12 per cent (versus 11, and 6). See SMP, p. 96; and Penang Master Plan, Annex, pp. 104, 118, 129. And see Survey of Unemployment, Table 5, 4, 1.

[3] They identify these assets: highly developed infrastructure, accumulated commercial assets, and the young, highly educated labor force. See Penang Master Plan, Vol. II, Pt. 1, pp. 2-3; and Vol. II, Pt. 2, p. 200.

[4] Penang Master Plan, Vol. II, Pt. 1, p. 27.

TABLE 32

MIDDLE CITY PROFILE: BUTTERWORTH

	District		City	
	Amount	Rank	Amount	Rank
1. TO61POPC[a]	8	109	19	23
2. TO61PROB	0	111	0	28
3. TO61ECFN	0	111	0	28
4. TO61URBN	0	111	19	25
5. TO61TOTL	8	110	19	23
6. 6165POPC	2,937	17	421	23
7. 6165PROB	0	111	0	28
8. 6165ECFN	27,816	4	26,407	2
9. 6165URBN	26,828	3	26,828	5
10. 6165TOTL	30,753	4	26,828	2
11. 6668POPC	1,766	25	575	22
12. 6668PROB	900	8	900	8
13. 6668ECFN	96,124	3	94,106	1
14. 6668URBN	95,581	2	95,581	2
15. 6668TOTL	98,790	3	95,581	2
16. TO65POPC	2,945	27	440	25
17. TO65PROB	0	111	0	28
18. TO65ECFN	27,816	4	26,407	2
19. TO65URBN	26,828	5	26,847	3
20. TO65TOTL	30,761	6	26,847	5
21. TO68POPC	4,721	29	1,015	24
22. TO68PROB	900	37	900	13
23. TO68ECFN	123,940	3	120,513	2
24. TO68URBN	122,409	2	122,428	2
25. TO68TOTL	129,562	3	122,428	2
26. 5760POPN (of 104)	110,836	18	42,405	11
27. 5760MALY (of 104)	54,253	20	10,190	11
28. 5760NONMaly (of 104)	56,583	20	32,215	11
29. 5760POPDensity (of 104)	1,097	3	'65	N.D.
30. 6760POPN (Estimated, City=6767)	212,078	8	50,398	12
31. 5760Percent URBan	38	14		
32. MANufacturing SALes ('67)	134,116	4		
33. 65Revenu+ ExpenLocalAuth	1,991	16	N.D.	N.D.
34. 65R+EXPer Person			N.D.	N.D.
35. 68HOTelRooMs				N.D.
36. JAn70UNEM-ployment			9,799	5 (of 21)
37. 1970 Population	161,605	16	50,398	11

[a]Vari bles 1-25, 32-34 M$000's.   Sources: See Appendix II.

In the urban areas the industry has been divided between that centering on processing industries which tend toward large-scale factory operation, and that
done on a small scale in small shops and in a variety of activities.[1] Small
manufacturing and service establishments dominate George Town and include,
inter alia, food, apparel, furniture, and light engineering. Oddly, industries
commonly associated with large ports, such as shipbuilding and fitting are not
part of Penang's scene,[2] although fisheries are important.[3]

With all of this, George Town not surprisingly ranked a lowly seventh
among cities in West Malaysia in gross sales of its own manufactured products--
the island district ranking ninth in 1967. But Butterworth/Prai ranked fourth,
with $151, 272, 000 in sales (as compared to Kuala Lumpur/Petaling Jaya's com-
bined $1, 064, 242, 000).[4] That meant that the Metropolitan Area's manufactur-
ing production was second in the nation, but only twice Ipoh's.

By contrast, the services and commercial establishment generally is
highly developed and comparatively large in Penang. Bank Negara estimates
that Penang's Commercial Banks had 13.4 per cent of Malaysian loans and
advances, 9.7 per cent of total deposits and 11.6 per cent of offices in 1969.[5]
In 1966 Penang's catering, retail and wholesale establishments accounted for
15.5 per cent of total sales in these businesses in West Malaysia. Penang's
retail sales per capita were 81 per cent of Selangor and Negeri Sembilan's and

---

[1]The large manufacturing and processing enterprises are Eastern Smelting Company, Malayawata Steel Berhad (in P.W. North--the only fully integrated
steel mill in Southeast Asia, producing cast iron and steel in various forms),
Straits Trading (tin smelting) in Butterworth, Prai Sugar (Malaysia's first and
largest sugar refinery with an investment of $22 million, and 320 workers),
Gilani Jute and textile mill, Federal Cables, and Min Ngai Knitting, also on the
Mainland. On the island, industry tends to be lighter, the larger operators
other than Eastern Smelting being Dragon and Pheonix Company, and Malayan
Marine Industries. (See University of Malaya, Department of Geography, "Phys-
ical Survey of Industries in Penang and Province Wellesley" [1966], passim.
See also Percy Philip Courtenay, "Penang: The Economic Geography of a Free
Port," unpublished Ph.D. thesis, University of London, 1961.)

[2]Ship-building materials have been traditionally scarce in Penang. But
Singapore's competition must be the main reason for this.

[3]Partaking of another of Penang's labor problems: inability to attract
laborers to certain jobs--whereby Japanese on contract man much of the tuna
fleet.

[4]See Table 13.

[5]N.B. This was down from 20.3 per cent but 9.4 per cent respectively
in 1961. (Quoted from Penang Master Plan, ibid., Table 45.)

more than twice the national average.[1] The fisheries industry is highly developed, with 1,658 licensed fishing-boats in 1967, and approximately, 1,000 men employed on trawlers alone, organized through government-inspired cooperatives.[2] A special industry in Butterworth should also be mentioned: the jet interceptor base of the Royal Australian Air Force which keeps cordial relations with the community and employs more than 2,000 townspeople.[3] The Australian Community lives on the island in large measure and has been a force, too, for the construction business there.

Robert Nathan observes that "to a large degree, private sector organizations concerned with development in Penang are trade-oriented. These organizations often reflect the points of view of large trading companies, shipping companies, etc."[4] This is considered a grave problem for Penang, in that the entrepôt trade is steadily declining, accumulated savings of Penang merchants are not being invested in developmental enterprises in the State to a fitting degree, and the absence of mass (and economies of agglomeration) in the manufacturing sector is discouraging to potential investors.

Such production patterns are a result of and in turn reinforce the areal sub-system of Penang, the major object of reformation, apart from local government, by the State government since 1969. Despite the large urban conurbation of Penang, and the smallness of the state, agriculture takes up about 68 per cent of the land area: 80 per cent on the mainland, and 50 per cent on the island. About 30 per cent of the island is covered by tropical forests and about 20 per cent cultivated in rubber. Province Wellesley is dominated by cultivated crops, especially padi and rubber. More than 80 per cent of the population, however, live in "gathered" settlements (i.e. not in dispersed villages or isolated small units), with densities ranging from 5,500 persons per square mile in villages to 18,000 in urbanized areas,[5] and so may be expected to be fairly urban in behavior and potential.

---

[1] Department of Statistics, Census of Distributive Trades (Kuala Lumpur: Department of Statistics, 1969), passim.

[2] In 1968 about 6,600 people in Penang were employed in marine fishing and associated industries, with landings grossing $46 million for non-tuna, and $21 million for tuna, according to the Fisheries Division of the Ministry of Agriculture and Cooperatives.

[3] Interview, Khoo Keat Theng, idem.

[4] Penang Master Plan, Vol. II, Pt. 1, pp. 53, 50-8, 144.

[5] Ishak, "Urbanization in Penang State," p. 3; and State of Penang, "Information for the Investor" (June, 1970), fugitive, p. 2.

Penang has inter-state arterial routes north and south passing through (roads) or near (railway) Butterworth, an efficient and frequent 24-hour ferry service between there and George Town, and a ring road around the island. The Butterworth/Prai area has spread from the harbor southeast and northward along the roads, with the industrial developments necessarily clustering around the port and rail (a spur of the main line) facilities, south and westward from the built-up area.

On the island, areal patterns in general are dominated by the City and the island circumference road. The city developed at the north-west corner of the island, pointing at Butterworth, with a fort commanding the harbor entrance, and jetties and commercial houses and banks along Beach street, and government buildings along the north side of the seafront. This colonial commercial and government area passes into a large Chinese and Indian commercial and residential area filling up the broadening triangle of city area towards the island's center, replete with shophouses, kongsi's and temples, the CBD, and fairly narrow streets often demonstrating functional specialization (as with Pitt Street's religious articles manufacturers and sellers--see Figure 29). Light to light-heavy industry is located primarily on the south side of town toward Jelutong, where the oil jetties are to be found. Dense shophouse land-use has spread along the arteries from the city center. To the northwest and west is a green residential belt containing beautiful examples of Malay, Colonial-adapted Malay, and Chinese homes, large schools and clubs, parks, and sporting facilities. Further toward the island's center is the village (middle city) of Ayer Itam, and beyond, Penang Hill served by a funicular. The north-west road leads past newer middle-class housing areas, swimming clubs, and the beaches and beach hotels for which Penang is famous.[1]

The problems of the Penang Metropolitan area's areal sub-system relate mainly to George Town. Butterworth has ample land for new development, large- and small-scaled; and it can be easily molded to future needs. There is room elsewhere on the island for varied development, and there is good infrastructure and a highly educated young population. George Town, on the other hand, has the old and now cramped pattern described above, while being asked to serve a multitude of commercial, governmental, manufacturing, housing, transportation, entertainment, educational and tourism functions at once.[2]

---

[1] For lengthier descriptions, see Courtenay, op. cit., passim; and J. Kuchler, Penang: Kulturlandschaftswandel und Ethnisch-Soziale Struktur Einter Insel Malaysias (Liebeg: Universitat Giessen, 1968), passim.

[2] Population density, of course, is greatest in the old commercial/residen-

Fig. 29.--George Town, Pitt Street

Fig. 30.--George Town, Bishop Street

Thus in 1966 W. D. McTaggart observed:

George Town, despite its lower rate of growth of population in recent years, has expanded enormously in terms of area utilized. This process has been particularly marked since Malaya gained independence in 1957, and the Malayan 'middle class' began to become numerically more important. A stream of suburban migration was started, fed chiefly by Chinese residents from the central parts of the town, but involving all groups and all income levels . . . In this way the town spread out to fill most of the available land between the former centre and Ayer Itam, and it has at the same time extended southwards and north-westwards along the coast line.[1]

This does not mean that housing is plentiful even now, especially at low cost, despite past housing schemes. The Nathan Master Plan of Penang suggests that as many as 10 per cent of the dwelling units in the city may be considered unfit for human habitation.[2] The water-borne sewerage system serves only about 65 per cent of the George Town City area.[3] Likewise, only about two-fifths of the city is zoned,[4] and there is only an incomplete land use survey for city area.[5]

Land circulation in and around George Town depends entirely on the roads. The heaviest traveled in 1964 were those linking the foreign commercial/

---

tial areas of the City--reaching 500 persons per acre in scattered centers of the Chinese town in 1957. The green belt and Ayer Itam sectors recorded the greatest rates of population increase 1947-57 (93 per cent), while the downtown dense sectors increased in population from 12 to 22.3 per cent in the same period. (See Chia Gek Sim, "Green Lane Suburb--A Geographical Study of a New Residential Area in Penang," University of Malaya, Department of Geography, thesis, 1967, Figures 3 and 4.) A 1964 analysis gives 303 as the highest density per acre--in an area immediately inward, from the foreign commercial, banking, and government neighborhoods. (See A. M. Munro, Penang Master Plan [Penang: State of Penang, 1964], "Housing and Density" map.)

[1]In "The Distribution of Ethnic Groups in George Town, Penang," Department of Geography, University of Malaya, 1966, fugitive, p. 5.

[2]With the housing shortfall on the island totalling as much as 30,092 units (three habitable rooms each), and in the mainland urban areas, 12,304. (See Penang Master Plan, Vol. III, pp. 34-43.)

[3]Through 16 pumping stations, whose effluent is discharged without treatment into the channel between the island and the mainland. Elsewhere septic tanks and night soil collectors are in use. (Ibid., p. 113.)

[4]What is zoned are the north waterfront and the green-belt areas from there past the race track and on either side of Green Lane to the Glugor Road. Naturally, the zoning classification breakdown makes careful distinctions among types of detached and semi-detached dwellings, and public institutional land use. There is no zoning nor control in the older downtown area now; that will await replanning of the inner city.

[5]Interview with Enche Ong, George Town, Town Planning Officer, August 26, 1970.

government area at the tip with the inner city, Ayer Itam, and Glugor (to the south), in that order.[1] This problem reflects the basic point-location pattern of the City and island: production facilities are between middle-class residences and the port and ferry; small-scale production for local consumption and associated dwelling (in shophouses) are at the center where a large mass of consumers live and to which the rest must come for all kinds of central business and governmental needs. The airport, which is taking on increasing importance, is on the south road. So are the Malayan Teachers' College, the new University of Penang, and the fisheries institutions. Tourists gravitate to the north beaches or the luxury hotels in and around the CBD.

The focus for the Penang Metropolitan area as a whole, however, is the port. The port of Penang offers facilities for all kinds to foreign freighters and passenger liners, as well as to coastal shippers. When, in 1968, the new Butterworth deep-water wharves were opened, Penang became the equal of any other port in Southeast Asia for the modern handling of general cargo, with competitive turn-around time, aided by completely computerized business arrangements.[2] Traffic[3] flowed through three handling installations: Butterworth and Prai on the mainland, handling most, and Swettenham Pier on the island. Swettenham Pier has two berths for ocean-going ships, and enjoyed 82 per cent occupancy in 1966, with 37 per cent of the cargo going over the side to lighters. Meanwhile, Prai and Butterworth as port sub-areas with five berths and large lighterage have found themselves in competition with one another (owing to the desire of the Penang Port Commission [PPC] to forbid lighter traffic making use of the Permatang Pauh area in the Prai River).[4] But business has not been

---

[1]Motor vehicles and cycles. See Munro, op. cit., "Traffic Density" maps.

[2]It can handle dry, liquid bulk, and general cargo, in addition to palletized and unitized cargo. It is readily convertible to container operations. See Nathan, Penang Master Plan, Vol. II, pp. 1-34.

[3]The 1968 total tonnage (in 000 revenue tons) gave general cargo 1,290.2 imported and 7701. exported. Bulk fuel oils were 696.2/0; ores exported 366.8; bulk vegetable oils were 9.1/17.4; and coal imported 25.6. (Ibid.)

[4]The PPC policy was designed to increase use of the Deep Water Wharves, the debt service on which had come into question because the additional one million tons of general cargo forecast in 1961 for the whole port in 1970 did not materialize. The new wharves were assessed to be economically viable only if one million tons of general cargo were handled annually through the five berths. Because of a shortfall overall in the port of at least .6 million tons, the PPC, by its licensing authority proposed to forbid mainland exports to be handled by lighters for ships in the roads or Butterworth. Strong objections by lighter and jetty

growing: Penang's freight tonnage was almost exactly the same in 1959 as 1967.[1] The non-realization of projected volumes for Penang's port may be directly related to the decline in the entrepôt function of the port, which in turn has happened because of tin-smelting development in South Thailand, Confrontation and the general malaise in Sumatran production of primary products for export, and the erosion of Penang's free-port status whereby trade has apparently been lost to Singapore.[2]

The port of Penang is also the key to Penang's centrality. That is true most completely for the declining international trade. Trade possibilities for the future may certainly exist, however.[3] In Malaysian national terms, Penang's hinterland extends northward through Perlis, and southward, for origin of exports, to a point somewhere not very far south of Ipoh.[4] The Malayan central mountain range will be the eastern boundary until the East-West Highway is completed. Then Kota Baharu and Kuala Trengganu will be approximately 250

---

operators persuaded a special investigative committee to disallow such draconian measures, a rare defeat for the PPC. (See Mohammad Osman bin Samsudin Cassim Committee , Report of the Committee to Study Problem Arising from the Commissioning of the Butterworth Deep Water Wharves [Kuala Lumpur: Government Printer, 1968], p. 8 et passim; Nathan Master Plan, Vol. II, p. 26; and Straits Echo, March 30, 1970, p. 3.)

[1]1959 = 2, 556, 241; 1967 = 2, 504, 028. Entrepôt dollar value declined from $332, 189, 000 to $87, 562, 000 from 1961-1967. (See Chairman of the Penang Branch of the States of Malaya Chamber of Commerce, "Notes on the Economic Situation in the State of Penang" [Engles Report] [Penang: Chamber of Commerce, 1969], p. 5.)

[2]To meet the last problem the PPC has made a concessionary reduction of 36 per cent in consolidated lighterage and handling charges for ready-packed re-export cargo along with free 14-day storage (instead of the previous three) in a bid to recapture some of the entrepôt trade of the past. (Far Eastern Economic Review, February 19, 1970, p. 47.)

[3]Penang's balance of trade with Sumatra in the first half of 1970 was -$77. 2 million. Increasing exports of technological and consumer items is a fair possibility here, in return for the tin, vegetable, spices, and rubber coming from Sumatra. (See Straits Echo, July 30, 1970, p. 12.)

[4]Robert Nathan (Penang Master Plan, Vol. II, pp. 41-45) notes from discussions with freight forwarders and the PPC that the hinterland extends in most cases no farther than Ipoh with exceptions of certain companies with strong commercial ties with Penang. Kampar (25 miles south of Ipoh) is the watershed in railway rates between Penang and Port Swettenham, and that for road traffic appears to be 30 miles south of Ipoh, near Tapah. All this notwithstanding the fact that differential port costs of Penang versus Port Swettenham favor Penang by as much as $1. 93 per ton on rubber and $2. 40 per ton on general cargo imports, with forwarding fees in Penang less as well.

and 150 miles respectively closer to the deep water port of Penang than they are at present to Port Swettenham. Their export business will have to grow enormously, however, for this to make much difference to Penang. Lastly, revived trade with North Sumatra is not to be written off, as in the cases of consumer goods and tourism.[1]

Penang serves northern Perak, Kedah, and Perlis as a high-order retail shopping center as well, and would be expected to be useful to East Coast cities in this manner when the road is completed. The Prai thermal electric generating plant serves the north and also sends power southward. Penang's large manufacturing enterprises operate on a national scale also: Eastern Smelting administers the national tin market, and has purchasing offices in Ipoh, Kampar, and Kuala Lumpur;[2] Malayan Sugar acquires raw sugar by sea and distributes processed sugar nation-wide (40-50 per cent in the northwest, 20 per cent in the Kuala Lumpur area);[3] Malayawata Steel, taking advantage of cheap labor and the transportation system offered by Penang, gets iron ore from Ipoh and Kedah primarily, and sells its products heavily in the Kuala Lumpur area.[4]

Development Policy

The Penang Metropolitan Area as a development policy object has of course been second only to Kuala Lumpur in importance and magnitude of expenditures and expectations over the years. The combination of George Town and Butterworth has attracted both high POPC and PROB expenditures and high ECFN expenditures, although, as a second city region it is a poor second in development policy attention.

Penang traditionally has had these strengths: (1) the City's population and economic mass, efficiency of organization, and expertise; (2) Penang's highly educated and available labor force; and (3) the reliable efficiency and power of the Penang Port Commission, and the large private companies. The general development problems of the State, as viewed by its government and

---

[1] In addition to daily MSA connections, Indonesia's Merpati-Nusantara airline flew 3 roundtrips between Penang and Medan per week in 1972. And the ADB in 1972 approved provision of technical assistance for a feasibility study of a ferry service between Belawan (Medan) and Penang. (ADB Press Release No. 37/72, October 6, 1972.)

[2] Interview with J. McKeown, Managing Director, Eastern Smelting, August 28, 1970.

[3] Interview with Lim Chiu-wah, Malayan Sugar Co., September 9, 1970.

[4] Interview with Ng Yook-thung, Malayawata Steel Co., September 9, 1970.

politicians, are (1) high rate of unemployment, (2) high rate of population increase, and as background, (3) dependence on traditional trading activities, and (4) scarcity of natural resources.[1] From the State's viewpoint, the answers to these local problems are heavy and light-heavy industrial development in combination with a realignment of traditional activities.

From the national viewpoint, the traditional answer to the problems has been medium-paced improvements of infrastructure, provision of welfare services, including hospitals, and approval of establishment of the industrial estates--without special incentives to manufacturers to set up there. With Penang's problems of distance from major peaks of population and consumption, and its traditional dependence on foreign trade, it is not surprising that the Center would not see it as a growth point, especially as Port Swettenham at the far end of the Kelang Valley development corridor appeared to be a better target of opportunity for development when Singapore's competition had to be met.

Thus, George Town received almost all of the mappable development expenditures on the island over the years, with high but decreasing relative amounts of them going to POPC. PROB expenditures held high in the three periods, and ECFN held low, the nadir for these two being 1961-65, and for the first, 1966-68. (See Table 30.) Butterworth, received most of the expenditures in Province Wellesley North also, but received few expenditures before 1961. In the First Malaysia Plan period, by contrast, it began to attract infrastructural investments heavily--for the railroad, Prai Power plant, and port. In the first three years of the FMP Butterworth/Prai received the highest mappable ECFN expenditures for a city in the country, the bulk going for the deep-water wharves, and in loans for industrial construction in the industrial estates.

In FMP planning documents, Penang received specific mention in connection with investments in the Prai thermal power station, road and water supply development, airport and railway improvements, industrial estate location development, and as the location for establishment of the U.N. Regional Center for Science and Mathematics.[2] Direct federal investment in the period went to

---

[1]State of Penang, "Briefing Points on Economic Development in the State of Penang in the 1970s, " fugitive (June 8, 1971), p. 1.

[2]Hence these federal expenditures occurred in 1968: for the state, $5.3 million for low-cost housing; $1.3 million for drainage and irrigation, and $1.2 million for other development works; while in George Town $642,049 for roads (loan), $195,210 for housing (loan); since 1964, $44 million for the Penang telecommunications exchange; and since 1966, $640,286 for coconut replanting and rehabilitation, $700,000 for a padi fertilizer subsidy scheme, $1 million for the

hospitals, sewerage ($1.5 million), power lines ($4.8 million), and as a loan to the Malayawata steel complex ($3.5 million), as well as to the Penang Port Commission. Federal expenditures for the Port during the FMP included $44.3 million in loans for the deep water wharves (to which were added $13 million from PPC reserves), and $1.75 million in grant and $1 million in loan for Weld Quay (to which were added $5.9 million for the ferry terminal from PPC reserves).[1]

The State of Penang, under the Alliance, was accused in the 1969 election campaign by the ultimately successful Gerakan Party of having perpetuated "12 years of misrule" in the state.[2] They meant inattention to Penang's basic state development problems, probably owing to close dependence on the national Alliance establishment. Indeed, development policy under the Alliance to 1969 followed a fairly conservative course.[3] From 1964 the State built new roads in rural areas on the mainland and the island, particularly around Prai and through Butterworth, in the south west of the island, the Southeast corner, and connecting Ayer Itam and Relau.[4] Since 1964, five housing schemes were completed at

---

Bumbong Lima Agricultural School, and $8.7 million for low-cost housing in George Town. (Source: EPU.)

Problems of federal perception of needs and ways of development in Penang have arisen in connection with the Rifle Range Road Flats scheme in Ayer Itam. Eight blocks of 17-storey flats were constructed with the use of a special prefabricated unit factory built on the site, which did not prove to be so economical that the factory could be used for other projects, as had been hoped. Residents were slow to enter the project (two of the eight blocks were filled fully in mid-1970); although near full occupancy seemed to be dependent on distance from the city and its environment--the scheme is inadequately served by bus service, a long way from central city employment, and fronts on an enormous Chinese cemetery. Rent has been seen to be excessive for the poor people for which the scheme was devised. Fifteen per cent of the residents were found unable to settle the $40 rent, including $9 for maintenance, after a short stay, owed partly to the need for $140 advance payment. The scheme seems to have been poorly located and coordinated so far as George Town's housing needs are concerned. It may be compared to the city high-rise low-cost housing scheme in Noordin Street Ghaut, which is located in the middle of Welt Quay and manufacturing employment opportunities, replaces slum dwellings, and is managed efficiently. (See Straits Echo, July 20, 1970, p. 3, and August 20, 1970, p. 13.)

[1] Private communication from Loo Hock-Beng, Assistant Secretary, PPC (January 24, 1969).

[2] See Far Eastern Economic Review, February 2, 1970, p. 35.

[3] Under the Second Malaysia Plan, the State managed these funds: $8.7 million for roads, $9 million for water supplies, $5.6 million for drainage and irrigation, $8.4 million for education, $4.1 million for health, and $2.4 million for electricity development. Straits Times, April 30, 1969, p. 3.

[4] Federal loans for these amounted to $11.4 million, with concentration in

an approximate cost of $3.6 million. [1]

Over the years, the City of George Town proceeded with housing schemes, the first of which had been completed in 1954 in Green Lane. [2] This work was dependent, however, on federal financial assistance in the form of loans. So in 1966 it was disappointing that the federal government turned down applications for financing of the Kedah Road Slum Clearance Scheme and for completion of the Trengganu Road Housing Scheme. [3] In 1968 a scheme for urban renewal was initiated for development of the Prangin Road/Maxwell Road area (the central bus station for private bus lines), with an allocation of $185,000. [4] In addition, the city constructed and reconstructed markets, the Town Hall, public lavatories, fire stations, laborers quarters, roads, Weld Quay, sewers, lighting, and so forth, at an allocation level of around $7.9 million, of which about $4.4 million came from the state and federal governments. [5] Total federal and State expenditures for low-cost housing in Penang State have been $39,830,300, of which $37,300,147 were urban. George Town has spent $7,790,477. [6]

Development policy expectations fulfillment is the most difficult matter to quantify in such a city. In productive terms, the Penang Metropolitan Area did not accomplish what its population and other sub-systems could have been expected to. Most of the indicators of expectation-fulfillment show Penang producing around 10 per cent of national totals, which is small considering her

---

Mak Mandin, Kampong Melayu, Jalan Chain Ferry. (See Department of Information, Penang, Penang Today: A Report on Government Achievements and Progress [Penang: State of Penang, 1969], "Roads, Bridges, and Buildings," p. 14.)

[1] Ibid., "Housing," p. 1.

[2] See Tan Gaik Lan, "The Economics of Low Cost Housing in Penang," Graduate Exercise, Faculty of Economics and Administration, University of Malaya, 1968/9, p. 10.

[3] George Town Planning and Building Department, Annual Report, 1966, p. G-6.

[4] Through 1968 the following allocations were made in the City Budget: Trengganu Road Housing Scheme, $2.98 million (of which $2.6 million federal loan, and $380,000 from George Town's reserves), Kampong Selut Scheme I and II, $1,090,000 ($400,000 federal), Kedah Road Housing Scheme, $4,795,014 ($3,880,000 federal), and other completions amounting to $400,000 in City revenue surpluses. (See George Town Planning and Building Department, Annual Report 1968, p. G-4.)

[5] George Town, City Budget 1968, Loans and Capital Accounts Estimates, Section 46 (1) (d), pp. 39-71.

[6] Nathan, Penang Master Plan, Vol. III, pp. 27-31.

almost 8 per cent of the population. Only in banking and commerce is her proportion of national production commensurate with what her traditions, economies of scale and agglomeration, and skills could be producing as a proportion of national totals, even considering the absence of large-scale immigration in the last decade. Penang's economic depression, unemployment, and low level of recent capital investment must be blamed. For example, Penang State produced 8.7 per cent of Malaysia's Gross Domestic Product in 1969, with, in 1967, 10 per cent of West Malaysia's contractors and subcontractors, and 11.6 per cent of the construction employment.[1] Penang State had over $14.5 million in Post Office Savings Bank deposits in 1968, which was 29 per cent of the national sum.[2] And lastly, the industrial estates on the mainland had the following facilities: Mak Mandin, 140 acres, rent per square foot of 50 cts, quit rent per annum per acre, $431; and Prai, 2,250 acres, rent of 55 cts per square foot, quit rent of $479, and, like Mak Mandin, NEB tariff rates, and a water rate of $1.00 per 1,000 gallons. These figures compare favorably with Kuala Lumpur's Batu Tiga (70 cts, $500 quit rent, $1.20 water rate), but unfavorably with Ipoh's Tasek (35-50 cts, $120 quit rent, $1.20 water rate).[3]

With this development history and sub-system set in mind, the Gerakan Party took over the Penang State Government in 1969, and the Second Malaysia Plan was promulgated in 1971. Both have proposed and, in the case of the former, undertaken significant changes in the scope and direction of national and Penang State development. The State has sought to revive the economy of the state by reordering the pattern of production, by introduction of new programs and development institutions, by itself actively attempting to attract investors to Penang, and by appealing to Penangites' innate sense of superiority and group identity to stir greater efforts in investment and promotion. The SMP, at the same time, speaks avidly of development policy designed to increase the welfare of the urban poor, and to improve employment opportunities. If anything, the SMP is regarded in Penang as too conservative.[4]

What is the new Penang State development strategy? Essentially it is to

---

[1] From 1966 to 1968 1,148 residential units were built in George Town, of which 462 were terraces and 420 were small detached and semi-detached. (See Nathan, Penang Master Plan, Vol. II, Part 1, pp. 27, 47.)

[2] Ibid., Vol. III, p. 182.   [3] MIDF.

[4] Although initial urban policy inputs will go to Kuala Lumpur, Penang hopes that more attention to its problems will be forthcoming under the Second Malaysia Plan. (Interview with Anwar Fazal, idem.)

mobilize all resources in the state and direct them to coordinated productive enterprises with an improved areal and administrative disposition. Five major items are stressed by the State: (1) <u>industrial development</u> in the two old industrial estates (Mak Mandin and Prai), in the new Bagan Serai Complex between them, and in Jalan Rifle Range (a garment factory) and the Taman Free School area (an electronics factory); (2) <u>free trade zones</u>, the three being at Bayan Lepas (221 acres eventually, 50 acres to start, at a cost of $700,000), near the airport where one electronics factory is already in operation--a joint state and private venture, at Prai (61 acres), where oil exploration and a spinning and weaving factory are already approved, and on Pulau Jerejak (261 acres), for specialized industries requiring deep water;[1] (3) <u>agro-based industries:</u> mushrooms, ginger, hogs, poultry, orchids; (4) <u>tourism:</u> development of the North Coast area and the Penang Hill Railway; and (5) <u>fishery development</u>. In addition, special projects such as the master Plan, the Penang Linkage (bridge) Study, the Sungei Prai Basin Drainage and Reclamation Project, extension of Penang airport (from 7,300 feet to 9,600 feet to runway), development of a new township in Province Wellesley North and a satellite town at Bayan Lepas are afoot.[2]

Administrative consolidation has facilitated areal/functional reorganization of the metropolitan area into a pattern which could be instructive for other cities: heavy industries and wood processing ones (to grow up with completion of the East-West Highway), and port facilities concentrate on the mainland. They have appropriate infra-structure, housing and amenities provided in association with the three industrial areas which will be interconnected beyond Butterworth, and linked perfectly with rail, sea, and road connections west and north-south. The mainland otherwise specialized in padi production and provision of increasing amounts of water and electricity to the island, itself, and surrounding areas. Labor intensive industries, particularly production for export in the airport Free Trade zone, locate on the island, but not in the city, as do tourist resort facilities, luxury housing, and agro-industries. In George Town, commerce, consumer manufacturing, low-cost housing, and government-- all needing its concentration of facilities and traditional associations--further converge.

---

[1] Free Trade zones have also been proposed for Subang (Kuala Lumpur), Port Swettenham, and Melaka. (See <u>Straits Times</u>, February 24, 1970, p. 2.; and August 18, 1970, p. 6.

[2] "Briefing Points," pp. 1-5.

Thus the whole--admitttedly small--state becomes organized around an urban core, which itself is bifurcated, and functionally organized to a rarely found degree. This disposition may soon begin to turn the sluggish progress and employment and isolation problems of the area into a new take-off; that is, if the government stays intact.[1] Further positive actions have included the establishment in 1970 of the Penang State Development Corporation which is responsible for agricultural, industrial, commercial, and residential develop- ment in the state and has powers to borrow by the issue of bonds and debentures, to lend to private and public agencies, and to enter into partnerships and joint ventures. Another has been the realignment of traffic flows in the CBD of George Town, the main object of which is to convert 26 two-way streets into one-way streets in order to alleviate congestion in the center of town.[2]

The Penang State government has a competitive and pugnacious attitude towards Kuala Lumpur and the federal government. This so far has produced a new mood and some sense of dynamism in Penang, and seemingly also increased federal attention to the state's development needs. The last piece to fit in the improved city-state structure will be the building of a bridge or other permanent link between the island and the mainland. This is now promised by the federal government, with preliminary investigations as well as increased ferry invest- ment proposed in the Second Malaysia Plan. On the other hand, state planners were not entirely satisfied with the SMP disbursements to Penang. (For exam- ple they were disappointed about low-cost housing development and land reclama- tion.) Yet they received commitments for a new hospital in Butterworth, devel- opment of the new township of Bagan Serai in Province Wellesley North, and $37 million for a new aerodrome in Bayan Lepas.[3] And infrastructural develop-

---

[1]Ironically the only major threat to the Gerakan-Lim Chong-eu govern- ment has come from dissident (and largely non-Penang) elements in the Party itself, whose major complaint, beyond ordinary intra-party fighting, was that the Gerakan was not, in effect, opposing the Alliance enough in Kuala Lumpur. That was hardly a useful criticism, of course, considering the needs of the State, amply demonstrated above, for Federal Government aid and cooperation in State and City development. (See Straits Times, September 28, 1971, pp. 8, 11.) Lim was also criticized for acquiescing to further erosion of Penang's free- port status, and for being arbitrary in the quit rent assessment storm. Neither issue bears on Penang's general development problems or plans.

[2]See State of Penang, "Information for the Investor," 1970, p. 25; and Penang Sunday Gazette, August 30, 1970, p. 2.

[3]See Straits Echo, August 11, 1970, p. 1. In October, 1972, the ADB approved a U.S. $10.9 million loan for Penang airport development. (ADB Press Release No. 40/72, October 19, 1972). This followed (or accompanied) a crisis

ment is heavily supported. [1]

The Development Policy System

In the Penang Metropolitan Area the federal and local governments seem to succeed in knowing where things are, where they want them, and in putting money and administrative power and authority as they like. The key factor in development, then, has been an essential disagreement between the central and state/city powers over the scope and direction of Penang's development. Whereas the (new) state government would have Penang turn into a super-efficient industrial, dormitory, port, and tourism center, the federal government has been inclined to see it as a welfare services and mostly small manufacturing area, in which high unemployment would be expected to persist. [2]

In the Penang of 1966-68, flows and blockages in the Development Policy System centered on Penang's traditional strengths and weaknesses--efficient government and financial flexibility in the public sector, a highly educated and ambitious population, room and opportunities for expansion, on the one hand; and high unemployment, a small consumer market, low private sector capitalization, and central government disdain, on the other. Urban malaise was a large problem, but George Town as a government was keeping up with some of

---

that year in which Thai International withdrew service to Penang because of a switch to use of DC-8's on its Bangkok-Penang-Singapore run--too large for Penang's present runway. After recriminations, the Butterworth Australian air base facilities were accepted for use, however inconvenient, illustrating Penang's determination to further tourism development (up 20 per cent a year in the last six years), and Thai International's appreciation of Penang's drawing power--also the good heartedness of the Malaysian and Royal Australian Air Forces.

[1]The East-West Highway receives $65 million for completion; the Port of Penang receives $18.5 million especially for ferry services; Penang Island receives $23.3 million for water supplies; and the University is allocated $18 million (versus $40 million for University Kebansaan in Kuala Lumpur[!]). And George Town is targeted for $3 million for sewerage system extension, $2 million for roads (versus $6 million for Kuala Lumpur, and $2 million for Ipoh); and Butterworth receives $1 million for acquisition of land and construction of approach roads to its port facilities. (See SMP, pp. 190, 221, 234-35; and Malaysia, 1971 Development Estimates [Kuala Lumpur: Government Printer, 1971], pp. 18, 77, 81, 94.)

[2]With the New Economic Policy, it will be interesting to see whether this significantly changes, and how, too, the East-West Highway is made to affect the area's development and its prospects for a permanent Island-Mainland linkage.

it,[1] and Butterworth booming. Likewise, urbanization was a problem, but not extremely. Unemployment, communal ill-feeling, squatting, and traffic congestion--all symptoms of "over-urbanization"--obtained. Developmental change, as noted, moved in the direction of infrastructural improvements (to the port, railway, industrial estates) which retained for Penang its second rank in Malaysian economic center terms, and on further improvements to Penang's excellent system of public services.

The blockages in Penang's DPS which the Gerakan Party has tried to correct are: (1) inadequate use of laborers highly qualified for modern technical industries; (2) inactive and undynamic local authorities (the Rural District Councils); (3) too outward-looking local capitalists; and (4) a set of poor environmental relationships: inadequate foreign and domestic investment in Penang industries, an underdeveloped agro-industrial hinterland in the state, and insufficient attraction of foreign resort-directed tourists.

The good flows in the system on which the post-1969 government (and the federal government under the SMP) seem to rely for success in their ventures are: (1) good intra-state governmental cooperation and communication; (2) flexibility of the population sub-system as to employment, residence, and style; (3) smooth operations of the port, tourist industry, banks and middle and upper class housing organizations; and (4) continued growth of demand and population in the state's hinterland to the north and south.

What of Penang in national development? It is a lowly second city in a country dominated in development policy by its capital, the Kuala Lumpur Metropolitan area, and is treated accordingly. Penang has the added handicap (or advantage) of a history of independence and arrogance. While the city area has always attracted significant POPC and PROB expenditures, and specific projects (ECFN, especially lately, in Butterworth), it is cramped by the smallness of the country and the limits of development in the modern Malaysian economy. This raises the essential question of scale. Clearly, Penang has attained a scale and sophistication of operation as an urban unit to support almost any kind of technological or heavy industrial function; and as a business and trade center its facilities are underutilized as it is. But little more can be done when the size and disposition of the country can only support one super city. Had Singapore remained in the Federation, Penang and Kuala Lumpur might be rivals for

---

[1] Physical development of the city's public sector (transport, water, health sanitation, education) was good; low-cost housing and productive facilities conditions in the private sector were bad and worsening.

second-city status, and have scaled their activities and aspirations accordingly. Without Singapore, Kuala Lumpur must somewhat artificially tend to "King City" proportions--raising a serious question of the viability of that also. Penang has nowhere to go; but she has the golden opportunity, especially considering her small population growth, to reorganize into a prosperous, happy, and dynamic medium-sized city whose prosperity is based on diverse and coordinated productive enterprises, within a city-state organization designed to get the most out of the area productively, and the most resources coming into the area from the outside.

CHAPTER VIII

CONCLUSION

The subject of this study has been the relationship in Malaysia of national area and of certain units of it, Middle Cities, to national development policy. The findings may be discussed in terms of _pattern_ and of _impact_ of this relationship over time. Pattern concerns where things are and why--specifically policy acts, with the perceptions underlying them. Impact concerns the difference these make on the landscape and the particular matter of policy goal formulation and fulfillment. With respect to the three initial questions of the study, then, one set of findings portrays the macro-area/development policy relationship, and another the micro-area/development policy relationship, stressing the rôle of Middle Cities in nationally defined development. From consideration of patterns and impact at these two scales, conclusions and recommendations are drawn on areal development strategy and further research needs.

Macro-Area and Development Policy

Area has not been a conscious, thoughtful concern in Malaysian development policy. In fact, the Malaysian government has had no systematic means of knowing exactly where it has been doing anything, at a particular moment or over time, in its development policy implementation. The general pattern of area in development policy in Malaysia, however, has had the following elements: (1) an implicit belief that traditional locations of economic activity are correct; (2) a growing concern for economic and social disparities among the Malay and non-Malay halves of the population, especially as associated with an urban/rural dichotomy; and (3) a vague but sufficient perception of "opportunity" development regions, such as the rice bowls (for water control), new land development areas, and, for urban amenities provision, the five major cities.

Through the First Malaysia Plan period, a major discrepancy in areal logic can be seen in the verbal emphasis on raising rural incomes through rural development, while very high urban and urban-related expenditures, both public and private, ensued. Information on where things are has been good; where

245

things have been desired to be has been clear; the problem has come in decisions about where to locate policy activity in the first place so that secondary effects could be achieved. Isolated land development schemes have not significantly raised rural incomes, nor prevented city-ward migration. The relationship between economic sectoral manipulation and areal dynamics has thus been poorly understood. The Malaysians, in the face of this, have exhibited notable flexibility and imagination in development policy conceptualization, especially within the Second Malaysia Plan. With their progressive movement in areal form of activity from concentration on points and lines to greater concern for small regions, integrated regional development and now urban/rural systems, we see perhaps some approach to a model for areal conceptualization in a maturing development policy.

In Malaysian development policy there is a special concern for scale of management unit--perhaps the most important aspect of Area in Policy--which has been reenforced by the differences and distances between East and West Malaysia. It is with administration that areal variation has had its greatest impact on development policy in Malaysia and through administrative innovations that much of the deliberate areal impact is made. Not only do the Borneo States function significantly differently from Malayan ones, but in general areal administrative forms have a fluidity in Malaysia which is striking and which must, in turn, influence the nature of development concepts in the capital. Because, for example, a Rajang Ports Commission can be created to compete (for trade and investment) with the Port of Kuching, the governments of Malaysia and Sarawak have the opportunity, and even obligation, to treat the Rajang River Valley as a region with interdependent parts. Because there is the opportunity to reorganize Penang into a city-state, that area should receive at least better planned attention and development expenditures than if George Town, and Butterworth and the State of Penang were all seen to be competing with one another and, respectively, with Kuala Lumpur, Petaling Jaya, and Selangor. Lastly, it is demonstrable that where units of a certain scale (states or municipalities, for instance) are governed by opposition (to the Alliance) parties, whose <u>raison</u> <u>d'être</u> is apparently to represent the interests of a special group, these governments can effectively attract relatively <u>more</u> development policy attention by making the concept of their areas especially alive (if only by being disagreeable) in the minds of the central policy-makers.[1]

---

[1]The converse, the "pork-barrel," or rewards for personal or political loyalty to the center on the part of local governments or individuals, seems to be minimal in Malaysia.

The impact of development policy on the landscape has been seen to be remarkably widespread in Malaysia. Impacts can be classified according to three kinds of change they engender: new change, continuing change, and countering change. Generally, Malaysian development policy causes far more continuing than new or countering change, which is understandable in the light of its duration and success. New change has been wrought in the physical environment by the control of water for drainage and irrigation, and by the opening of new land. These have increased Malaysia's ability to feed herself and provide agricultural jobs. The impact areas have been the traditional intensive rice growing regions of Northeast and Northwest Malaya on the one hand, and the wild areas of central and south-central Malaya and interior Sabah on the other. The land-development schemes were intended to reverse or diminish the rural-urban migration flow as well, but did not.

Cases of impacts which counter apparent trends in Malaysia are found in the system of Malaysian cities, but are not geographically widespread either. Policy has tended to support certain traditionally magnetic cities (George Town, Melaka, Kuching) beyond their declining relative needs for POPC and PROB investments, while comparatively ignoring and depriving others with greater potential (Johore Baharu) or need (Kota Baharu, Sandakan).

Impacts of development policy which reinforce on-going change, on the other hand, are everywhere. In general, the areal impact of development policy in Malaysia has been one which has supported increasing similarity within the system of units of like scale (for instance cities) but increasing heterogeneity among the sets of units of different types. This is reinforced by the relative homogeneity itself of development policy over districts and cities, as shown in the cluster analyses. However, with industrialization and modernization there is a tendency for a few areas to become increasingly specialized in a small country such as Malaysia. Again, this is reinforced by development policy, which gives particular combinations of expenditures to Kuala Lumpur, Kuching, Penang, Kinta, and so on.

Spectacular economic success has resulted, but associated with discontent among the races related to polarization of systemic conditions among three kinds of generalized areas: cities and towns (Chinese-Indian) versus primary product extraction areas (Indian-Chinese) versus subsistence agricultural areas (Malay). These areas have always and in some ways increasingly been set apart from one another in terms of living conditions, opportunity, mood, and productivity. [1] That Malaysian development policy might now be designed to reverse this by urbanizing the Malay urban-ward migrants is the most startling and interesting notion on the present and future area/development policy relationship in Malaysia. And it will be a case of a counterchange with high import to Malaysia and potentially great significance in general for the evolution of areal development strategy in the Third World.

Middle Cities in National Development

Cities and city-regions occupy a central position in the areal pattern of development and development policy in Malaysia. They not only receive relatively large amounts of funds, but are the loci of administration and those modern sectors on which development ultimately depends. The functions that middle cities, most prominently the dynamic ones, perform in and for national development, and in part as an impact of infrastructure policy, in order of apparent importance in the national view are: (1) production and handling for export; (2) high productivity industrial production for domestic consumption with associated employment; (3) mobilization of financial, administrative, educational and entrepreneurial resources from national and internal sources; (4) housing development administration; (5) provision of high and middle order services to rural areas, increasingly as the agriculture modernizes; (6) providing physical arrangements for convenient provision of welfare and other social policy incremental inputs; (7) cultural modernization; and (8) focusing of political-popular-administrative self-help dynamism.

The impact of urban reality on policy, meanwhile, has been simple. One reason there has been no specifically urban policy until the advent of the Second Malaysia Plan has been that while Malaysia has become comparatively highly urbanized, large urban malaise and self-development problems have not arisen. Therefore programs for popular welfare, such as provision of health services, have been national in scope, and follow fairly closely the distribution of population. Cities until 1970 were regarded simply as those places to which people went from the problem areas, i.e. the subsistence agriculture sector, and as such, were seen as places that should have been able to take care of themselves

---

[1] Of course the tin and rubber areas are "urbanized" to a fair degree, and are therefore more similar to cities than subsistence areas. But they do not enjoy the increasing complexity and density of modern activity that is the crux of development, and cannot. Rural areas are likewise more modern than they used to be, but perhaps also more justifiably discontented.

and their own. The problem, once it was realized, was that they didn't take care of themselves, in the cases of most undynamic cities, and called out for more support from the state and national governments to spur development; and they did not take care of their own Malays in the style enjoyed by urban non-Malays. The reality of these points, and the failure of rural development programs to significantly raise incomes and prospects of Malays combined to yield an urban policy of limited but important scope. With "urban development" (treating malaise) still not an overriding problem, makers of the new policy now see cities as working machines for the modernizing of attitudes and life styles, particularly of the Malays who have migrated from the countryside. The danger of this policy, of course, is that in turning to the cities to change the Malays, the cities, as somewhat delicate productive and social systems with old traditions, may instead be changed, and the policy frustrated at the same time that the national economy is done harm. For example the policy currently concentrates on Kuala Lumpur. It will encourage more Malays to migrate into the city with high expectations of satisfaction. Their inevitable early disappointment, combined with probable physical deterioration of certain neighborhoods can only anger them. At the same time, the non-Malay and already established Malay businessmen will look with disfavor at government intervention in the hitherto free enterprise system of the urban and primary products export sectors of the capital. An alternative strategy is discussed below.

A large variety of development inputs is directed at Middle Cities in Malaysia. Certain generalizations emerge from examination of the nine city areas. First, local governments, including localized semi-autonomous authorities, are key factors in their development policy systems. With better resources, connections, and motivation, they bring more national development activity to their areas (e.g. industrial estates, port development, employment opportunities), and generate their own contributions. When stagnant or depressed, they can be negative forces in city development and in the contributions of the city to national development (e.g. by resisting state take-over, or failing to keep the city attractive for investment--in part the case of Kota Baharu).

Second, export and manufacturing functions of cities accompany, perhaps to a degree generate, dynamism. Cities above the "threshold of dynamism"[1]

---

[1]This Threshold does not neatly correspond to the manufacturing industries thresholds calculated by J. J. O'Callaghan ("Town Sizes," passim) because of the variable significance of primary products processing. He suggests, however, that cities over 90,000 in population represent thresholds for many "national" activities such as skilled manufacturing as for sugar, textiles, chemicals,

seem to have generative powers of self-development and attract large POPC, PROB, and ECFN federal expenditures, though in widely differing balances. Their urban malaise, though absolutely greater like their size, is proportionally less than that of undynamic cities. Most important perhaps, their governments have the impression they can mold their cities to meet modern challenges and opportunities.

Third, geographical factors such as basic location, but especially the superb national transportation systems, seem to perpetuate the dynamism, even in East Malaysia, of the industrial commercial centers. Hence the production sub-systems are depressed in the smaller, less central, and agriculture-oriented cities (Keluang, Sandakan,[1] Kota Baharu, and Alor Setar). And fourth, high urban unemployment is general (though greater in larger cities), but so are centralized and traditional urban land-use patterns--high central densities with mixed manufacturing, commercial, living, government and transportation functions, and shophouse architecture--which give the Development Policy Systems of the cities cores of efficient manufacturing, trade, entertainment, and living facilities, that are adaptable and resilient.

What work well in the middle city Development Policy sub-systems are: (1) the welfare ministries, being centralized, hierarchical, standardized, professional, and in possession through their state networks of good information, including that bearing on political necessity; (2) the semi-autonomous authorities, owing especially to their independent sources of revenue and business functions; (3) opposition governments in cities (Kota Baharu to a degree, Ipoh, Keluang); (4) state-controlled city government, in its own terms, when the city houses the state government (Alor Setar, George Town, excepting Melaka); (5) local transportation and intra-regional connections and circulation; (6) the city-owned electricity and water services, particularly as generators of city revenues; and (7) the civil services generally.

What do not work well are: (1) local government financing, excepting that of four Municipalities; (2) state-city relations, of an integrative and development-imaginative sort (except in Penang, and somewhat in Kuching); (3) pri-

---

and equipment. Middle cities below this figure (below the rank of 6 in 1970 population) but still called dynamic (Kuching, Sandakan, Kota Kinabalu and--taken by itself--Butterworth) are so for special reasons, of which isolated hinterland service and primary products handling are the most obvious.

[1]Here the gigantic timber export business has provided the dynamism. If it declines, large-scale estate agriculture may be a factor for dynamism, with oil production in the future.

vate sector--population sub-system relations (employment, low-cost housing, savings-mobilization); (4) public infra-structural development not managed by authorities (e.g. Rifle Range Road flats Penang, the Sandakan Port, the early stages of the Muda Irrigation project); and (5) control of the areal development of cities.

One may further generalize, referring to Figure One, on the following Malaysian Development Policy System elements. Power flows poorly. Information flows downward well and in statistical form upward well, but upward poorly in the case of qualitative judgements. Projects have the problem of several governments and government departments bearing on them all at once--yielding blockages unless they are strictly locally operated (e.g. George Town sewerage versus its water supply, the former being federally financed and inadequate). System environments vary tremendously in extent and effect on cities in development. States, as funding and containing environments (i.e. not controlled by forces within the city), can be seen as instruments for special mobilization of federal as well as local resources, if they make enough noise (Sarawak, Penang). Large, usually foreign-financed projects create their own (generated) activity regions which then can impinge, not necessarily beneficially, on others (Muda on Alor Setar, Jenga Triangle on Kuantan, East-West north highway eventually on Penang and Kota Baharu).

The production sub-system of Middle Cities is really two sub-sub-systems: the larger-scale western organized and export (from the city) oriented, and the small-scale, family business and service.[1] Both have locational attributes, but the former is the more amenable to general policy and causes fewer internal problems. The government sub-system of cities, with the significant exceptions of the Municipalities other than Melaka, plus Petaling Jaya and, to a degree, Sandakan, have not been significantly and directly involved with national development policy needs or imperatives. They have to struggle to find means to repair malaise and are dependent on their state governments for city development initiatives and direction. Developmental change in city regions is extremely variable, with large differences in rate and direction. Many cities do not develop as effectively or directly in the interests of national development as they might (Kota Baharu, Melaka are slumped, even for undynamic cities; Sandakan has large unfilled needs--for a port, skilled labor, water supply--that hamper its productivity).

---

[1] Cf. Gerald Hickey, remarks at SEADAG Urban Development Seminar, Asia House, New York, July, 1968, with reference to Hue and Saigon. (Report, [New York: Asia Society, 1968], passim.)

Areal Development Strategy

An areal strategy is one by which policy decisions are made about where things ought to be. Policy decisions and the strategies they serve may be classified according to pattern--the underlying concepts of areal form and intent, as discussed above--and according to the kinds of impacts they are intended to have. Such classification is central to the geography of policy. We have seen that Malaysian development policy heavily concentrated on point and line form concepts and Economic-Functional and Population Coverage areal concepts--phasing toward the organization of development policy activity on the basis of larger regional concepts, Problem Area expenditures and innovative development administration. The intended impacts of such policy have been increasing production and productivity and improved circulation in and among the modern sectors of the economy (which happen to be areally clearly delimited), and provision of welfare to large urban and new agricultural opportunities to rural populations. Operational lessons for a Malaysian areal development strategy are as follows:

A. Larger Middle cities work better for developmental change.[1]

B. Among areal administrative possibilities, self-financing, functionally and areally specific, but controlled, semi-public authorities seem to be desirable.

C. Discrepancies between national and local (city) developmental needs and ambitions are political questions. It is an attribute of dynamic centers to acquire political power, often but not necessarily in an opposition role. A central Government ignores this pull or influence of dynamic areas at its peril.

D. But politically derived city development inputs are a very different matter from those for regional, especially rural or road development. Excessive locally inspired demands for the latter may conflict seriously with national needs; although the local and regional benefits and "regional development" advantages could be considerable. Thus regions centered conceptually on cities, and variable and flexible in their functional bounding, may be the most reliable policy targets, even for purely rural expenditures. Policy directed to regions otherwise defined has had many pitfalls, particularly administrative.[2]

---

[1] The size limits of middle cities in this study have been 25,000 to 400,000. But definitional emphasis falls on independence from and middle size by comparison to Kuala Lumpur, which, of course, seems to have functioned excellently in its role as capital and proto "Million City."

[2] Not the least of the pitfalls can be temptation to raise the scale of plan-

E. Large-scale agricultural development projects may best be administered through development authorities devoted to their integrated operation. (Viz. Muda and Kemubu versus Jengka Triangle.) Yet it is hopeless to conceive of a complex project invoking human productivity changes without the modernizing forces, development inputs and throughputs that are best organized in urban environments, such as training, marketing, and engineering, for instance in Alor Setar and Kota Baharu in the coming years. (Thus Jengka is basically for subsistence, albeit newly advantaged, small farming.)

F. Malaysian development policy has traditionally been directed at national economic growth. This has led to the development of the Kuala Lumpur region--assisted strongly by private sector investment (whose only concern, of course, has been economic advantage) and by the absence of Singapore in Malaysia. Pioneer industry and other incentives in a policy which might have sought to counter this trend have not seriously affected such centralization, as the rhetoric of development policy has looked to backward areas ("development regions"), rural versus urban, and general welfare development goals. Nor has the distribution of expenditures in national development policy been greatly changed. It may be very difficult, practically, and even dangerous to reverse this particular trend.

G. On the other hand there is a tendency to continue putting POPC and even PROB expenditures into secondary old established large centers and to ignore newer and smaller ones, even if they are the fastest growing. This seems to inhibit the development of the deprived cities and their regions. Except in magnitude of expenditures, then, the approach to cities in national development has not systematically differentiated between those before and those beyond the "threshold of Dynamism." For those beyond the threshold, increased specialization may dictate special expenditures (like the Penang bridge). For the suffering ones, an explanation for their lack of dynamism must be sought before an expenditure or administrative solution can be applied. The "Growth Pole" literature so far does not supply much helpful guidance here as the cases where strategies suggested by it have been applied also do not. Conceivably, certain cities, because of near-by rivals, or obsolete functions may effectively have to be abandoned, the population assisted to move and not grow. But no Malaysian city really finds itself in this position now. Possibilities for down-

---

ning to elude essential problems. Jane Jacobs evokes someone's observation that often a region is "an area safely larger than the last one to whose problems we found no solution." (In The Death and Life of Great American Cities [New York: Random House, 1961], p. 410.)

grading in the future could be Kangar, Labuan, Mersing, and, as to many past or supposed functions, Melaka.

Of the many problems and discrepancies suggested in these operational conclusions and through the manuscript, the most important one for future Malaysian development is that of differing levels of income and opportunity among rural rich and poor, and urban rich and poor--most significantly as between Malays and non-Malays. The change in development policy strategy to remedy this specific fault has been discussed above, and may be wanting. An alternative approach that is suggested by this study would be to concentrate government attention, especially capital investment and management, in the undynamic cities instead of Kuala Lumpur and/or new towns. These demonstrably need new investments and newly conceived urban development programs. They are not places where unemployment is worst, and therefore with expanding programs and economies, could be better expected to absorb new urban workers and entrepreneurs. They are in a better position to serve the purpose of bringing urban and rural values and styles together; for they primarily have agricultural hinterland and service center functions.

The argument against such an approach is that these urban areas do not have the buying power, the economic mass, to support new urban enterprises, while the Kelang Valley does. In other words it is not by accident that they are undynamic. The answer to that is that judicious capital investments and incentives to dispersion of the growing manufacturing and services sectors should provide many new jobs in an expanding economy, if careful policy attention is paid to possible specialization of the cities, to the workings of their development policy systems, and to transport and other external considerations.[1] A few of the dynamic cities monopolize higher order functions, and are supreme as population agglomerations, and as generators of new economic activity. They can and should be encouraged to grow in size and sophistication. But that does not mean that lower order "non-national" functions, such as manufacturing for immediate consumption and provision of many services including government, cannot be dispersed far farther than they are in Malaysia today--in a program of systematic development of the undynamic cities as areas where new

---

[1] It must be emphasized that this suggestion treats the special problem of Malay deprivation in Malaysia. Investment in undynamic cities as a solution for general economic development or urbanization problems is not necessarily a promising strategy, anywhere else; although "threshold of dynamism" analysis may be useful at a certain stage when a growth center strategy is evolved in countries with severe problems associated with marginal urban migrant populations.

Malay entrepreneurs could be expected to be more effective, and less of a threat to the present system.

Further Research

Comparative examination and classification of areal policy strategies--of differing geographies of policy--would be an important next step in the evolution of this sub-field of geography. But data and methodological constraints may be severe. In this study, it has been possible to fairly exactly determine the areal concepts and intents in policy, because of the simplicity of the policy for development of Malaysia, and the high articulation of it in documents. Macro-areal impacts, too, have been relatively easy to map, with the use of simple machine quantitative analysis. The analytical techniques were more successful, too, because the units of analysis--districts and Middle Cities--were at once easily comparable, and already in use as units of analysis with attendant data sets. It has not been possible to analyze areal patterns of expectations fulfillment with much authority, however. That is because goals are vague; data are of variable quality and availability; and the concept of expectation fulfillment itself is difficult. And for similar reasons the development policy systems of cities have not been elucidated as helpfully as one wished.

Therefore further endeavors might be in two strands. First is an extension of these techniques and questions farther afield in policy studies, so that taxonomies of policy geographies might be developed. Second is an expansion specifically of geographical research on development policy, so that (1) comparative insights may be gained, (2) the micro-analysis of units in policy activity might be perfected, (3) elements of the non-active policy elements, such as expectations fulfillment, might be better integrated into the analysis, and (4) more definite policy recommendations might be proferred.

The more exciting and ultimately important research would combine a study of impacts in and through area and the dynamics of areal organization and working out of policy, with examination of the comparative significance of the exogeneous forces associated with these. Likely candidates for such research are foreign policies of superpowers generally, and defense or foreign assistance policies in particular. The whole arena of non-governmental policy activity, that of large multi-national corporations for example, would be equally challenging, and more interesting, perhaps in that their actual policies and activities are somewhat secret. That makes studying them critical though unfortunately improbable.

So little is known, finally, about the nature and roles of cities in development in Asia and the area/development policy relationship that far more research and methodological development must take place before more than dubious conclusions can be drawn and more than peripheral operational advice yielded. Among this study's limitations have been ones of underdeveloped methodology, as well as incomplete data. Research in political geography might concentrate heavily on the following topics:

A. The areal pattern of past development policy, where more complete operational data may be available, in countries having had varying degrees and types of devotion to the national development cause.

B. Urban settlements as changing sets of loci of development expectations fulfillment, stressing functional and scale types in relation to one another, and inter-systemic relationships.

C. The limits of possible impacts of policies owed to the nature of the larger system(s) into which they are thrust, and aspects of which are out of the policy-maker's control.

D. The distribution and interaction of powers to areal units of administration, stressing interaction of semi-public, public, and private operators in the same fields, and overall coordination.

E. The political factor in explicit and implicit areal policy, particularly the competition of local versus national or regional perceptions and interests, and the roles of particular leaders.

F. Employment, development expenditures, and productivity relationships in cities, as a means to approach the development of a quantitative model of the development policy system.

APPENDIX I

DEVELOPMENT EXPENDITURES TO 1975--

BY BUDGET LINE

TABLE 33

MALAYSIA: GOVERNMENT DEVELOPMENT EXPENDITURES 1949-1968[1]

Development Budget Item	1961 to 1965 No.	FMP No.	Rural -- Urban	Con- cep- tual Area Code	To 1961		1961-1965	
					Area Specific	Total	Area Specific	Total
Judicial	100	101	--	1	107,778	107,778	603,636	603,636
Prime Minister	101	100	--	3	937,721	4,496,881	6,917,665	7,899,660
Statistics	102	102	--	3	140,853	999,769	802,378	802,378
Radio	103	105	U	1	1,802,403	6,395,285	9,800,670	17,203,426
Television	104	106	U	1	---	---	5,269,073	9,361,710
Information	105	107	--	1	108,874	340,527	3,229,989	3,242,822
Min. of Local Gov't	106	108	U	2	19,857,336	38,483,839	3,221,273	5,269,859
Housing	107	109	U	2	4,765,512	42,885,373	13,100,000	49,385,454
Melaka	108	110	U	2	1,070,000	1,070,000	886,500	886,500
George Town	109	111	U	2	28,240,000	28,240,000	9,140,000	9,140,000
Chemistry	110	103	--	3	44,028	44,028	23,041	23,041
Printing	111	104	U	3	117,854	117,854	1,778,494	1,778,494
Prisons	112	114	--	1	1,907,197	2,100,685	5,979,030	5,979,030
Federal Capital	113	112	U	2	17,500,000	17,500,000	14,350,000	14,350,000
Ipoh	--	113	U	2	---	---	---	---
Police	114	115	--	1	52,819,719	54,729,178	45,894,257	87,711,588
Immigration	116	116	--	3	---	---	---	---
Min. of Culture	118	118	--	1	---	---	---	---
Treasury	119	119	--	3	---	41,000,000	---	5,000,000
Customs	120	120	--	3	6,459,928	6,720,238	2,863,796	3,190,336
Min. of Commerce & Industry	121	121	U	3	12,396,075	244,259,193	85,231,897	271,007,378
Education	122	122	--	1	42,742,466	91,475,347	37,375,049	235,029,665
Medical & Health	123	123	--	1	20,007,765	47,448,891	93,288,571	102,174,967
Labour	124	124	--	3	21,209	142,659	373,538	2,203,213
Social Welfare	125	125	U	2	748,595	1,463,925	5,076,370	5,537,227
National & Rural Development	126	126	R	2	466,792	27,758,572	167,029,507	157,345,700
Geological Survey	127	128	--	3	---	4,407,770	195,156	428,459
Min. of Lands & Mines	--	127	--	3	---	---	---	---
Mines	128	129	--	3	---	249,993	---	436,775
Survey	129	130	--	3	1,227,758	7,635,983	3,812,861	5,792,089
Aborigines	130	131	R	2	---	---	---	2,558,298
Forestry	132	132	R	3	2,440,002	3,156,131	953,221	3,209,189
Agriculture	133	133	R	3	1,575,374	32,073,300	2,732,876	23,252,228
Cooperatives	134	134	--	1	---	412,948	---	1,500,054

TABLE 33--Continued

1966-1968		1966-1968 Regions			1949-1968 Total		Per Cent Shortfall 1961-1968[2]
Area Specific	Total	Malaya	Sabah	Sarawak	Area Specific	Total	
3,634,266	3,634,266	2,340,000	1,294,266	---	4,345,680	4,345,680	59.3
---	1,730,328	1,730,328	---	---	7,855,386	14,126,869	50.6
902,540	1,838,722	1,838,722	---	---	1,845,771	3,640,869	26.6
1,401,161	23,741,001	21,215,709	447,698	2,077,594	13,004,234	47,539,712	46.1
128,048	1,172,036	552,036	620,000	---	5,397,121	10,533,746	46.1
1,410,232	1,410,232	1,253,616	87,660	68,956	4,749,095	4,993,581	56.4
4,523,856	4,523,856	2,500,856	---	2,023,000	27,602,465	48,277,554	42.4
39,480,492	88,714,562	87,314,562	---	1,400,000	57,346,004	180,984,389	17.5
---	---	---	---	---	1,956,000	1,956,000	---
1,500,000	1,500,000	1,500,000	---	---	38,880,000	38,880,000	---
284,460	284,460	284,460	---	---	351,529	351,529	---
256,465	931,794	675,329	---	256,465	2,152,813	2,828,142	30.9
4,614,344	5,587,345	1,649,644	757,550	3,180,151	12,500,571	13,667,060	53.9
2,550,000	2,550,000	2,550,000	---	---	34,400,000	34,400,000	26.5
200,000	200,000	200,000	---	---	200,000	200,000	---
2,150,212	61,094,644	48,490,259	4,794,890	7,809,495	100,864,188	203,535,410	36.5
455,948	693,475	639,475	---	---	455,948	639,475	48.1
3,388,817	3,388,817	3,388,817	---	---	3,388,817	3,388,817	49.2
2,192,297	2,192,297	2,192,297	---	---	2,192,297	48,192,297	13.7
7,113	2,677,525	2,677,525	---	---	9,330,837	12,588,099	57.1
63,067,680	238,263,786	204,981,279	4,900,000	28,382,507	160,695,652	753,530,557	18.1
57,991,704	167,273,986	138,839,392	10,123,907	18,310,687	138,109,219	493,778,998	35.2
90,425,198	96,832,409	80,134,104	5,370,824	11,327,481	203,721,534	246,456,267	35.2
197,344	356,528	356,528	---	---	592,091	2,702,400	64.8
1,151,745	1,881,728	1,499,488	191,349	190,891	6,976,710	8,882,880	56.1
---	207,155,885	200,886,905	2,029,112	4,239,868	167,496,299	392,260,157	28.0
199,209	360,862	360,862	---	---	394,365	5,197,091	59.9
311,525	8,241,682	7,305,898	---	935,784	311,525	8,241,682	49.0
---	---	---	---	---	---	686,768	56.3
---	2,087,027	932,349	448,670	706,008	5,040,619	15,515,099	48.9
---	2,817,205	2,817,205	---	---	---	5,375,503	8.6
58,542	2,510,028	1,965,386	1,027	---	3,451,765	8,875,348	43.5
1,012,359	37,751,513	23,341,880	2,442,493	125,529	5,320,609	93,077,041	46.1
---	7,902,628	7,777,369	125,259	---	---	9,815,630	57.4

TABLE 33--Continued

Development Budget Item	1961 to 1965 No.	FMP No.	Rural -- Urban	Con- cep- tual Area Code	To 1961 Area Specific	Total	1961-1965 Area Specific	Total
Drainage & Irrigation	135	135	R	3	19, 431, 183	33, 979, 546	59, 767, 452	78, 082, 194
Fisheries	136	136	R	3	130, 000	4, 774, 337	1, 321, 849	2, 646, 707
Veterinary	137	137	R	3	---	2, 065, 656	4, 083, 910	10, 814, 553
Roads & Bridges	138	138	--	3	62, 567, 490	101, 845, 500	7, 306, 673	334, 484, 976
Water Supplies	139	139	--	1	59, 404, 831	93, 280, 320	50, 750, 248	111, 461, 487
Gov't Buildings	140	140	U	3	25, 224, 525	67, 654, 559	40, 019, 248	41, 876, 485
Public Works Plant	141	141	--	3	270, 072	35, 510, 161	---	80, 008, 194
Postal Services	142	142	--	1	30, 021	1, 468, 410	4, 507, 411	4, 942, 265
Gov't Housing	143	143	U	3	5, 066, 023	85, 426, 067	11, 961, 600	11, 961, 600
Telecommuni- cations	144	144	--	1	11, 361, 157	90, 574, 691	10, 403, 196	102, 206, 123
Railways	145	145	--	3	---	126, 676, 342	5, 650, 000	17, 697, 000
Ports	146	146	U	3	25, 682, 694	30, 167, 314	50, 439, 340	51, 096, 083
Civil Aviation	147	147	U	3	10, 392, 213	21, 980, 253	47, 440, 143	63, 681, 232
Meteorology	148	148	--	3	58, 184	329, 983	32, 690	499, 832
Marine	149	149	--	3	135, 704	6, 696, 100	981, 325	4, 580, 262
External Affairs	150	150	--	3	---	8, 194, 743	---	7, 534, 467
Total					437, 259, 336	1, 416, 339, 129	814, 593, 933	1, 955, 876, 636
Urban Total					152, 863, 230	585, 642, 662	297, 714, 608	552, 535, 448
Rural Total					24, 043, 351	103, 807, 542	235, 888, 815	277, 908, 869
No. 1 (POPC) Total					190, 292, 211	388, 334, 060	267, 101, 130	681, 416, 773
No. 2 (PROB) Total					72, 648, 235	157, 400, 709	212, 803, 650	244, 473, 038
No. 3 (ECFN) Total					174, 318, 890	870, 604, 360	334, 689, 153	1, 029, 986, 825

[1]Some rounded, and not including expenditures of authorities when self-generated.

[2]Economic Planning Unit, "An Interim Report on the Problem of Shortfall Development Estimates, 1961-1968" (Kuala Lumpur: Prime Minister's Office, 1969), fugitive.

TABLE 33--Continued

1966-1968		1966-1968 Regions			1949-1968 Total		Per Cent Shortfall 1961-1968[2]
Area Specific	Total	Malaya	Sabah	Sarawak	Area Specific	Total	
160,613,554	171,602,691	165,695,993	---	3,073,968	239,812,189	283,664,431	19.6
435,770	3,463,747	2,776,475	---	687,272	1,887,619	10,884,791	77.3
---	6,768,481	5,902,606	---	865,875	4,083,910	19,648,690	42.5
95,160,100	161,067,742	77,026,087	40,671,832	43,369,823	165,034,263	597,398,218	24.3
30,228,068	49,285,490	44,096,145	2,040,000	3,149,345	140,383,147	254,027,297	40.9
14,907,489	13,391,028	10,495,624	720,529	2,174,875	80,151,262	122,922,072	46.4
---	4,280,448	1,009,348	2,295,268	975,832	270,072	119,798,803	30.9
351,036	2,524,403	2,242,568	188,365	93,470	4,888,468	8,935,078	59.4
---	3,899,140	3,224,080	675,060	---	17,027,623	101,286,807	45.8
1,336,030	62,211,986	48,180,351	6,546,014	7,485,621	23,100,383	254,992,800	35.2
4,250,000	6,745,000	6,335,000	410,000	---	9,900,000	151,118,342	33.5
44,118,096	44,512,046	42,514,414	34,186	1,963,446	120,240,130	125,775,443	21.0
6,765,953	40,235,547	30,863,745	4,432,892	4,938,910	64,598,309	125,897,032	29.3
1,880	449,479	449,479	---	---	92,754	1,279,294	59.0
661,628	5,056,317	1,840,978	2,139,447	1,075,892	1,778,657	16,332,679	52.5
---	3,452,602	3,452,612	---	---	---	19,181,812	43.9
642,318,048	1,300,297,785	93,788,298	150,888,745			4,932,608,039	
	1,560,192,774				1,894,177,930		1929.50
180,050,985	465,516,524	410,087,122	12,021,714	43,407,688	630,628,323		41.95
						1,603,894,134	(Avg.)
162,120,225	432,069,550	403,386,450	4,472,632	8,992,512	422,052,391	813,784,961	
197,059,116	486,059,243	400,160,010	32,396,433	53,502,800	654,452,457		
						1,556,010,076	
49,406,093	309,343,236	299,269,016	2,220,461	7,853,759	334,857,478	711,216,483	
395,859,952	764,790,295	600,868,759	59,171,404	89,532,185	904,867,995		
						2,665,381,480	

TABLE 34

MALAYSIA: PLANNED GOVERNMENT DEVELOPMENT EXPENDITURES 1971-1975[1]

Development Budget Item	No.	Rural / Urban	Conceptual Area Code	1971-1975				1966-1970
				Malaya	Sabah	Sarawak	Total	Total
Judicial	101	--	1	8,330,000	550,000	740,000	9,620,000	331,428
Prime Minister	100	--	1	26,550,000	100,000	6,000,000	32,650,000	14,807,921
Statistics	102	--	3	---	---	---	---	2,486,750
Radio / Television / Information	103	U	1	47,783,000	27,667,000	8,622,000	84,072,000	56,656,390
Local Gov't	105	U	2	11,153,081	---	---	11,153,081	1,438,115
Housing	112	U	2	193,697,580	---	---	193,697,580	160,023,472
Melaka	109	U	2	1,400,000	---	---	1,400,000	---
George Town	107	U	2	3,000,000	---	---	3,000,000	2,500,000
Chemistry	111		3	1,240,000	610,000	---	1,850,000	741,895
Printing	110	U	3	3,680,000	---	400,000	4,080,000	1,211,202
Prisons	113		1	20,050,000	400,000	1,060,000	21,510,000	6,370,144
Federal Capital	106	U	2	15,040,000	---	---	15,040,000	3,000,000
Ipoh	108	U	2	5,900,000	---	---	5,900,000	---
Police	115		1	181,000,000	30,000,000	39,000,000	250,000,000	140,657,228
Immigration	114		3	1,768,750	75,000	460,000	2,303,730	1,386,636
Culture	104		1	5,510,010	430,000	010	5,940,020	8,662,410
Treasury	117		3	209,350,000	---	---	209,350,000	10,000,000
Customs	118		3	11,930,000	600,000	010	12,530,010	4,101,393
Commerce & Industry	119	U	3	411,208,080	660,000	61,860,000	473,728,080	590,547,819[2]
Education	120		1	370,110,000	36,000,000	42,370,000	448,480,000	303,495,456[2]
Medical & Health	121		1	170,260,000	25,000,010	17,570,010	212,830,020	165,866,202

Labour	122	-	3	5,020,000	250,000	---	5,270,000	632,567
Social Welfare	123	U	2	10,930,000	90,000	480,000	11,500,000	3,822,532
National & Rural Development	124	R	2	925,200,010	1,000,000	3,000,000	929,200,010	428,076,292
Geological Survey	131	-	3	495,000	180,000	---	675,000	432,970
Lands & Mines	126	-	3	132,110,000	---	---	132,110,000	22,635,090
Survey	132	-	3	680,000	200,000	2,530,000	3,410,000	2,465,050[2]
Aborigines	133	R	2	7,380,000	---	---	7,380,000	5,087,464[2]
Forestry	134	R	3	4,360,000	2,000,000	1,500,000	7,860,000	6,055,757
Agriculture	127	R	3	73,460,000	19,000,000	2,670,011	95,130,011	64,999,229
Cooperatives	125	-	1	1,100,000	---	100,000	1,200,000	1,495,962
Drainage & Irrigation	128	R	3	205,000,000	250,000	12,930,000	218,180,000	342,903,147
Fisheries	129	R	3	36,500,000	---	1,610,000	38,110,000	4,804,008
Veterinary	130	R	3	26,350,010	1,000,000	730,000	28,080,010	13,253,115
Roads & Bridges	135	-	3	452,200,010	82,338,000	53,000,000	587,538,010	279,758,958[2]
Water Supplies	136	-	1	127,498,596	---	010	127,498,606	162,510,990
Gov't Buildings	137	U	3	50,360,000	8,090,000	4,800,000	63,250,000	19,061,617
Public Works Plant	138	-	3	31,000,000	---	16,780,000	47,780,000	20,697,444
Postal Service	139	-	1	15,160,010	1,500,000	2,320,000	18,980,010	4,237,042
Gov't Housing	140	U	3	2,500,000	1,000,000	010	3,500,020	4,830,854
Telecommunications	141	-	1	222,950,010	38,440,000	37,000,000	298,390,010	150,658,702
Railways	142	-	3	85,700,030	---	---	85,700,030	15,462,000
Ports	143	U	3	86,500,000	50,200,000	38,590,000	175,290,000	68,312,300
Civil Aviation	144	U	3	49,760,000	45,400,000	12,400,000	107,560,010	118,671,660
Meteorology	145	-	3	3,500,000	---	---	3,500,000	389,449
Marine	146	-	3	61,180,010	3,400,000	1,500,000	66,080,010	2,873,880
External Affairs	147	-	3	10,000,000	---	---	10,000,000	6,000,000[3]

TABLE 34--Continued

Development Budget Item	No.	Rural -- Urban	Conceptual Area Code	1971-1975				1966-1970 Total
				Malaya	Sabah	Sarawak	Total	
Total				4,325,854,187	376,430,010	370,022,061	5,072,306,258	3,224,412,540[3]
Urban Total				892,911,741	133,107,000	127,152,010	1,153,170,771	1,030,075,961
Rural Total				1,278,250,020	23,250,000	22,440,011	1,323,940,031	865,179,012
No. 1 (POPC) Total				1,196,301,626	160,087,010	154,782,030	1,511,170,666	1,015,749,875
No. 2 (PROB) Total				1,173,700,671	1,090,000	3,480,000	1,178,270,671	603,947,875
No. 3 (ECFN) Total				1,955,851,890	215,253,000	211,760,031	2,382,864,921	1,604,714,790[3]

[1] Source: Malaysia, Development Estimates 1971 (Kuala Lumpur: Government Printer, 1970), passim.

[2] A discrepancy in the 1971 Estimates necessitates the use of this figure from Malaysia, Development Estimates 1970 (Kuala Lumpur: Government Printer, 1969), pp. 37, 54, 78.

[3] Approximate.

APPENDIX II

NOTES ON DATA

APPENDIX II

NOTES ON DATA

Notes on Matrices

The basic data for analysis of Policy in Area national patterns comprised three matrices, for state, district, and city areas. With machine calculations, from these were derived the correlation coefficients, factor scores, clusters, and rankings that appear in the earlier tables. Data in the matrices and in Table 33 are subject to the following qualifications:

1. District figures contain those of their contained cities.

2. The 1966-68 (FMP) figures only contain state expenditures when listed in the Federal FMP documents, e.g. for water projects.

3. FMP figures contain expenditures for rural health clinics through 1969.

4. FMP figures contain MIDF loans from the beginning of their existence to April 1970.

5. 1961-65 figures contain FLDA expenditures from their beginning to June, 1963. There are no areal-specific FLDA figures for the FMP period.

6. FMP figures include mapped secondary school construction and higher education projects. There were no area-specific data on primary school construction.

7. Military expenditures are not included.

Data in the matrices came from the following sources:

Federation of Malaya, Estimates of Federal Revenue and Expenditures. Kuala Lumpur: Government Printer, 1959. Pp. 281-305.

_____, Federal Estimates. Kuala Lumpur: Government Printer, 1949-1956. Passim.

_____, Financial Statements. Kuala Lumpur: Government Printer, 1961. Pp. 101-13.

_____, Provisional Development Estimates. Kuala Lumpur: Government Printer, 1961. P. 316, et passim.

_____, Reports of the Drainage and Irrigation Department 1958-1960. Kuala Lumpur: Public Works Department, 1961. Pp. 86-93.

Malaysia, Development Estimates. Kuala Lumpur: Government Printer, 1965, 1970. Pp. 80-96, and 6-121 respectively.

_____, Financial Statements. Kuala Lumpur: Government Printer, 1965. Pp. 315-57.

North Borneo, Annual Reports. Jesselton: Government Printer, 1951-55, 1963. Pp. 106, 197-98, 161-62, 156-58; 54-55, 229-30 for respective years.

_____, Financial Statements. Jesselton: Government Printer, 1956-61. Pp. 29-32, 31-34, 31-36, 33-38, 33-40, 33-40, for respective years.

Sarawak, Report on Development. Kuching: Government Printer, 1956, 1961. Appendix IV, pp. xx-xxxviii, and pp. 9-19, for respective years.

_____, Financial Report. Kuching: Government Printer, 1962, 1963. Pp. 58-70, and 58-71 respectively.

For the state development expenditures columns of the state data matrix, figures were taken from each state's Anggaran Hasil dan Perbelanjaan Biasa bagi Tahun of the following years off the following pages:

Sarawak. 1970, pp. 113-59.

Sabah. 1970, pp. 157-92.

Johore. 1970, pp. 113-23.

Kedah. 1970, pp. 80-85.

Kelantan. 1967, pp. 65-77; 1968, pp. 65-77; 1969, pp. 65-77.

Melaka. 1968, pp. 57-66; 1970, pp. 65-74.

Negeri Sembilan. 1967, pp. 79-92; 1968, pp. 85-96; 1970, pp. 93-106.

Pahang. 1969, pp. 109-18.

Penang. 1966, pp. 76-85; 1969, pp. 84-94.

Perak. 1970, pp. 113-28.

Perlis. 1970, pp. 40-43.

Selangor. 1967, pp. 73-84; 1969, pp. 75-87.

Trengganu. 1967, pp. 125-41; 1968, pp. 125-37; 1969, pp. 123-37.

Notes on Figures

Photographs are by the author.

Figure

2. Report of the Royal Commission of Enquiry to Investigate into the Workings of Local Authorities in West Malaysia (Nahappan). Kuala Lumpur: Government Printer, 1968. Passim.

3. 1971 Population and Housing Census of Malaysia: Field Count Survey. Kuala Lumpur: Department of Statistics, 1971. Passim.

4-5. Same as for Figures 2 and 3.

6. Malaysia, Rubber Statistics Handbook for West Malaysia, 1968. Kuala Lumpur: Department of Statistics, 1968. P. 27.

_____, Survey of Manufacturing Industry in West Malaysia. Kuala Lumpur: Department of Statistics, 1968. Passim.

National Electricity Board, private communication.

Robert Nathan Co., Malaysian Transport Survey. Kuala Lumpur: EPU, 1968. Pp. G-237, 149.

Sabah Electricity Board, private communication.

Sarawak, Report on the Industrial Survey 1962. Kuching: Government Printer, 1964. Passim.

_____, Annual Bulletin of Statistics 1968. Kuching: Department of Statistics, 1968. Pp. 35-36.

7. Malaysia, Atlas Kebangsaan, in draft, 1970.

Malaysia-Singapore Airlines, private communication.

Robert Nathan, Malaysian Transport Survey, plates AIV-1, 4, 6.

Sabah Marine Department, private communication.

Sarawak, Department of Royal Customs and Excise, private communication.

8-19. Same sources as for matrices.

28. Penang State Government.

Notes on Tables

Table
1. From matrices, Federation of Malaya, Report on the Population Census 1957, Kuala Lumpur: Department of Statistics, 1958, passim; Departments of Statistics of Sabah and Sarawak; and Nahappan Report.

2. First Malaysia Plan. Pp. 28-29.

3. Economic Planning Unit.

4. Same as Table 1.

5. Snodgrass, op. cit., p. 7; and Department of Statistics.

6. Malaysia, Mid-Term Review of the First Malaysia Plan, p. 8; and Second Malaysia Plan, pp. 68-71.

7. Development Administration Unit.

8. State Matrix, and see Table 7 footnotes.

9. Same as Table 1, and from Economic Planning Unit.

10. State Matrix.

11-12. Same as Table 1.

13. Same as Table 1, and Federation of Malaya, Report on the 1947 Census, Kuala Lumpur: Government Printer, 1947, passim; and Census of Manufacturing Industries in West Malaysia 1968, Kuala Lumpur: Department of Statistics, 1971, pp. 33-36.

14. Same as Table 1.

15. Same as Tables 1 and 9.

16. Same as Table 1, and Table 9, and Bank Negara Malaysia, Ministry of Labour, Development Administration Unit.

17, 19, 21, 23, 25, 27. Respective city governments, private communications.

18, 20, 22, 24, 26, 28, 30, 32. Same as Table 17.

29. Municipality of George Town, Accounts 1966, 1967, 1968.

31. Robert Nathan, Penang Master Plan. George Town: State of Penang, 1970.

33-34. Same as Table 1.

BIBLIOGRAPHY

BIBLIOGRAPHY

On the Geography of Policy

Adelman, Irma. Practical Approaches to Development Planning: Korea's Second Five Year Plan. Baltimore: John Hopkins Press, 1968.

Adelman, Irma, and Morns, Cynthia Taft. Society, Politics, and Economic Development. Baltimore: Johns Hopkins Press, 1967.

Alonso, William. "Industrial Location and Regional Policy in Economic Development." Working Paper Number 74. Department of City and Regional Planning and Center for Planning and Development Research, University of California at Berkeley, February, 1968. Fugitive.

_____. "Urban and Regional Imbalances in Economic Development." Economic Development and Cultural Change, XVII (October, 1968), 1-14.

Anderson, Nels, ed. Urbanism and Urbanization. Leiden: Bull, 1964.

Bauer, Raymond A., and Gerzen, Kenneth J. The Study of Policy Formation. New York: Free Press, 1968.

Beaujeu-Garnier, Jacqueline, and Chabot, G. Urban Geography. New York: Wiley, 1967.

Berry, B. J. L., ed. City Classification Handbook. New York: Wiley, 1972.

Bhat, L. S. Some Aspects of Regional Planning in India. New Delhi: Indian Statistical Institute, 1963.

Brewis, T. N., and Paquet, G. "A Systematic View of Regional Development and Planning." Urban Studies, IV (January, 1967), 286-92.

Brodbeck, May, ed. Readings in the Philosophy of the Social Sciences. New York: Macmillan, 1968.

Chambre, Henri. L'Aménagement du Territoire en URSS. Paris: Mouton, 1959.

Clarkson, James D. "Ecology and Spatial Analysis." Annals of the Association of American Geographers, LX (December, 1970), 700-716.

Cohen, Saul B. "Toward a Geography of Policy." Economic Geography, XLII (January, 1966), iii.

Cohen, Saul B., and Rosenthal, Lewis D. "A Geographical Model for Political Systems Analysis." Geographical Review, LXI (January, 1971), 5-31.

Cole, John P., and King, C. A. M. Quantitative Geography. London: Wiley, 1968.

Contori, Louis J., and Speigel, Stephen. The International Politics of Regions. Englewood Cliffs: Prentice-Hall, 1970.

Crouch, Winston. Agricultural Cities: Paradoxes in the Politics of a Metropolis. Los Angeles: University of California, Department of Political Science, 1964.

Daland, Robert T., ed. Comparative Urban Research: The Administration and Politics of Cities. Beverly Hills: Sage Publications, 1969.

Dwyer, D. J. The City as a Centre for Change. Hong Kong: Hong Kong University Press, 1972.

Ellis, David O., and Ludwig, Fred J. Systems Philosophy. Englewood Cliffs: Prentice-Hall, 1962.

Esman, Milton J. "The Politics of Development Administration." Approaches to Development: Politics, Administration and Change. Edited by J. D. Montgomery and William Siffin. New York: McGraw-Hill, 1966.

Eulau, Heinze, and Eyestone, Robert. "Policy Maps of City Councils and Policy Outcomes: A Developmental Analysis." The American Political Science Review, LXII (March, 1968), 124-43.

Fesler, James W. Area and Administration. Tuskaloosa: University of Alabama Press, 1949.

Fisher, Jack C. Yugoslavia: A Multinational State. San Francisco: Chandler, 1966.

Foster, C. D., and Smith, J. F. "Allocations of Central Government Budgets over City Regions." Urban Studies, VI (June, 1969), 210-26.

Franck, Thomas M. Why Federations Fail: An Enquiry into the Requisites for Successful Federalism. New York: New York University Press, 1968.

Frankel, Joseph. The Making of Foreign Policy: An Analysis of Decision Making. London: Oxford University Press, 1963.

Freeman, T. W. Geography and Planning. London: Hutchinson, 1964.

_____. Geography and Regional Administration. London: Hutchinson, 1968.

Friedmann, John. "Cities in Social Transformation." Comparative Studies in Society and History, IV (1961-62), 86-103.

_____. Regional Development Policy. Cambridge: MIT Press, 1966.

_____. "Two Concepts of Urbanization: A Comment." Urban Affairs Quarterly, I (June, 1966), 78-84.

Friedmann, John, and Alonso, William. Regional Development and Policy. Cambridge: MIT Press, 1964.

Friedmann, John, and Stohr, Walter. "The Uses of Regional Science: Policy Planning in Chile." Papers of the Regional Science Association, XVI (1966), 207-22.

Ginsburg, Norton S. "Area." International Encyclopedia of the Social Sciences. 2d edition. Vol. I, pp. 398-401.

_____. "The Great City in Southeast Asia." American Journal of Sociology, LX (March, 1955), 455-62.

_____. "Planning the Future of the Asian City." The City as a Center of Change in Asia. Edited by D. J. Dwyer. Hong Kong: Hong Kong University Press, 1972.

_____. "The Regional Concept and Planning Regions." Regional Planning. Edited by the United Nations. New York: United Nations, 1959.

Golay, Frank H. The Philippines: Public Policy and National Economic Development. Ithaca: Cornell University Press, 1961.

Gross, Bertram. The Administration of Economic Development; Principles and Fallacies. New York: United Nations, 1966.

Haar, C.; Higgins, Benjamin; and Rodwin, Lloyd. "Economic and Physical Planning: Coordination in Developing Areas." Journal of the American Institute of Planners, XXIV (January, 1958), 167-73.

Hance, William. Population, Migration, and Urbanization in Africa. New York: Columbia University Press, 1970.

Hanson, Niles M., ed. Growth Centers in Regional Economic Development. New York: Free Press, 1972.

Hartshorne, Richard. "The Functional Approach in Political Geography." Annals of the Association of American Geographers, XL (April, 1950), 95-130.

Harvey, David. Explanation in Geography. New York: St. Martin's Press, 1969.

Hauser, Philip. Handbook for Social Research in Urban Areas. New York: United Nations, 1965.

_____. Urbanization in Latin America. Paris: United Nations, 1961.

Hazelhurst, Leighton W. "The Middle-Range City in India." Asian Survey, VIII (July, 1968), 539-52.

Herrick, Bruce H. Urban Migration and Economic Development in Chile. Cambridge: MIT Press, 1965.

Hicks, Ursula K. Development Finance: Planning and Control. London: Oxford University Press, 1965.

Hirshman, Albert. The Strategy of Economic Development. New Haven: Yale University Press, 1958.

Horvath, Ronald J. "In Search of a Theory of Urbanization: Notes on the Colonial City." East Lakes Geographer: The Pre-Industrial City, V (December, 1969), 69-82.

Hoselitz, Bert F. "Generative and Parasitic Cities." Economic Development and Cultural Change, III (April, 1955), 278-94.

Ilchman, Warren F., and Bhargava, R. C. "Balanced Thought and Economic Growth." Economic Development and Cultural Change, XIV (July, 1966), 385-99.

Ilchman, Warren F., and Uphoff, Norman T. The Political Economy of Change. Berkeley: University of California Press, 1969.

Isard, Walter, and Cumberland, J. H., eds. Regional Economic Planning: Techniques of Analysis. Paris: O. E. C. D., 1960.

Jacobs, Jane. The Death and Life of Great American Cities. New York: Random House, 1961.

Jakobsen, Leo, and Prakash, Ved. "Urbanization and Regional Planning in India." Urban Affairs Quarterly, II (March, 1967), 36-65.

Jayme, Vicente R. "The Mindanao Development Authority: A New Concept in Philippine Economic Development." Philippine Journal of Public Administration, V (October, 1961), 321-39.

Johnson, E. A. J. Market Towns and Spatial Development in India. New Delhi: National Council of Applied Economic Research, 1965.

_____. The Organization of Space in Developing Countries. Cambridge: Harvard University Press, 1970.

Kamerschen, David R. "Further Analysis of Over Urbanization." Economic Development and Cultural Change, XVII (January, 1969), 235-53.

Kaplan, Milton. The New Urban Debate. Washington: United States Agency for International Development, 1968.

Kasperson, Roger, and Menghi, Julian V., eds. The Structure of Political Geography. Chicago: Aldine, 1969.

King, Leslie J. Statistical Analysis in Geography. Englewood Cliffs: Prentice-Hall, 1969.

Kuklinski, Antoni, ed. Growth Poles and Growth Centres in Regional Planning. Hague: Mouton, 1972.

Laird, William E., and Rinehart, James R. "Regional Development in Developing Nations." The Developing Economies, VII (March, 1969), 22-34.

La Palombara, Joseph. Bureaucracy and Political Development. Princeton: Princeton University Press, 1963.

Lasswell, Harold. "Policy Sciences." International Encyclopedia of the Social Sciences. 2d edition. Vol. XII, pp. 181-89.

Lasswell, Harold. "The Policy Sciences of Development." World Politics, XVII (January, 1965), 286-309.

Lerner, Daniel, and Lasswell, Harold, eds. The Policy Sciences. Stanford: Stanford University Press, 1951.

Leven, Charles; Legler, J. B.; and Shapiro, P. An Analytical Framework for Regional Development Policy. Cambridge: MIT Press, 1970.

Lipton, Michael. "Strategy for Agriculture: Urban Bias and Rural Planning." The Crisis in Indian Planning. Edited by Paul Streeten and Michael Lipton. London: Oxford University Press, 1968.

Livingstone, I., ed. Economic Policy for Development. Harmondsworth: Penguin, 1971.

Maass, Arthur. Area and Power. Glencoe: The Free Press, 1959.

Maddick, Henry. Democracy, Decentralization and Development. Bombay: Asia Publishing House, 1963.

McGee, T. G. The Southeast Asian City. New York: Praeger, 1967.

McLoughlin, J. B. Urban and Regional Planning: A Systems Approach. London: Faber and Faber, 1969.

Mennes, L.; Tinbergen, J.; and Waardenburg, J. The Element of Space in Development Planning. Amsterdam: North Holland, 1969.

Mikesell, Marvin. "The Borderlands of Geography as a Social Science." Interdisciplinary Relationships in the Social Sciences. Edited by Musafer and Carolyn W. Sharif. Chicago: Aldine, 1969.

Mobogunji, A. L. "Urbanization in Nigeria--A Constraint on Economic Development." Economic Development and Cultural Change, XIII (April, 1965), 413-38.

Myrdal, Gunnar. Asian Drama. New York: Pantheon, 1968.

Nichols, V. "Growth Poles: An Evaluation of Their Propulsive Effect." Environmental Planning, I (1969).

Olson, Mancur. "Rapid Growth as a Destabilizing Force." Journal of Economic History, XXVII (December, 1963), 529-52.

Osborn, James. Reports of the SEADAG Urban Development Seminar. New York: The Asia Society, 1967-69.

Papenoe, David. "On the Meaning of 'Urban' in Urban Studies." Urban Affairs Quarterly, I (September, 1965), 12-33.

Pederson, Paul O. "Innovation Diffusion within and between National Urban Systems." Geographical Analysis, II (October, 1970), 203-54.

Perloff, Harvey; Dunn, Edgar; Lampard, Eric; and Muth, Richard. Regions, Resources, and Economic Growth. Baltimore: Johns Hopkins University Press, 1960.

Prescott, J. R. V. The Geography of State Policies. London: Hutchinson, 1968.

Reiner, Thomas A. "Subnational and National Planning Decision Criteria." Papers of the Regional Science Association, XIV (1964), 107-36.

Riggs, Fred W. "Economic Development and Local Administration: A Study in Circular Causation." Philippine Journal of Public Administration, III (January, 1959), 86-146.

Rivkin, Malcolm. Area Development for National Growth. New York: Praeger, 1965.

Robock, Stefan. Brazil's Developing Northeast. Washington: Brookings, 1963.

Rodwin, Lloyd. "Metropolitan Policy for Developing Areas." Regional Economic Planning: Techniques of Analysis. Edited by Walter Isard and J. H. Cumberland. Paris: O.E.C.D., 1960.

_____. Nations and Cities: A Comparison of Strategies for Urban Growth. New York: Houghton Mifflin, 1970.

Roth, Irwin. "Industrial Location and Indian Government Policy." Asian Survey, X (May, 1970), 383-96.

Rubin, Jerrold, and Friedman, H. P. "A Cluster Analysis System and Taxonomy System for Grouping and Classifying Data." Journal of Theoretical Biology, XV (1967), 103-44.

Rummel, R. J. Applied Factor Analysis. Evanston: Northwestern University Press, 1970.

Samonte, Abelardo. "Decentralization and Development: Some Basic Issues." Philippine Journal of Public Administration, XI (April, 1967), 128-37.

Schmandt, Henry J. "Toward Comparability in Metropolitan Research." Comparative Research in Community Politics. Edited by Thomas R. Dye. Athens: University of Georgia Press, 1967.

Schurmann, H. Franz. Ideology and Organization in Communist China. Berkeley: University of California Press, 1966.

Soja, Edward. The Geography of Modernization in Kenya. Syracuse: Syracuse University Press, 1968.

Solo, Robert A. Economic Organizations and Social Systems. New York: Bobbs-Merrill, 1967.

Stanford Research Institute. Costs of Urban Infrastructure for Industry as Related to City Size in Developing Countries: Indian Case Studies. Menlo Park: Stanford Research Institute, 1968.

Tyron, R. C. "Domain Sampling Formulation of Cluster and Factor Analysis." Psychometrika, XXIV, 113-35.

United Nations. Decentralization for National and Local Development. New York: United Nations, 1962.

United Nations. Handbook of Public Administration. New York: United Nations, 1961.

_____. Regional Planning. New York: United Nations, 1959.

_____. Urbanization: Development Policies and Planning. New York: United Nations, 1968.

United States Natural Resources Committee. Regional Factors in National Planning. Washington: United States Government Printing Office, 1945.

Waardenburg, J. G. "Space in Development Programming." Papers of the Regional Science Association, XVIII (1966), 91-110.

Ward, Benjamin. Greek Regional Development. Athens: Center of Economic Research, n.d.

Whitney, J. B. R. China: Area, Administration and Nation Building. Research Paper No. 123. Chicago: University of Chicago, Department of Geography, 1970.

Whittlesey, Derwent. "The Inpress of Effective Central Authority upon the Landscape." Annals of the Association of American Geographers, XXV (April, 1935), 85-97.

Wiles, P. J. D. The Political Economy of Communism. Cambridge: Harvard University Press, 1962.

Williamson, Jeffery G. "Regional Inequality and the Process of National Development." Economic Development and Cultural Change, XIII (July, 1965), 3-84.

Withington, W. A. "The Intermediate City in the Developing World of Southeast Asia." SEADAG Discussion Paper. New York: The Asia Society, 1970.

Wohlstetter, Albert. "Illusions of Distance." Foreign Affairs, XLVI (January, 1968), 242-55.

Wu Yuan-li. The Spatial Economy of Communist China. New York: Praeger, 1967.

Young, Oran. "Professor Russett: Industrious Tailor to a Naked Emperor." World Politics, XXI (April, 1969), 486-511.

On Malaysia

Allen, D. F. Report of the Major Ports of Malaya. Kuala Lumpur: Government Printer, 1951.

Allen, G. C., and Donnithorne, Audrey. Western Enterprise in Indonesia and Malaya. London: Allen and Unwin, 1954.

Allen, Richard. Malaysia: Prospect and Retrospect. London: Oxford University Press, 1968.

Baker, M. H. Sabah: The First Ten Years. Singapore: University of Singapore, Department of History, 1965.

Barber, Noel. The War of the Running Dogs: The Malayan Emergency 1948-1960. London: William Collins, 1971.

Bastin, John, and Winks, R. W., eds. Malaysia: Selected Historical Readings. London: Oxford University Press, 1966.

Beyer, John C. "Regional Inequalities and Economic Growth in Malaysia." Yorkshire Bulletin of Economic and Social Research, XXI (May, 1969), 17-30.

Bilainkin, George. Hail Penang! London: Sampson Low, Marston, 1932.

Borneo Bulletin, 1968-1970.

Borneo Housing Mortgage Finance. Annual Report. Kota Kinabalu: BHMF, 1969.

Broek, Jan O. M. "Trade and Trade Centers of Sarawak." Department of Geography, University of Minnesota, n.d. Fugitive.

Caldwell, J. C. "New and Old Malaya: Aspects of Demographic Change in a High Growth Rate Multi-Racial Society." Population Review, VIII (July, 1964), 29-36.

Chatfield, Godfrey. Sabah: A General Geography. London: University of London Press, 1965.

Chia Gek-sim. "Green Lane Suburb--A Geographical Study of a New Residential Area in Penang." Thesis, University of Malaya, Department of Geography, 1967.

Cole, Fay-Cooper. The Peoples of Malaysia. Princeton: Van Nostrand, 1945.

Comber, L. F. Chinese Secret Societies in Malaya. New York: Augustin, 1959.

Commission of Enquiry to Enquire into the Affairs of the City Council of George Town, Penang. Part One of Report of the Commission. Alor Setar: Government Printer, 1967.

Concannon, T. A. L. "Town Planning in Malaya." Journal of the Town Planning Institute, XLIV (1958), 241-44.

Courtenay, Percy Philip. A Geography of Trade and Development in Malaya. London: Bell, 1972.

_____. "Penang: The Economic Geography of a Free Port." Unpublished PhD Thesis, University of London, 1961.

Cowan, C. D. Nineteenth Century Malaya. London: Oxford University Press, 1961.

Crosson, Pierre. "Planning Data and Information Flows in Malaysia." Philippine Economic Journal, IV (1965), 226-48.

Crosson, Pierre. Economic Growth in Malaysia. Jerusalem: Israel Programme for Scientific Translation, 1965.

Douglas, J. N. H. "Political Geography and Administrative Areas." Essays in Political Geography. Edited by C. A. Fisher. London: Methuen, 1968.

Drake, P. J. Financial Development in Malaya and Singapore. Canberra: Australian National University Press, 1969.

Edwards, C. T. Public Finance in Malaya and Singapore. Canberra: Australian National University Press, 1970.

Elliston, G. P. The Marine Fishing Industry of Sarawak. Hull: University of Hull, Department of Geography, 1967.

Emerson, Rupert. Malaysia: A Study in Direct and Indirect Rule. Kuala Lumpur: University of Malaya Press, 1964 (first published in 1937).

Esman, M. J. Administration and Development in Malaysia. Ithaca: Cornell University Press, 1972.

Far Eastern Economic Review. Yearbook 1968. Hong Kong: Far Eastern Economic Review, 1969.

Federation of Malaya. Draft Development Plan. Kuala Lumpur: Government Printer, 1950.

_____. Financial Statements. Kuala Lumpur: Government Printer, 1948-1963.

_____. Interim Review of Development in Malaya under the Second Five-Year Plan. Kuala Lumpur: Government Printer, 1963.

_____. The Municipal Ordinance. Kuala Lumpur: Government Printer, 1959.

_____. Progress Report on the Development Plan for the Federation of Malaya 1950-1952. Kuala Lumpur: Government Printer, 1953.

_____. Report of the Commission of Enquiry, North Borneo, and Sarawak (Cobbold Commission). Kuala Lumpur: Government Printer, 1962.

_____. Report on Economic Planning in the Federation of Malaya, 1956. Kuala Lumpur: Government Printer, 1957.

_____. A Report on the 1947 Census of Population. Kuala Lumpur: Government Printer, 1947.

_____. Report on the 1957 Census of Population. Kuala Lumpur: Government Printer, 1958.

_____. Second Five Year Plan. Kuala Lumpur: Government Printer, 1961.

Federation of Malaya, Drainage and Irrigation Department. Reports 1958-63, 1961-63, (then Malaysia) 1964-66. Kuala Lumpur: Public Works Department, 1960-1966.

Fisher, C. A. "Malaysia: A Study in the Political Geography of Decolonization." Essays in Political Geography. Edited by C. A. Fisher. London: Methuen, 1968.

_____. "The Problem of Malayan Unity in Its Geographical Setting." Geographical Essays on British Tropical Lands. Edited by C. A. Fisher and R. W. Steel. London: George Philip, 1956.

_____. "The Railway Geography of British Malaya" The Scottish Geographical Magazine, LXIV (1948), 123-36.

_____. South-East Asia. London: Methuen, 1964.

Fryer, D. W. "National Development Plans and the Budget: Public Sector Resources for Urbanization." SEADAG Discussion Paper. New York: The Asia Society, 1969.

George Town City Council. Accounts 1966-1969. George Town: George Town, 1967-1970.

_____. Penang Past and Present. George Town: George Town, 1966.

George Town City Council, Planning and Building Department. Annual Reports 1966-1969. George Town: George Town, 1966-1969.

Ginsburg, N. S., and Roberts, C. F. Malaya. Seattle: University of Washington Press, 1958.

Glaskin, G. M. The Beach of Passionate Love. London: Barrie and Rockliff, 1961.

Gosling, L. A. Peter. "The Location of 'Problem' Areas in Rural Malaya." Essays in Geography and National Development. Edited by N. S. Ginsburg. Research Paper No. 62. Chicago: University of Chicago, Department of Geography, 1960.

Gullick, S. M. Malaya. London: Ernest Benn, 1963.

Guyot, James. "Creeping Urbanism and Political Development in Malaysia." Chapel Hill: Comparative Urban Studies Group, 1967. Fugitive.

Hall, D. G. B. A History of South-East Asia. London: Methuen, 1964.

Hamzah Sendut. "The Patterns of Urbanization in Malaya." Journal of Tropical Geography, XVI (1962), 114-30.

_____. "The Resettlement Villages in Malaya." Geography, XLVII (January, 1962), 41-46.

Hawkins, Gerald. "First Steps in Malayan Local Government." Pacific Affairs, XXVI (July, 1953), 155-58.

Haynes, Kingsley E. "Growth Poles and the Hierarchy of Cities: Some References to Malaysia." SEADAG Discussion Paper. New York: The Asia Society, 1970.

Hicklin, Hugh. Sarawak and Its Government. Kuching: Government Printer, 1954.

Hughes, William. "Social Benefits through Improved Transport in Malaya."
Transport and National Goals. Edited by Edwin T. Hoefele. Washington:
Brookings, 1969.

Hunting Technical Services - Binnie and Partners. Johore Tenggara Regional
Master Plan. Kuala Lumpur: Hunting/Binnie, 1971.

Ibrahim, Mohd. "Role of Agency Houses in the Marketing of Consumer Products in Malaya." Graduation Exercise, Faculty of Economics and Administration, University of Malaya, 1966/7.

International Bank for Reconstruction and Development. Current Economic
Position and Prospects of Malaysia. Washington: IBRD, 1968.

_____. The Economic Development of Malaya. Baltimore: The Johns Hop-
kins University Press, 1955.

Ipoh Municipal Council. Annual Reports 1966, 1967, 1968. Ipoh: Municipal
Council, 1966-68.

_____. Ipoh: The Town that Tin Built. Ipoh: Phoenix Publications, 1962.

Irwin, Graham. Nineteenth-Century Borneo: A Study in Diplomatic Rivalry.
Singapore: Donald Moore, 1955.

Ishak, Mohd. Ariff. "Urbanization in Penang State, with Special Reference to
Problems of Physical Planning." George Town: Government of Penang,
1970.

Jackson, James C. Sarawak. London: University of London Press, 1968.

Jones, S. W. Public Administration in Malaya. London: Royal Institute of
International Affairs, 1952.

Kuching Municipality. Annual Reports, 1966-1968. Kuching: Municipality,
1967-69.

Kuching Port Authority. Report and Accounts for the Year 1966. Kuching:
Port Authority, 1967.

Kuchler, J. Penang: Kulturlandschaftswandel und Ethnisch-Soziale Struktur
Einter Insel Malaysias. Liebeg: Universitat Giessen, 1968.

Lee Yong-leng. North Borneo (Sabah): A Study in Settlement Geography. Singapore: Eastern Universities Press, 1965.

_____. Population and Settlement in Sarawak. Singapore: Asia-Pacific
Press, 1970.

Leinbach, Thomas. "Transportation and Modernization in Malaya." Unpublished PhD Thesis, Department of Geography, Pennsylvania State University, 1971.

Lim, C. "Geographical Influences in Planning for Urban Penang." Unpublished
M.A. Thesis, University of Malaya (Singapore), Department of Geography, 1955.

Lim Chang-yah. Economic Development of Modern Malaya. Kuala Lumpur: Oxford University Press, 1967.

Lim Heng-boon. "Federal-State Financial Relations in West Malaysia." Graduation Exercise, Faculty of Economics and Administration, University of Malaya, 1968/9.

Lim Tay-boh. Problems of the Malayan Economy. Singapore: Donald Moore, 1960.

The Malay Mail (Kuala Lumpur), 1965-1972.

_____. Malaysia Year Book, 1971. Kuala Lumpur: Straits Times Press, 1971.

Malaya Economic Secretariat. A Plan of Development for Malaya 1956-1960. Kuala Lumpur: Government Printer, 1956.

Malayan Agreement Concluded between the United Kingdom of Great Britain and North Ireland, the Federation of Malaya, North Borneo, Sarawak, and Singapore. Command Paper 2094. London: Her Majesty's Stationery Office, July, 1963.

Malaysia. Budget Summary of Federal Government Expenditures, 1969. Kuala Lumpur: Government Printer, 1969.

_____. Development Estimates 1964-1972. Kuala Lumpur: Government Printer, 1963-1971.

_____. The Expenditure Budget of the Federal Government 1971. Kuala Lumpur: Government Printer, 1971.

_____. Federal Constitution. Kuala Lumpur: Government Printer, 1970.

_____. Financial Statements 1965. Kuala Lumpur: Government Printer, 1967.

_____. First Malaysia Plan 1966-1970. Kuala Lumpur: Government Printer, 1965.

_____. Mid-Term Review of the First Malaysia Plan. Kuala Lumpur: Government Printer, 1969.

_____. A New Industrial Development Strategy. Kuala Lumpur: Government Printer, 1969.

_____. Report of the Inter-Governmental Committee 1962. Kuala Lumpur: Government Printer, 1963.

_____. Report of the Royal Commission of Enquiry to Investigate into the Workings of Local Authorities in West Malaysia (Nahappan Report). Kuala Lumpur: Government Printer, 1968.

_____. Report of the Royal Commission on the Revision of Salaries and Conditions of Service in the Public Service (Suffian Report). Kuala Lumpur: Government Printer, 1967.

Malaysia. The Second Malaysia Plan. Kuala Lumpur: Government Printer, 1971.

_____. "Treasury Memorandum on the Development Estimates of the Government of Malaysia, 1971." Kuala Lumpur: Treasury, 1971.

Malaysia, Department of Statistics. Census of Distributive Trades. Kuala Lumpur: Department of Statistics, 1966.

_____. Census of Manufacturing Industries in West Malaysia 1968. Kuala Lumpur: Department of Statistics, 1971.

_____. 1971 Population and Housing Census of Malaysia, Field Count Summary. Kuala Lumpur: Department of Statistics, 1971.

_____. Oil Palm Coconut and Tea Statistics. Kuala Lumpur: Department of Statistics, 1968.

_____. Report on Employment, Unemployment, and Underemployment. Kuala Lumpur: Department of Statistics, 1962.

_____. Rubber Statistics Handbook. Kuala Lumpur: Department of Statistics, 1968.

_____. Socio-Economic Survey of Households - West Malaysia. Kuala Lumpur: Department of Statistics, 1970.

_____. Survey of the Manufacturing Industry in West Malaysia. Kuala Lumpur: Department of Statistics, 1965 and 1968.

_____. Urban Conurbations - Population and Households in Ten Gazetted Towns and Their Adjoining Built-up Areas. Kuala Lumpur: Department of Statistics, 1971.

Malaysia, Development Administration Unit. Organization of the Government of Malaysia. Kuala Lumpur: Government Printer, 1967.

_____. "The Problem of Shortfalls." 1969. (Mimeographed.) Fugitive.

_____. "State Expenditures: An Analysis." 1969. (Mimeographed.) Fugitive.

Malaysia, Economic Planning Unit. Land Capability Classification Reports. Kuala Lumpur: Economic Planning Unit, 1969-1971.

_____. "Rail Origin and Destination Study." 1967. (Mimeographed.) Fugitive.

_____. "Some Data on Distribution of Economic Activity in West Malaysia." N.d. (Mimeographed.) Fugitive.

Malaysia, Federal Industrial Development Authority. An Industrial Potentiality Study of Kedah and Perlis. Kuala Lumpur: FIDA, 1968.

Malaysia, Federal Land Development Authority. "Land Settlement in Malaysia under the FLDA." 1966. (Mimeographed.) Fugitive.

Malaysia, Industrial Development Finance Ltd. Annual Report and Accounts 1960-70. Kuala Lumpur: MIDFL, 1961-1971.

Malaysia, National Family Planning Board. "Report on the West Malaysia Family Survey 1966/7." 1968. Fugitive.

Malaysia, Rubber Industry Replanting Fund. Report on Operations for the Year 1967. Kuala Lumpur: Government Printer, 1968.

McGee, T. G. "Down but Not Out." Far Eastern Economic Review, June 5, 1969, pp. 566-68.

_____. "The Malayan Elections of 1959: A Study in Political Geography." Journal of Tropical Geography, XXII (October, 1962), 70-99.

McHale, T. R. Rubber and the Malaysian Economy. Kuala Lumpur: Malaysian Publishing, 1966.

McTaggart, W. D. "The Distribution of Ethnic Groups in George Town, Penang." University of Malaya, Department of Geography, 1966. (Mimeographed.) Fugitive.

_____. "The Grading of Social Areas in George Town, Penang." Journal of Tropical Geography, XXVI (December, 1966), 40-46.

_____. "Industrialization in West Malaysia 1968." Occasional Paper No. 2. Center for Asian Studies, Arizona State University, 1972.

_____. "Malaya and Its Geographical Interpretation: A Review Article." Malayan Economic Review, IX (1964), 83-91.

_____. "The May 1969 Disturbances in Malaysia: Impact of a Conflict on Developmental Patterns." 1972. Fugitive.

Means, Gordon. "Eastern Malaysia: The Politics of Federalism." Asian Survey, VIII (April, 1968), 289-308.

_____. Malaysian Politics. New York: New York University Press, 1970.

Milne, R. S. Government and Politics in Malaysia. Berkeley: University of California Press, 1967.

_____. "Political Parties in Sarawak and Sabah." Journal of Southeast Asian History, III (September, 1965), 104-17.

Milne, R. S., and Ratnam, K. J. "Patterns and Peculiarities of Voting in Sabah." Asian Survey, IX (May, 1969), 373-81.

Morgan, James. "Malaysia: Bracing for a Long Haul." Far Eastern Economic Review, October 9, 1971, p. 18.

Muda Agricultural Development Authority. "Proposal: Organization and Management Policy." Alor Setar: MADA, 1970.

Munro, A. M. Penang Master Plan. George Town: State of Penang, 1964.

Nathan, Robert, and Associates. Penang Master Plan. George Town: State of Penang, 1971.

_____. Transport Development in Malaysia (Malaysia Transport Study). Kuala Lumpur: Prime Minister's Office, 1968.

Ness, Gayl. Bureaucracy and Rural Development in Malaysia. Berkeley: University of California Press, 1967.

New Nation (Singapore), 1971.

Nicholls, J. "Keluang Town Plan: Report on Survey Description of Plan." Johore Baharu: Town and Country Planning Department, State of Johore, 1958.

North Borneo. Reconstruction and Development Plan 1948-1955. Jesselton: Government Printer, 1948.

Ongkili, J. P. The Borneo Response to Malaysia 1961-1963. Singapore: Donald Moore, 1966.

Ooi Jin-bee. Land, People and Economy in Malaya. London: Longmans, 1963.

Osborn, James. "Field Observations on Urban Policy, Research, and Data Availability in Southeast Asia." New York: The Asia Society, 1968.

Osborne, Milton E. Singapore and Malaysia. Data Paper Number 53. Ithaca: Cornell Southeast Asia Program, 1964.

Osman, Mohd. bin Samsudin Cassim (Committee). Report of the Committee to Study Problems Arising from the Commissioning of the Butterworth Deep Water Wharves. Kuala Lumpur: Government Printer, 1968.

Pahang Tenggara Regional Masterplanning Study (J. J. O'Callaghan). "Apparent Cost Differences in Manufacturing Activities in Different States in West Malaysia." 1971. (Mimeographed.) Fugitive.

_____. "Town Sizes and Thresholds for Manufacturing Activities in West Malaysia." 1971. (Mimeographed.) Fugitive.

Penang. "Briefing Points on Economic Development in the State of Penang in the 1970's." 1971. (Mimeographed.) Fugitive.

_____. "Information for the Investor." 1970. Fugitive.

_____. Penang Today: A Report on Government Achievements and Progress. George Town: Department of Information of the State of Penang, 1969.

Penang Port Commission. Thirteenth Annual Administration Report and Accounts. George Town: PPC, 1968.

Perak River Hydro-Electric Power Company, Ltd. Report and Accounts 1969. London, 1969.

Purcell, Victor. The Chinese in Malaya. London: Oxford University Press, 1948.

Purcell, Victor. The Memoires of a Malayan Official. London: Cassell, 1965.

Rabushka, Alvin. "Racial Stereotypes in Malaya." Asian Survey, XI (July, 1971), 709-16.

Ratnam, K. J., and Milne, R. S. The Malayan Parliamentary Election of 1964. Singapore: University of Malaya Press, 1967.

Razak, Tun Abdul. Budget Address. Kuala Lumpur: Government Printer, 1970.

Reece, Bob. "Alliance Troubles." Far Eastern Economic Review, June 18, 1970, pp. 7-8.

Reinhardt, J. M. "Administrative Policy and Practice in Sarawak: Continuity and Change under the Brookes." Journal of Asian Studies, XXIX (August, 1970), 851-62.

Runciman, Sir Steven. The White Rajahs: A History of Sarawak from 1841 to 1946. Cambridge: Cambridge University Press, 1960.

Sabah. Annual Bulletin of Statistics 1969. Kota Kinabalu: Department of Statistics, 1969.

_____. Sabah since Malaysia 1963-1968. Kota Kinabalu: Government Printer, 1969.

_____. Survey of Housing Structures, Housing Units and Households in Urban Areas, Sabah. Kota Kinabalu: Department of Statistics, 1968.

Sadka, Emily. The Protected Malay States 1874-1895. Singapore: University of Malaya Press, 1968.

Sandakan Chamber of Commerce. Newsletter. 1970.

Sandhu, K. S. "Emergency Resettlement in Malaya." Journal of Tropical Geography, XVIII (August, 1964), 157-83.

Sarawak. Annual Bulletin of Statistics 1968. Kuching: Department of Statistics, 1968.

_____. Annual Report, 1962. Kuching: Government Printer, 1963.

_____. Financial Statements 1968. Kuching: Government Printer, 1969.

_____. Kuching Water Board Annual Report 1967. Kuching: Government Printer, 1968.

_____. Local Authority Approved Estimates of Revenue and Expenditure for the Year 1969. Kuching: Government Printer, 1969.

_____. Report on the Industrial Survey of 1962. Kuching: Government Printer, 1964.

_____. Revised Development Plan. Kuching: Government Printer, 1952.

Sarawak. Sarawak Development Plan 1959-1963. Kuching: Government Printer, 1959.

_____. Sarawak Development Plan 1964-1968. Kuching: Government Printer, 1963.

Sarawak, Public Works Department. Annual Reports, 1966-68. Kuching: Government Printer, 1967-70.

Sarawak, State Development Office. Report on Development, 1959, 1961. Kuching: Government Printer, 1960, 1962.

Sarawak Tribune, 1970.

Scott, James E. Beliefs of an Elite. New Haven: Yale University Press, 1968.

Sheridan, L. A. Malaya and Singapore and Borneo Territories: The Development of Their Law and Constitutions. London: Stevens, 1961.

Silcock, T. H. The Commonwealth Economy of Southeast Asia. London: Cambridge University Press, 1959.

_____, ed. Readings in Malayan Economics. Singapore: Eastern Universities Press, 1961.

Silcock, T. H., and Fisk, E. K., eds. The Political Economy of Independent Malaya. Berkeley: University of California Press, 1963.

Simandjuntak, B. Malayan Federalism 1945-1963. London: Oxford University Press, 1969.

Snodgrass, D. R. "Capital Stock and Malayan Economic Growth: A Preliminary Analysis." Malaysian Economic Review, XI (1966), 63-85.

_____. "Some Development Implications of Political Integration and Disintegration in Malaysia." Government and Economic Development.. Edited by Gustav Ranis. New Haven: Yale University Press, 1971.

States of Malaysia. Anggaran Kumpulan Wang Pembangunan Negeri, 1966-1970. Kuala Lumpur: Government Printer, 1966-70.

Stone, Horace. From Malacca to Malaysia. London: Harrap, 1966.

The Straits Echo (Penang), 1964-1972.

The Straits Times (Kuala Lumpur), 1960-1972.

The Sunday Gazette (Kuala Lumpur), 1964-1972.

The Sunday Times (Kuala Lumpur), 1960-1972.

Sumitro Djojohadikusumo. Trade and Aid in South-East Asia: Malaysia and Singapore. Melbourne: Cheshire, 1968.

Swettenham, Sir Frank. British Malaya. London: Allen and Unwin, 1948.

Tan Giak-lan. "The Economics of Low Cost Housing in Penang." Graduation Exercise, Faculty of Economics and Administration, University of Malaya, 1968/9.

Tarling, Nicholas. British Policy in the Malay Peninsula and Archipelago 1824-1871. Kuala Lumpur: Oxford University Press, 1969 (first published in 1957).

_____. "Intervention and Non-Intervention in Malaya." Journal of Asian Studies, XXI (December, 1962), 523-27.

Tate, D. J. M. The Making of Modern South-East Asia. Vol. I: The European Conquest. Kuala Lumpur: Oxford University Press, 1971.

Thio, Eunice. British Policy in the Malay Peninsula 1880-1910. Singapore: University of Malaya Press, 1969.

Tilman, R. O. Bureaucratic Transition in Malaya. Durham: Duke University Commonwealth Studies Center, 1964.

Tregonning, K. G. "American Activity in North Borneo 1865-81." Pacific Historical Review, XXIII (November, 1954), 357-72.

_____. The British in Malaya: The First 40 Years. Tucson: University of Arizona Press, 1965.

_____. "The Founding and Development of Penang 1786-1826." Unpublished PhD Thesis, University of Malaya (Singapore), 1958.

_____. A History of Modern Sabah. Singapore: University of Malaya Press, 1965.

_____. Home Port Singapore. Singapore: Oxford University Press, 1967.

Valentine, Laurie, and Davies. Sandakan Traffic Study. 1969. Fugitive.

Vasil, R. K. Politics in a Plural Society: A Study of Non-Communal Parties in West Malaysia. Kuala Lumpur: Oxford University Press, 1971.

Wageningen Agricultural University Study Team. "Regional Planning Study of the First Division of Sarawak--Interim Report, Notes for Discussion." 1970. Fugitive.

Wang Gungwu. Malaysia: A Survey. New York: Praeger, 1964.

Waterston, Albert. Development Planning: Lessons of Experience. Baltimore: Johns Hopkins University Press, 1965.

Wheatley, Paul. The Golden Khersonese. Kuala Lumpur: University of Malaya, 1961.

Wheelwright, E. L. Industrialization in Malaysia. Melbourne: Melbourne University Press, 1965.

te, Sir Bruce, and Partners/Sabah Public Works Department. Report on the Development of Sandakan Harbour. 1963. Fugitive.

ikkramatileke, R. "State-aided Rural Land Colonization in Malaya: An Appraisal of the FLDA Programme." Annals of the Association of American Geographers, LV (September, 1965), 377-403.

_____. "Federal Land Development in West Malaysia." Pacific Viewpoint (May, 1972), 62-86.

ndstedt, R. I. A History of Malaya. Singapore: Maricam and Sons, 1962.

isconsin, University of. Economic Interdependence in Southeast Asia. Washington: United States Agency for International Development, 1970.

oodcock, George. The British in the Far East. London: Weidenfield and Nicolson, 1969.

Wh

v

—

Wi

w

p